CONGREGATIONAL STUDIE

This book presents th⁓ ⁓⁓⁓ ⁓⁓ introduction to congregational studies in the UK ⁓⁓⁓ ⁓⁓ays, it explores the difference that the incr⁓⁓ ⁓⁓⁓ ⁓⁓y is making to life in Christian congregations, and compares the the very different scenario that exists in the USA.

Contributions from leading scholars in the field include rich case studies of local communities and theoretical analyses which reflect on issues of method and develop broader understandings. Congregational studies is revealed as a rich and growing field of interest to scholars across many disciplines as well as to those involved in congregational life.

Explorations in Practical, Pastoral and Empirical Theology

Series Editors: Leslie J. Francis, University of Wales, Bangor, UK and
Jeff Astley, University of Durham and Director of the North of England
Institute for Christian Education, UK

Theological reflection on the church's practice is now recognized as a significant element in theological studies in the academy and seminary. Ashgate's new series in practical, pastoral and empirical theology seeks to foster this resurgence of interest and encourage new developments in practical and applied aspects of theology worldwide. This timely series draws together a wide range of disciplinary approaches and empirical studies to embrace contemporary developments including: the expansion of research in empirical theology, psychological theology, ministry studies, public theology, Christian education and faith development; key issues of contemporary society such as health, ethics and the environment; and more traditional areas of concern such as pastoral care and counselling.

Other titles in this series:

God, Human Nature and Education for Peace
New Approaches to Moral and Religious Maturity
Karl Ernst Nipkow
0 7546 0863 8 (Hbk); 0 7546 0872 7 (Pbk)

Sin and Forgiveness
New Responses in a Changing World
Kay Carmichael
0 7546 3405 1 (Hbk); 0 7546 3406 X (Pbk)

A Christian Theology of Place
John Inge
0 7546 3498 1 (Hbk); 0 7546 3499 X (Pbk)

Divine Revelation and Human Learning
A Christian Theory of Knowledge
David Heywood
0 7546 0850 6 (Hbk)

Women's Faith Development
Patterns and Processes
Nicola Slee
0 7546 0885 9 (Hbk); 0 7546 0886 7 (Pbk)

Congregational Studies in the UK

Christianity in a Post-Christian Context

Edited by

MATHEW GUEST, KARIN TUSTING AND
LINDA WOODHEAD

ASHGATE

Published by
Ashgate Publishing Limited
Gower House
Croft Road
Aldershot
Hants GU11 3HR
England

Ashgate Publishing Company
Suite 420
101 Cherry Street
Burlington, VT 05401-4405
USA

Ashgate website: http://www.ashgate.com

British Library Cataloguing in Publication Data
Congregational studies in the UK : Christianity in a post-Christian context. – (Explorations in practical, pastoral and empirical theology)
   1. Religious gatherings – Great Britain – Christianity
   2. Parishes – Great Britain 3. Sociology, Christian
      I. Guest, Mathew II. Tusting, Karin, 1973– III. Woodhead, Linda
      250

Library of Congress Cataloging-in-Publication Data
Congregational studies in the UK : Christianity in a post-Christian context / edited by Mathew Guest, Karin Tusting, and Linda Woodhead.
      p. cm. – (Explorations in practical, pastoral, and empirical theology)
      Includes bibliographical references and index.
      ISBN 0-7546-3288-1 (alk. paper) – ISBN 0-7546-3289-X (pbk: alk. paper)
      1. Great Britain–Church history–20th century. 2. Christian sociology–Great Britain. 3. Church growth–Great Britain. I. Guest, Mathew. II. Tusting, Karin, 1973– III. Woodhead, Linda. IV. Series.

BR759.C64 2004
274.1'82–dc22

2003063023

ISBN 0 7546 3288 1 (Hbk)
ISBN 0 7546 3289 X (Pbk)

Typeset by Tradespools, Frome, Somerset
Printed and bound in Great Britain by Antony Rowe Ltd, Chippenham, Wilts

Contents

Contributors

Kristin Aune is completing a PhD thesis on gender in contemporary British evangelicalism at King's College, London. She is the author of *Single Women: Challenge to the Church?* (Paternoster, 2002), 'Evangelicals and Gender' in Iain Taylor (ed.) *Not Evangelical Enough* (Paternoster, 2003) and editor of *On Revival: A Critical Examination* (with Andrew Walker; Paternoster, 2003). She is Assistant Director of Youth and Community Work at Ridley Hall, Cambridge.

Helen Cameron is a tutor at The Wesley Centre, Oxford Brookes University and Cliff College, Sheffield. She is currently a Visiting Fellow at the Centre for Civil Society at the London School of Economics. She has carried out extensive empirical research into congregations, drawing theoretical and methodological insights from organizational studies.

Paul Chambers is a Research Fellow at the Centre for Civil Society Studies, University of Glamorgan. His PhD research was based on an ethnographic study of growth and decline among Christian congregations in Swansea, South Wales. He is the author of *Religion, Secularization and Social Change in Wales: Congregational Studies in a Post-Christian Society* (University of Wales Press, 2004).

Simon Coleman is Reader in Anthropology at the University of Durham. He has written extensively on the charismatic evangelical movement in Europe, focusing particularly on the prosperity-based 'Faith' movement. He is the author of *The Globalisation of Charismatic Christianity: Spreading the Gospel of Prosperity* (Cambridge University Press, 2000), and editor of *Pilgrim Voices: Narrative and Authorship in Christian Pilgrimage* (with John Elsner; Berghahn, 2002), *Tourism: Between Place and Performance* (with Mike Crang; Berghahn, 2002), and *The Cultures of Creationism: Antievolution in English-speaking Countries* (with Leslie Carlin; Ashgate, 2003).

Peter Collins is Lecturer in Anthropology at the University of Durham. He has published widely on British Quakerism, as well as on the Shakers, ritual and symbolism. He has recently edited *Religion, Identity and Change: Perspectives on Global Transformations* (with Simon Coleman; Ashgate, 2004).

Douglas Davies is Professor in the Study of Religion in the Dept of Theology at the University of Durham where he is also Director of the 'Clergy and British Society' Project. His recent publications include *The Mormon Culture of*

Salvation (Ashgate, 2002), *Death, Ritual and Belief* (2nd edn, Continuum, 2002), and *Anthropology and Theology* (Berg, 2002). He was co-director of the Rural Church Project, the extensive empirical findings of which are published in *Church and Religion in Rural England* (T & T Clark, 1991).

Arthur Farnsley is a Senior Research Associate of The Polis Center, at Indiana University/Purdue University, Indianapolis. He is the author of *Southern Baptist Politics* (Pennsylvania State University Press, 1994) and contributing author, with Nancy Ammerman, of *Congregation and Community* (Rutgers University Press, 1997), one of the most innovative large-scale studies of congregations in the contemporary USA.

Mathew Guest is Senior Research Associate to the 'Clergy and British Society' Project, based in the Theology Dept at the University of Durham. His doctoral research explored recent changes in evangelicalism through the lens of a congregational study, based in Northern England. He has published on contemporary British evangelicalism and post-evangelicalism, focusing on the 'alternative' worship movement. He is co-author of *Modern Christianity: Reviewing its Place in Britain Today* (with Douglas Davies; South Street Press, 2000).

Timothy Jenkins is Lecturer in the Faculty of Divinity at the University of Cambridge. He has recently produced one of the most original treatments of religion in England: *Religion in English Everyday Life: An Ethnographic Approach* (Berghahn, 1999).

Peter McGrail is Lecturer in Catholic Studies at Liverpool Hope University College, and has recently completed a PhD thesis at The University of Birmingham on the religious and social functions of the ritual of First Communion in Liverpool.

Philip Richter is Educational Development Officer at the Southern Theological Education and Training Scheme, Salisbury. He has published widely in the sociology of religion, focusing on mainstream church culture and shifting patterns of attendance. He is co-author of *Gone But Not Forgotten: Church Leaving and Returning* (with Leslie Francis; Darton, Longman and Todd, 1998).

Martin Stringer is Lecturer in the Sociology and Anthropology of Religion in the Dept of Theology at the University of Birmingham. He has published extensively on the ethnographic study of congregations, focusing particularly on experiences of worship. He is the author of *On the Perception of Worship: The Ethnography of Worship in Four Christian Congregations in Manchester* (Birmingham University Press, 1999).

Karin Tusting is a Research Associate at the Literacy Research Centre, Lancaster University. Before this she was a member of the team working on the Kendal Project, also at Lancaster. Her doctoral research was a study of the role of written texts in processes of identity construction and maintenance in a Roman Catholic parish community. She is the author of *Exploring French Text Analysis* (with Robert Crawshaw; Routledge, 2000) and has chapters in *Situated Literacies* (edited by David Barton, Mary Hamilton and Roz Ivanic; Routledge, 2000).

Frances Ward received her doctorate from the Dept of Religions and Theology at the University of Manchester. Her research used the poststructuralist theories of Michel Foucault in an analysis of the distribution of power in an Anglican congregation. She is currently working as a parish priest in Bury, Greater Manchester.

Linda Woodhead is Senior Lecturer in Christian Studies in the Dept of Religious Studies at Lancaster University. She has published widely on the study of religion and spirituality in the modern world. She is the author of *An Introduction to Christianity* (Cambridge University Press, 2004) and editor of *Religion in Modern Times: An Interpretive Anthology* (with Paul Heelas; Blackwell, 2000); *Peter Berger and the Study of Religion* (Routledge, 2001); *Religions in the Modern World. Traditions and Transformations* (Routledge, 2001) and *Reinventing Christianity: Nineteenth Century Contexts* (Ashgate, 2001). She is currently completing a book on the findings of the Kendal Project: *The Spiritual Revolution: Why Religion is Giving Way to Spirituality* (with Paul Heelas, Ben Seel, Bronislaw Szerszynski and Karin Tusting; Blackwell, 2004).

Introduction

Although congregational studies have been undertaken in Britain at least as long as in North America, the field in the UK is less recognized, less resourced, less institutionally embedded and less prolific. It is always in danger of being dismissed as the poor relation or marginalized as an academic novelty. Yet despite the disadvantages under which it labours, it contains surprising riches.

This book arises out of our own discovery of these riches. In the year 2000 the editors of this book all found themselves engaged in congregational studies. Karin Tusting and Linda Woodhead were starting research within the 25 congregations in Kendal, Cumbria, as part of the Kendal Project, a broad empirical study of religion within this locality (see Chapter 1). Mathew Guest was immersed in doctoral research in an evangelical congregation in York, a city on the other side of Britain (see Chapter 5). Since we were all based at Lancaster University, we met regularly to swap notes and to discuss relevant work being carried out elsewhere. We began to hear of a significant number of related studies across the UK. When we organized a conference in 2001 to bring those working in the area together, we realized just how much interesting but often unrecognized research was under way.

But that was not all. By then we had also become interested in the history of congregational studies in the UK. In a collaborative attempt to reconstruct this history, we undertook a literature review. Our main findings are conveyed in Chapter 1, which offers an account of the development of congregational studies as a fertile endeavour across the disciplines. We were surprised at just how much interesting work we found, and just how long it had been going on.

Guessing that we were not the only ones ignorant of this rich seam of work, we decided to put together a book that would help publicize it more widely. This volume is the result. Its aims are simple: to recover the main lines of development of the history of congregational studies in the UK, to showcase some of the most interesting recent work in the area, and to take stock of the field as a whole.

Given that congregational studies in North America have a much higher profile than those in Britain, an obvious way in which to take stock of the field is by comparison. In this way the less well known may be illuminated by contrast with the more familiar.

The first two chapters of this book provide some of the detail on the basis of which such comparison can be made. As Chapter 1 argues, one of the most striking contrasts is that between the predominantly 'extrinsic' nature of congregational studies in the USA and the more 'intrinsic' nature of the field in the UK. Thus recent UK studies tend to be concerned with studying congregations purely for the sake of understanding them as socio-religious phenomena, while US studies often relate such understanding to, and place it in the service of, broader issues and agendas. While many UK scholars are hesitant to generalize beyond their own findings, their counterparts in the USA often work within larger horizons. Particularly common among American scholars is a concern with church growth and/or with the role of the churches in sustaining social goods. While social concern used to be presented in terms of the maintenance of a healthy 'civil society', it is now as likely to be couched in terms of the churches' role in providing 'social capital' or in preventing the 'breakdown of community'. A lot of theoretical water may have passed under the bridge between Bellah *et al.*'s *Habits of the Heart* (1985) and Putnam's *Bowling Alone* (2000), but an underlying anxiety about the health of American society appears to have remained an abiding preoccupation.

As we also see in Chapter 1, however, there has not always been such a difference between congregational studies in the USA and the UK. The earliest crop of congregational studies in the UK often had similar extrinsic preoccupations. They too were concerned to take the temperature of society, and they too made connections between the health of the churches and that of the general culture. The most important were the crop of community studies which appeared during the 1950s and 1960s, many of which took congregations very seriously. Broadly socialist in ideology, these studies were often undertaken by sociologists at the margins of the academy, and many were driven by concern that an organic society was breaking down and giving way to a more mechanistic and impersonal one as industrial–commercial interests rode roughshod over authentic human community. The authors saw post-war society as characterized by rapid and dangerous change, and regarded the churches as part of the traditional order that was increasingly under threat. What they did not yet know for sure was that the brief post-war increase in church attendance was about to give way to a precipitous decline that would more than halve national attendance figures in just three decades.

With the decline of the churches came a declining interest in the role of congregations in British society, and a period of relative quiescence in congregational studies. The churches now seemed peripheral to the most important social changes, from the sexual revolution and the reshaping of popular culture to the rise of new forms of late-industrial economic activity. The most important political, cultural and economic upheavals of the last quarter of the twentieth century could, according to popular and academic wisdom, be studied without reference to Christianity. Even the sociology of religion was primarily concerned with speculating on the reasons for secularization, while its more empirical endeavours tended to be confined to new religious movements and 'sects'. In North America, by contrast, where congregations were seen as far more central to society, they continued to attract a correspondingly greater interest.

While a concern with the churches' role in society was thus shared on both sides of the Atlantic for a time, the American concern with church growth never achieved the same level of significance in Britain. What James Hopewell (1987) called the 'mechanistic' type of congregational study, the main concern of which was the identification of those features of congregational life that were conducive to growth, never took root in the UK. There seem to be at least three explanations for this.

The first has to do with the much greater influence of evangelical Christianity in the USA. Given its defining concern with evangelism and conversion, evangelicalism has always measured its success in terms of numbers. By contrast, and despite the influence of church-growth theory since the late 1970s, many UK churches find such a concern with what they often refer to disparagingly as 'bums on pews' misconceived. Some will say that 'success' has nothing to do with the Gospel, whose fruit is more likely to be suffering, humiliation and failure. Others believe that conversion is a matter for God, not church leaders, and that the Holy Spirit blows where it wills. These differences are mainly theological. But they are greatly reinforced when they are related to ecclesiastical–institutional differences.

For the second reason why church-growth literature is not significantly represented in the UK is that it is more common for British churches to operate within a parochial system and to display 'communal' rather than 'associational' characteristics. The congregation, in other words, is not a self-contained unit concerned with those who have 'converted' into its membership, but a wider unit whose life is identified with that of the society around it, the locality which it serves. 'Success' is therefore to be measured in terms of the health of the wider society rather than in terms of levels of church membership.

Third and finally, as Philip Richter explains in Chapter 12, the lack of concern with church growth in the UK can be ascribed to the fact that so many congregations in Britain belong to wider denominations. As such, they tend to have limited individual autonomy. Their policies, finances, ministries and forms of organization are decided at national or international rather than local level. There is therefore less room and less incentive for individual congregations to develop strategies for expansion than in the USA, where congregations compete more openly with one another in a less centrally regulated market. (In recent years, this situation has been complicated further by globalization, which has, as Simon Coleman argues in Chapter 3, challenged existing congregational identities throughout the Western world.)

When congregational studies did eventually re-emerge in the UK during the 1980s, they did so in rather a different guise from what had gone before. Pragmatic concerns with the health of church and/or society were now far less prominent. There was a new interest in studying congregations, but this time for their own sake. Here, it was felt, were social groups with rich and intriguing lives. What were they all about? How did they attract and retain members? What were their beliefs and values? How did they sustain their difference from the rest of society? How did they engage with a society that was now largely indifferent or hostile to their activities? Why were many declining? These issues were now considered of sufficient interest in and of themselves, irrespective of more pragmatic concerns.

If there was a new interest in congregations, and a new sense of freedom regarding the questions that might be asked about them, there was also a new openness about the methods that might be used to study them. The chapters in Part Three of this volume give a good impression of the liveliness of the current methodological debate, which seems more explicit and more preoccupying than in congregational studies based in North America. There is an experimental feel to the field in Britain today, as different scholars work with different methods and different theoretical approaches. In this volume, Helen Cameron makes use of theoretical resources from organizational studies, asking of congregations questions usually confronted by practitioners and consultants within management science and public policy research. Douglas Davies draws from the rather more established discipline of theology, exploring the interplay between notions of leadership and community through an examination of 'occasional' congregations. Kristin Aune draws attention to the role played by gender in congregations, as in social life in general, in establishing identity, framing social conflicts and producing local meanings. Frances Ward advocates an approach which owes more to current trends in social science, and is perhaps more revealing of the overall direction being taken by many British congregational studies today. Both 'intrinsic' and post-critical, her study of a congregation in Manchester generates important reflections on the complexities and – in her words – the 'messiness' of studying congregations using ethnographic methods.

The more empirically focused studies in Part Two display an equally wide range of approaches. Confronting the traditional sociological question of secularization but in relation to local culture, Paul Chambers offers an analysis of declining congregations in South Wales and their confrontation with new evangelical strategies of growth. Mathew Guest's analysis of a large Anglican evangelical church uses sociological tools of enquiry to explore how conflict and decline are managed through the control of public discourse. Peter McGrail uses ethnographic methods to study changes in a Catholic Field Day in one parish over time, demonstrating how broader changes in church and society play out in this distinctive local event. Peter Collins borrows tools from narrative theory in his discussion of story as a constituent of congregational culture among English Quakers. And Timothy Jenkins employs a classically ethnographic approach in his analysis of findings from a study of Bristol, favouring the development of indigenous categories and the painting of congregational cultures in relation to locally forged webs of significance.

The sheer variety of interests and methods represented by the different chapters in this volume strongly suggests that congregational studies in the UK is currently in a lively, exploratory phase. This makes it hard to generalize about overall characteristics and to predict future trends. The majority of these studies are intrinsic. But some recent and ongoing projects suggest the renaissance of somewhat wider and more pragmatic agendas. The Kendal Project, whose findings are soon to be published (Heelas and Woodhead, 2004), was a wide-ranging multi-focused survey of religion and spirituality in a single locality which included a comprehensive study of all the congregations in the town. Its concern was not only to understand and categorize congregations, but to look for correlations between their rates of growth and decline and (a) different forms of congregational life and (b) wider socio-cultural trends and developments (see www.kendalproject.org.uk). Then there is the ongoing study of the churches and society in Manchester which began in 2002, which is funded by the William Temple Foundation, and which even hints at a return to a post-war concern with the churches and social welfare. In this case, however, the driver comes in part from regeneration schemes and new governmental initiatives designed to channel welfare through existing 'community' structures – an initiative inspired by practice in the USA (see www.wtf.org.uk).

This last development reminds us of the key role that funding inevitably plays in shaping congregational studies. As Arthur Farnsley argues in Chapter 2, many of the most important differences between congregational studies on either side of the Atlantic can be explained in terms of their different institutional placements and different funding opportunities. Congregational studies have flourished in the USA in recent decades partly because massive funding has been available. Such funding comes both from the churches and, even more importantly, from large charitable trusts concerned with the health of (Christian) America. Neither source is available in the UK. Here, the largest research funding bodies are government-funded, and have little interest in religion and the churches. Nor do the churches in the UK fund research. Unlike several other state churches in Europe, the Church of England has no research division, nor a significant history of making funds available to academics to undertake study of its activities. Its official think-tanks tend to be theological and non-empirical in orientation.

The result of this lack of funding for congregational studies in the UK is that such studies tend to be undertaken solely by academics in a variety of different university departments – including sociology, theology, religious studies, organizational studies and gender studies. Hence some of the variety so evident in this volume. And hence the general lack of pragmatic concern and the tendency towards an intrinsic rather than extrinsic approach. This necessity is often turned into a virtue. It is likely that the academics who undertake congregational studies in the UK would be suspicious of the threat to academic freedom that would result if their work were to be accountable to a charitable trust or ecclesiastical body. Yet, as Martin Stringer argues in Chapter 14, objectivity is always compromised and qualified. It is qualified by the assumptions, pressures and demands of the British higher education system itself, and it is qualified by accountability to the congregations that are studied.

As yet, the issue of accountability to a congregation tends not to be a complicating factor, since few congregations in the UK fund or participate in such research themselves. In contrast to the US situation, only a handful of congregations have been studied or audited either from the inside or outside. Few British seminaries train their students in congregational studies, and few clergy initiate such studies. When a scholar approaches a congregation in the UK, he or she is therefore usually in virgin territory, with no clear expectations or responsibilities on either side. This does not, of course, erase the issue of accountability, but it does allow a certain latitude in relation both to the questions that may be asked and the answers and interpretations that may, eventually, be offered.

All of which helps explain one final major difference between congregational studies on either side of the Atlantic. It is a difference of tone as much as substance, and it is a difference that can perhaps be best captured in a series of somewhat loose adjectives. Congregational studies in the UK today feel a little more critical, more irreverent, more ironic, and more irresponsible than their American counterparts. The latter tend to be more serious, more substantial, more respectful of what is studied and more 'consequential'. Thus, for example, a number of recent studies in the UK, including some in this volume, draw critical attention to the way in which power is used and abused in churches. Some look at the way in which such power is used to reinforce male dominance, others at how congregations fail to displace white dominance. Still others are concerned with how and why congregations have declined, and how – for example – their maintenance of hierarchical power structures and their identification with an ethic of respectability may have alienated many baby boomers and their offspring. In the USA, by contrast, there is a much more widespread assumption that congregations, as forms of 'community', are necessarily 'good', that their healthy functioning is important for the healthy functioning of society, and that it is an important task for congregational studies to suggest how they may be nourished and sustained. There also tends to be less reflection on whose interests are served through this process. Moreover, in the USA church growth is more likely to be considered desirable per se, and where such growth is concerned the end may be thought to justify the means.

What is clear is that the distinctive features of congregational studies in the UK have a great deal to do with the distinctive features of the social and religious landscape in which they take place. As the subtitle of this volume indicates, the single most salient feature of this landscape is undoubtedly the rapid decline in church attendance during recent decades. Far from killing off congregational studies, however, this appears to have opened up a new phase in its existence. We have a phase in which congregations can be studied for their own sake, as well as for what they can tell us about religious decline and social change. To some extent congregations are now treated like the small, exotic cultures that used to tempt anthropologists overseas. Today, there is a similar sense that the strange cultural lives of congregations ought to be studied and recorded before they too become extinct, crushed by the onslaught of a more powerful, secularizing or 'spiritualizing' culture.

In North America things are clearly very different. Here too congregational studies are shaped by their environment. But congregations are in a much stronger position, as are congregational studies. The broader horizon of some studies of congregations wins them a wider audience and allows them to achieve a more far-reaching significance than many of their UK equivalents. The fact that congregational studies is seen as having a direct relevance for church life and growth means that it is taken seriously within as well as outside the churches. And the central position of congregations within US culture means that some of the best work in this field is also able to shed light on the wider culture, just as some of the best studies of American culture and society have made a point of taking congregations seriously. In their scope, and their willingness to take seriously the question 'so what?', such studies still have a lot to teach their counterparts in Britain.

Yet as this volume demonstrates, the work that is going on in the UK has a significance and integrity of its own. In many ways it fits its culture and its times in a sensitive and appropriate manner, just as the shape of congregational studies in the USA fits theirs. One of our fondest memories from the conference which launched the book was of the American scholar Arthur Farnsley exclaiming in exasperation as we considered yet another tiny, shrinking congregation: 'hey guys, what's the point, it's cooked!' His diagnosis was almost certainly correct in a number of cases. Yet, as some of us argued at the time, it may be just as interesting to study dying congregations as flourishing ones. There is much to be learned from them: about the state of contemporary Christianity, contemporary society, and the position of a certain style of religion within that society. The study of such congregations may, for example, help place secularization theory on a firmer empirical foundation than has previously been the case. And the window of opportunity for studying these congregations is likely to be a small one – if current trends continue. On the other hand, the relatively rare examples of flourishing British congregations are equally fascinating, and expose just as many issues which need to be understood and explained, not least the reasons they buck dominant de-Christianizing trends. If it can overcome the many handicaps it faces, congregational studies in the UK may therefore be entering a rich new phase in its development.

References

Bellah, R. N., Madsen, R., Sullivan, W. M., Swidler, A. and Tipton, S. M. (1985), *Habits of the Heart. Individualism and Commitment in American Life*, Berkeley, Los Angeles and London: University of California Press.

Heelas, P. and Woodhead, L. (with Seel, B., Szerszynski, B. and Tusting, K.) *The Spiritual Revolution: Why Religion is Giving Way to Spirituality*, Oxford, UK and Malden, MA: Blackwell.

Hopewell, J. F. (1987), *Congregation: Stories and Structures*, London: SCM Press.

Putnam, R. (2000), *Bowling Alone: The Collapse and Revival of American Community*, New York and London: Simon and Schuster.

PART ONE
THE
EMERGING FIELD

Chapter 1

Congregational Studies: Taking Stock

Linda Woodhead, Mathew Guest and Karin Tusting

By the mid-1980s the field of congregational studies in the English-speaking world had produced a sufficiently rich crop for Hopewell (1987) to offer a typological survey. Hopewell divided the studies into four types: contextual, mechanistic, organic and cultural. He himself championed and helped to shape the last approach, particularly within ecclesiastical and theological circles. Since Hopewell wrote, the field has grown considerably, and has taken directions he could not have anticipated. It is now fed by many disciplines including theology, religious studies, sociology, anthropology, organizational studies, linguistics, social theory and gender studies. It takes shape in many institutional settings, not only in theological colleges, seminaries and churches, but in university departments and by way of funded research projects. Its practitioners range from clergy and lay people seeking to understand and resource their own congregations, to social scientists seeking to discern the fate of 'community' in late-capitalist societies.

This chapter provides a fresh survey of congregational studies which takes account of developments in the last couple of decades, and modifies and develops Hopewell's typology in light of them.[1] It focuses primarily on congregational studies from the UK, including books, influential articles and PhD theses.[2] Coverage of congregational studies in the USA is limited to studies that have been influential on both sides of the Atlantic.[3]

The typology offered here divides congregational studies into two main categories, extrinsic and intrinsic, and a number of subcategories:

---

[1] This chapter is based on a survey of relevant literature undertaken by the authors, its bibliography compiled with the advice of several long-standing experts in the field. We would particularly like to thank David Martin and Mike Hornsby-Smith for their invaluable assistance.

[2] Our main criteria of selection were influence in the wider field and the quality of the study: we were particularly concerned to include those studies that had contributed something new to the field.

[3] There is no comprehensive historical account of congregational studies in the USA, though a sketch is offered in Wind and Lewis (1994, Vol II, pp. 1–20) and, of course, in Hopewell (1987).

Extrinsic Studies	Intrinsic Studies
Communitarian	Self-contained
Church-growth	Typologizing
Organizational	Contextualizing
Church-health	Multi-focused
Theological	

Extrinsic congregational studies are those whose study of a congregation or congregations has some broader good, such as a concern to assess the role of congregations in the generation of social capital, or a desire to enrich theological reflection with 'congregational voices'. Intrinsic studies are those that study congregations for their own sake and for the sake of understanding them. Some intrinsic studies focus narrowly on a congregation or congregations alone, others focus more broadly on congregations in relation to their wider context. Obviously, both of these categories are ideal-types, since most extrinsic studies also seek to achieve some understanding for its own sake, and most intrinsic studies have some wider agenda, even if this remains unspecified. But the fact remains that peculiarities of overall aim, method and style allow most congregational studies to be placed within one of these two main types.

This chapter traces the development of both types of congregational study in Britain and argues that a first phase of activity which was primarily extrinsic in orientation has given way since the 1970s to a second phase that is characterized by a predominantly intrinsic approach. It compares this situation with that in the United States, suggesting that the field there has been more progressive in its development and has tended to adopt a largely extrinsic approach throughout. In its conclusion the chapter attempts to explain this contrast by reference to the very different religious contexts in which congregational studies now takes place on either side of the Atlantic.

Extrinsic Studies

Communitarian

The first significant congregational studies in the UK appeared in the 1950s. Though they were written from a variety of perspectives and had very different aims, many shared the assumption that community was in danger of breaking down under the pressures of modernization, particularly rapid industrialization and urbanization. Attention therefore turned to congregations as exemplars of community, as 'intermediate institutions' whose health was intimately bound up with that of civil society, and as places where claims about the breakdown or survival of community could be tested. These were the first 'extrinsic' studies of congregations. Their motive was to understand and help preserve healthy human community.

This communitarian agenda was shared by two superficially very different sorts of congregational study. The first, mainly secular, took place under the auspices of 'community studies'. In the UK the Institute of Community Studies was established in 1953 (Willmott, 1985). Its methods were informed by anthropology and sociology, but its aim was to influence public policy. It was influenced by the politics of the 'post-war consensus' and the establishment of the British welfare state. Studies associated with this movement typically took a town or suburb as a focus and engaged in intensive (usually team-based) research in that locale over a number of years. The better-known studies include Williams (1956), Young and Willmott (1957) and Stacey (1960). Their aim was to build up what would now be called a 'thick' description of the community, and to assess the impact of social change. Study of religion – almost exclusively of Christian churches and chapels – was often an integral part of the task. The primary interest was not congregational life per se, but the role and place of congregations within the wider community. (While such studies have a great deal in common with the American tradition of community studies which perhaps begins with the Lynds' pioneering portrait of Middletown (1929), the latter sought 'maximum objectivity' through the adoption of 'the approach of the cultural anthropologist', (p. 3), and did not entirely share the socio-political agenda of later British community studies. It was, in other words, more 'intrinsic' than 'extrinsic'.)

The second, contemporaneous, form of congregational study in the UK also had a left-wing bias, but was Christian rather than secular in origin and motivation. It shared the sense that modern Western society was in danger of becoming atomized and individualistic and that men and women craved a fellowship that was rapidly disappearing, but sought the solution not in public policy but in Christian churches. Here, it was argued, could be found the true community around which society could be re-formed. This was as much a programme as a hypothesis, and its proponents tended to be priests within a broadly Catholic tradition of Christianity (which included Anglo-Catholics from the Anglican Church as well as Roman Catholics).[4] In the 1950s, a number began to publish studies of their own congregations and initiatives within them. The Abbé Michonneau's *Revolution in a City Parish* was translated into English in 1950, and inspired a number of British studies, including Southcott's *The Parish Comes Alive* (1956). Southcott quotes with approval Michonneau's exhortation that 'every parish [should] strive to make its liturgy splendid and full of meaning ... [that] each parish [should] strive to make of itself a real community' (p. 19), and he documents the attempted implementation of this programme in his (Anglican) parish in Halton, Leeds. While Southcott does not offer a comprehensive congregational study, he describes and records the main services, regular activities, chief organizations and initiatives of his parish. His intention is to inspire other clergy, and thereby spearhead a movement of community renewal both in church and wider

---

[4] The roots of this movement can be traced as far back as the late nineteenth century in the work of Christian socialist writers like F. D. Maurice, but they took shape in the first part of the twentieth in a pan-European call for 'liturgical renewal'.

society.[5] Related issues are addressed in Wickham's *Church and People in an Industrial City* (1957). Wickham explores how churches may facilitate urban mission by offering an effective response to the fragmentation of community in industrial Sheffield. While again not concerned with congregational specifics – presenting an historical rather than a sociological account – he conceives an ecclesiological agenda which has congregational reform at its centre (Wickham, 1957, p. 225).

From the Roman Catholic side, Ward's study of a Catholic parish in Liverpool (Ward, 1958; 1961) drew on observation, document analysis and informal interviewing in a more rigorous way than Southcott, reflecting the achievements of the growing field of Roman Catholic sociology in Europe. Ward found parishioners to have a strong individual ('vertical') identification with the parish, but weak communal ('horizontal') social bonds between one another. This was explained in terms of the ecclesiastical organization of the parish; strong individual relationships between priests and people, fostered particularly by a system of regular parish visiting; and the structure of parish societies formed largely from a small core of parish activists. Ward's (1958) conclusion draws out a number of points relating the research to contemporary conditions in urban communities and questioning the long-term viability of 'the parish' as an organizational unit in these settings. In the USA at the same time, the most significant Roman Catholic congregational study was Fichter's intensive study of a parish in New Orleans, which drew on detailed factual data concerning the parish, its priests and people and an account of religious attitudes (1951). While the full study was never published, Fichter (1954) contains reflections on various aspects of parish life arising from the study. Both of these works remain influential today.

In the UK the tradition of Roman Catholic sociology has been advanced by Hornsby-Smith. In *The Changing Parish* (1989) he constructs ideal-types of parish, priest and parishioner for the pre- and post-Vatican II periods in the Church, drawing largely on two previously published studies: one of a traditional parish in the North Midlands studied by Leslie (1986), and one of (his own) parish as described by its former parish priest (O'Sullivan, 1979), in which post-Vatican II liturgical and administrative changes were experienced as positive charismatic renewal. These data are brought together with other academic studies and reports from the USA, Australia, continental Europe and the Philippines to produce a picture of the parish as a focus of conflict between rival models of the Church. More recently Tusting (2000) addresses the role of written text in the construction of identity in a Catholic parish, again proceeding from participant observation in several of the communities which make up a large parish. Her study considers the roles of different types of written text in the construction of community identities. Both the latter studies

---

[5] Gray (1986) provides a history of the 'parish communion' movement in the Church of England, and suggests reasons for its demise. See also Penhale (1986), who offers a comprehensive bibliography of works dealing with Anglo-Catholic congregations (pp. 159–60).

move away from earlier extrinsic concerns about the health of church and society towards an 'intrinsic' desire to understand contemporary Catholic congregations for their own sake.

Church-growth

If the characteristic contribution to the development of congregational studies on the part of British Catholic Christianity was made by community-focused studies, the equivalent contribution from American evangelical Protestantism came from church-growth literature. This too had its origins in the 1950s, and generated an extrinsic form of congregational study. In this case, however, the preoccupation was not with the health of communities, whether local, civic or national, but with the size of congregations and the salvation of souls. The desirability of church growth is axiomatic within the evangelical worldview, with each new individual brought into the church representing another soul brought within the ambit of salvation. Research is therefore focused on investigating the factors which cause growth and decline in order to offer practical guidance on how to maximize church numbers.

Church-growth literature not only originated in the USA, but has always been more influential there than in Europe. Its pioneer was McGavran, who devised the key principles of 'church-growth' in his *Bridges of God* (1955; also McGavran, 1959). Subsequent studies, mostly focusing on churches in the USA, have developed and refined his approach (see, for example, Belew, 1971; Wagner, 1976). As Hopewell recognized, such studies typically assume that congregations may be understood in 'mechanistic' terms – as machines which function according to particular rules. While different writers formulate these rules differently – Wimber, for example, develops Wagner's principles to include the importance of a present-day, charismatic encounter with Christ (Wimber, 1985) – all agree that it is by grasping such rules and adjusting practices accordingly that congregations will grow (for example, Wagner, 1976, p. 159).

Church-growth studies fall into two categories. First, there are those that look at individual congregations in order to discern the empirical evidence on which to base prescriptions for growth. Such evidence, including both attendance levels and attitudinal data, is generally presented in statistical form, offering numerical evidence to support church-growth theories. Second, there are those studies that observe the implementation of church-growth principles by individual churches, and draw conclusions about their efficacy.

The church-growth type of extrinsic study has had a significant but limited impact within the UK. The first church-growth conference was sponsored by the London Bible College in 1978, and Peter Wagner was its guest speaker. The British Church Growth Association was formed three years later. Since then, many evangelical churches have taken up principles from church-growth literature in attempts to enlarge their congregational body, and a few evangelical theologians have developed ideas imported from the USA in light of their own experience (for example, Watson, 1976; Gibbs, 1981). Occasionally such works are used to shed light on parochial particularities and serve as a kind of congregational study. Other scholars, working in conjunction with churches, have taken on the mechanistic understanding of congregational life advocated by church-growth theorists, while downplaying the American emphasis upon numerical expansion. As such, their work falls into the category of 'church-health', which is explored below, rather than 'church-growth'. Reed's study of how particular congregations develop and transform themselves (*The Dynamics of Religion: Process and Movement in Christian Churches*, 1978) represents an interesting synthesis of both the communitarian and church-growth forms of extrinsic study, since it combines ideas drawn from church-growth literature with a focus on identifying a congregation's responsibility to its wider community.

Organizational Studies

Since the 1980s, studies of congregations from a church-growth perspective have been supplemented by those emerging from the field of organizational studies. Whereas the former tend to be written by active churchmen, the latter generally derive from university departments of management science or applied social science. There are, nevertheless, some interesting similarities in approach. First, both church-growth literature and organizational studies are interested in the effective achievement of goals wider than that of 'understanding' alone. It is this which places them both in the category of 'extrinsic' congregational studies, even though organizational studies tend to be more explicit about what these goals might be, and more systematic in their definition of them. Second, in their preoccupation with efficiency, both types of study focus on the internal operation of congregations rather than on their relationships with wider contexts.

Harris's work is the classic example in the UK. She locates herself within the broad area of 'social administration' (see, for example, *Organising God's Work: Challenges for Churches and Synagogues*, Harris, 1998a), and is therefore committed to a set of issues derived from the concerns of social policy-makers. Although she is concerned to shed light on our understanding of congregations as organizations, she has also focused on the development of 'usable' theory – ideas that may be usefully implemented by decision-makers, whether they are the leaders of organizations or those who work in social policy administration. Congregational studies inspired by this approach display a similar focus on pragmatic objectives and their practical workability, whether in relation to the church as a welfare provider (Harris, 1995; Cameron, 1998) or the management of voluntary work within congregational contexts (Cameron, 1999; see Chapter 10 of this volume).

In their concern with wider questions about how social groups function, some organizational studies of congregations take up part of the agenda of earlier community studies. However, they do not share the latter's social vision, nor the theological agenda of their Catholic counterparts. Moreover, they tend to treat religion as epiphenomenal when it comes to the functioning of congregations. Harris, for example, speaks of the 'religion factor' (Harris, 1995) as though it were a peripheral component rather than an essential aspect of congregational identity. This approach derives from the underlying assumption that congregations are governed by the same principles as other, non-religious, organizations, and should therefore be subject to the same kind of analysis (Harris, 1998a). In this approach, church members may be considered as 'clients' (Cameron, 2000), and churches as 'voluntary associations' (Harris, 1998b).

Church-health

As mentioned above, the evangelical-inspired church-growth approach has been appropriated only selectively in the UK, and has tended to transmute into an extrinsic approach with a focus on 'church-health' rather than numerical growth. A good example is Lovell and Widdecombe's *Churches and Communities. An Approach to Development in the Local Church* (1978), which focuses on how congregations might develop through a 'non-directive' approach to community development, stressing member empowerment over the paternalistic authority of leaders. The authors conclude that the sixteen churches that took part in their 'action research' benefited from this approach, but that this benefit must be understood in wider terms than church growth alone. It is presented in terms of a healthier pattern of active and collaborative lay/clergy decision-making, an enhancement of relations with local communities and other churches through open discussion, and an engagement with local communities without an overt intent to proselytize.

It is on the other side of the Atlantic that the church-health approach has really flourished, particularly since the 1980s. The pioneering work was Dudley's edited collection, *Building Effective Ministry: Theory and Practice in the Local Church* (1983), which evolved from an experiment carried out in 1981 when a team of scholars and experts descended en masse on 'Wiltshire Church' in the USA. The book is a pioneering example of collaboration between those involved in congregational study, including academics from a range of disciplines, church-growth experts and those active in parish ministry. *Building Effective Ministry* was presented not just as a study for its own sake, but as a practical tool capable of aiding and encouraging others to study their own congregation. The approach was developed in the *Handbook for Congregational Studies*, edited by Carroll *et al.* (1987), several of whose contributors had been involved in the original Wiltshire project. It too was collaborative and inter-disciplinary, incorporated a theological perspective, and was designed as a practical tool for church health and renewal. A revised form of the handbook appeared in 1998, edited by Ammerman *et al.*, entitled *Studying Congregations: A New Handbook*. The latter builds on its predecessor by proposing six 'frames' through which congregations should be approached: theology, ecology (context), culture and identity, process/dynamics, resources and leadership.

A church-health approach also characterizes Ammerman *et al.*'s *Congregation and Community* (1997a), which brings together the findings of a team of scholars engaged in the 'Congregations in Changing Communities' project. Together they observed 23 Christian congregations across the USA and gathered questionnaire responses from 1,995 members. The book consists of detailed descriptions of these congregations, with a particular focus on the ways in which they have responded to change in the wider communities in which they are situated. Its broad conclusion is that those churches that have been willing and able to adapt have remained healthy, while those which have not have suffered, and that both church leaders and laity play a significant role within this process. Ammerman relates her findings to the continuing debate about the health of community in American society.

The church-health approach has had a major impact in the USA, not least by presenting congregational studies as a practical tool which may be employed by clergy and laity as well as specialists and academics. The fruits are evident in the large numbers of projects now carried out by congregations and clergy, and in the growing numbers of MMin and DMin dissertations which build on this approach.[6] As an alternative to the more mechanistic and evangelical church-growth approach, the church-health approach seems better suited to the ecclesiastical climate of the UK. The fact that it has been slow to catch on must therefore be ascribed to other factors, including the general reluctance of the major denominations to engage with congregational studies and to make provision for the subject in their seminaries and training courses. Gradually, however, things are beginning to change. For example, a team of British scholars, some of whom are represented in this volume, are currently planning a handbook for congregational studies that owes much to the inspiration of Carroll and Ammerman, but which is designed for the British context.

Theological

An important development which paralleled the production of extrinsic congregational studies was the growth of 'practical' or 'pastoral' theology in the UK after the 1960s. In part this was a response to the entrance of new secular professionals into the pastoral arena. The rise of liberation theology and other more contextual forms of theological reflection also fed practical theology and helped shape its agenda.

In general, practical theology has encouraged congregational studies by insisting that theology must be done not 'from above' (doctrine imposed on experience) but from below (doctrine explored from the starting point of lived experience), and that the congregation is the core site of Christian experience. A good example of this approach is Browning's *A Fundamental Practical Theology* (1991). This advocates a theological method which begins with a description of a congregation and the situation in which it finds itself, goes on to examine relevant resources from the tradition, and ends with a conversation between the two. The book itself contains studies of a number of congregations in order to illustrate the method proposed. In the UK, Graham's *Transforming Practice: Pastoral Theology in an Age of Uncertainty* (1996) develops

---

[6] A further area of development in the USA has used psychological theory to shed light on pastoral issues within congregations. See, for example, Capps (1983, 1990) and Moore (1998).

Browning's work from a feminist and postmodern perspective by arguing that attention to the practice of the faith-community can form the basis of a feminist pastoral theology which takes into account the situated nature of all knowledge and the diversity and fragmentation within and outside these communities, differences that are often overlooked by traditional practical theology.

In the theological realm the rise of feminist theology is also beginning to have some impact on congregational studies. Though feminist theologians have long insisted that theology should arise from women's as well as men's experience, it is only recently that academic theologians like Fulkerson (1994) have interpreted this to mean that they should actually listen to women's voices within Christian congregations. While Fulkerson offers not so much a study of a congregation as of the beliefs and discourses of the women within it, there are some signs that her work is beginning to stimulate a new engagement between theology and congregational studies in the UK. Ward (2000) offers a highly informative empirical study of a congregation in Manchester, England, while seeking to discover what it can reveal of 'the body of Christ' (see also Chapter 9). Clark-King (2003) interviewed working-class women from congregations in Byker, Newcastle, about their religious beliefs and spiritual lives, comparing what she found with the claims about 'women's experience' that are made in academic feminist theology (see also Aune in Chapter 13).

Intrinsic Studies

Clearly a number of extrinsic studies offer such rich descriptions of congregations that they are capable of standing on their own, irrespective of their wider purpose. As such, they might be said to exemplify an intrinsic as well as an extrinsic approach. This section discusses studies that are more narrowly intrinsic; that is, they aim to provide a portrait and analysis of a congregation (or congregations) on its (or their) own terms and for its (or their) own sake.

Self-contained

Hopewell's highly original *Congregation: Stories and Structures* (1987) has been influential on both sides of the Atlantic. In some ways the book is characterized by an extrinsic church-health approach, for part of its aim is to bring new life to congregations by enabling them to understand themselves better. Hopewell also retains at least a residual theological purpose, for he believes that the unique story of each congregation represents 'the immediate outworking of human community redeemed by Christ' (p. 11). But his fascination with parishes for their own sake tends to override any extrinsic aim. The 'symbolic' or 'cultural' approach which he advocates arises from his belief that every congregation has its own meaning, expressed in a story: 'I have begun to see how astonishingly thick and meaning-laden is the actual life of a single local church' (p. 3). Hopewell begins with observations of different parishes, and offers a myth or story which captures their distinctiveness. His approach is to treat the congregation as a self-contained entity, rather than attempt to relate it to wider contexts.[7]

A similar approach, albeit with a less prominent theological agenda, is evident in another influential American study, Ammerman's *Bible Believers* (1987). The aim of Ammerman's participant observation at 'Southside Gospel Church' was simply to 'listen to how one group of fundamentalists defines itself and how it gives order to the world' (p. 9). Like Hopewell, she sought to uncover the group's shared meanings and assumptions and to see how these are supported by its members' everyday practices and interactions.

This focus on the life and 'culture' of a congregation is also characteristic of many of the congregational studies that have been produced in the UK since the 1980s. Some take in a range of congregations, while others look at a smaller number (or just one) in greater depth.[8]

One of the best examples of the former is Francis's *Church Watch: Christianity in the Countryside* (1996). Francis and his team of ordinand researchers studied the churches in ten rural deaneries (subdivisions of an Anglican diocese) in England in the late 1980s and early 1990s. Researchers attended all the services at a church on a given weekend and, guided by a checklist, observed as many aspects as possible of service, congregation and setting. In *Church Watch* Francis simply gathers together these descriptions (no doubt with skilful editing) and offers them, without comment, to the reader. Analysis is confined to a short postscript at the end of the book, where he does no more than pose a series of questions about the challenges that these rural churches face and the ways in which they may – or may not – be equipped to face them. Francis's emphasis 'is on *displaying* the strengths and weaknesses of rural chapels and rural churches rather than *judging* their performance', and on showing 'how things really are in the present' (pp. viii, x; original emphases). In this way, Francis moves away from the extrinsic, ecclesiological concerns of the *Faith in the Countryside* report, published six years earlier, and from the survey techniques of the Rural Church Project, published by Davies, Watkins and Winter as *Church and Religion in Rural England* in 1991. All tap into a topical concern about religion in rural contexts, but Francis's study favours the

---

[7] While Hopewell's influence is widespread in congregational studies, only a few authors (for example, Wind, 1993) have followed his approach comprehensively.

[8] Some self-contained intrinsic studies also include an historical dimension. In the UK nearly every local church has a pamphlet on the history of church and parish, often written by a local historian. Studies that take the history up to the present are far less common. In the USA an interesting example is furnished by Wind and Lewis's edited collection *American Congregations* (1994, Vol. 1), which offers historical portraits of twelve religious communities, both Christian and non-Christian. Dolan's *The American Catholic Parish: A History from 1850 to the Present* (2 vols, 1987) is similar in approach, while his *The American Catholic Experience* (1992) draws on local materials to tell the story of five hundred years of American Catholicism from the perspective of the ordinary parishioner.

presentation of self-contained congregational profiles, seeking understanding for understanding's sake.

Several of the more in-depth self-contained studies of congregational life that have appeared in the UK in recent years pay particular attention to matters of worship, ritual and 'performance'. For example, in *On the Perception of Worship* (1999) Stringer explores the ways in which members of four congregations in Manchester, England, experience and understand their worship. He identifies key elements in each: narrative and story in a liberal intellectual Baptist congregation; habit and tradition in a Roman Catholic church; the conversion experience in a charismatic community; and festival in an Anglican inner-city church. Stringer analyses worship as the site in which these key elements are re-enacted and reconstituted over time, a process shaped by local congregational cultures as well as by trends in liturgy and tradition. In this way he builds on studies such as Cotton and Stevenson's *On the Receiving End* (1996), which explores Christian worship in terms of the experiences of individual participants. Stringer's concern, however, is not with individuals alone but with congregational cultures, accessed through participant observation and analysed using anthropological theories of meaning and ritual significance.

A focus on ritual praxis is also important in Coleman's study of the Word of Life Ministry in Sweden (Coleman, 2000). His concern is to characterize the 'habitus' or 'embodied disposition' of this large and successful charismatic congregation. He presents a wide-ranging study which offers 'an ethnographic appreciation of charismatic constructions of the person, of sociality, even of space and time' (p. 6). He considers not only the beliefs, narratives and practices of the community, but their material culture as well, including their art, architecture and deployment of money, demonstrating the importance of a globalizing context in shaping the charismatic identity of this particular congregation.

Retaining an interest in charismatic groups, but taking power as his conceptual focus, Percy has recently published a congregational study of the Toronto Airport Church, home of the infamous Toronto Blessing (Percy, 2004). He draws on empirical and theoretical material offered in previous works, including empirical data on congregations in northern England (Percy, 1996; 1998). The charismatic evangelical tradition is also the subject of Guest's study of a thriving Anglican congregation in northern England (2002b). Guest analyses how the value changes associated with late modernity are managed and contained within a congregational setting, paying particular attention to the role of small groups and the establishment of 'alternative', post-evangelical groups as sites for the negotiation of evangelical identity (see also Guest, 2002a). He also addresses the role of the public discourse of the congregation as both a mirror of congregational identity and a tool used in the minimization of internal conflict (see Chapter 5).[9]

---

[9] Stromberg presents a comparable argument in his study of Immanuel Church, Stockholm (Stromberg, 1986).

Typologizing

There are, of course, few congregational studies that do not offer or assume some categorization of congregations. The simplest are based on denominational categories (Lutheran, Anglican, Catholic, and so on) or the categories of churchmanship (liberal, conservative, radical, for example). When a study encompasses several congregations, it is sometimes possible to offer a fresh typology which attempts to shed new light by cutting the cake in a somewhat different way. In some cases this may constitute a, or even *the*, main contribution of the work.

The most influential cluster of typologizing studies come from the USA and take their rise from what Marty called the 'great divide' between liberal and evangelical. In his study of a congregation in Mendocino, north California, Warner (1988) proposed a typology which cross-cut horizontal categories of liberal and evangelical with vertical ones of 'institutional' and 'nascent' orientation.[10] This typology is developed from an earlier version proposed by Roozen, McKinney and Carroll in *Varieties of Religious Presence* (1984). The two may be correlated in the following way:

Warner		**Roozen** *et al.*
Institutional liberalism	=	The 'civic' orientation
Institutional evangelicalism	=	The 'sanctuary' orientation
Nascent liberalism	=	The 'activist' orientation
Nascent evangelicalism	=	The 'evangelistic' orientation

In an article arising from the 'Congregations in Changing Communities' research project, Ammerman (1997b) offers a further variation by categorizing American Christians as 'Activist', 'Golden Rule' or 'Evangelical'. Activists characterize the Christian life in terms of social action and working for justice, Golden Rule Christians in terms of doing good deeds, and Evangelical Christians in terms of 'being saved'.

Becker has recently proposed a further development of this typology in her *Congregations in Conflict* (1999). On the basis of her study of 23 different congregations in the USA, Becker concluded that most internal conflict was directly related to clashes between different local understandings of congregational identity. She identifies four main understandings:

1 'House of worship': congregation as provider of religious goods and services to individuals;
2 'Family': congregation as provider of close-knit and supportive relationships for members;

---

[10] Although Warner studied only one congregation, he studied it over several phases of its historical development, during which it moved through different 'types' of churchmanship.

3 'Community': congregation as a democratic forum which supports its members while also expressing their values in social programmes;
4 'Leader': congregation as an activist, mission-focused community of values led by pastor or denomination.[11]

Becker suggests that the most intractable conflicts occur when two or more of these types are represented in a single congregation.

In the UK, Woodhead and Heelas (2000) have proposed an alternative three-fold typology which distinguishes between religions of difference, religions of humanity and spiritualities of life. The first locate authority in external forms of transcendent obligation, the last in the depths of inner subjectivity, and religions of humanity locate authority in 'the human' and human values. Although this typology was developed in order to make sense of religions in the modern world more generally, it can also be applied to Christian congregations, and is beginning to be used in this way (see, for example, Aune, Chapter 13 and Heelas and Woodhead, 2004).

Contextualizing

Contextualizing intrinsic studies are those which seek to relate congregations to their wider socio-cultural contexts, but have no wider or pragmatic agenda. They generally seek to illuminate both church and wider society with reference to one another. Contextualizing studies are the most obviously sociological of congregational studies, particularly those large-scale studies that situate congregations in relation to broad social trends. Smaller-scale contextualizing studies seek only to relate the congregation to its local context, and these tend to adopt anthropological methods. Both forms of study have been well represented in Britain since the 1970s.

Small-scale – local context One of the earliest small-scale contextualizing studies in the UK came out of the Scottish context in the early 1970s. Directed by the sociologist of religion Sissons, *The Social Significance of Church Membership in the Burgh of Falkirk* (1973) was a thorough study of all the congregations in the town and made use of both quantitative and qualitative research methods.[12] It was a collaborative project commissioned by the General Assembly of the Church of Scotland and the departments of Social Anthropology and Christian Ethics and Practical Theology at the University of

---

[11] Becker notes that this typology is close to that of Mock (1992). Mock, in turn, derives his categories from Roozen *et al.* (1984).

[12] This study stands within a tradition that may be traced back much further, at least to Chalmers's *The Christian and Civic Economy of Large Towns* (1821). Chalmers used social scientific methods and gathered statistics from the Glasgow area to demonstrate the correlation between working-class culture and the growing irreligion associated with city life (Brown, 2001, p. 23). Highly respected among evangelical churchmen, Chalmers's methods of interpretation influenced the presentation of the 1851 census on religious worship.

Edinburgh. As well as providing detailed information about the life and beliefs of the congregations in Falkirk, the study looked for correlations between church membership and a range of variables, including class, work and politics. The study was influenced by Lenski's research in Detroit (1963), which found that 'the religious factor' was key to the acquisition of social and economic values, especially in combination with other social factors such as ethnicity and communalism. Though ethnicity and communalism were not major factors in Falkirk, Sissons found a significant correlation between church membership and socio-economic status, political attitudes, involvement in voluntary associations and attitudes to work. He also discovered significant differences not only between denominations, but also between two main forms of church membership: 'communal' and 'associational', a contrast which builds on Troeltsch's model of church and sect and Tonnies's (1955) distinction between *Gemeinschaft* and *Gesellschaft* (community and association).

The small-scale sociological approach was advanced in Britain by a number of works, including Clark's *Between Pulpit and Pew* (1982), which offered a contextualizing study of a Yorkshire fishing village. Clark traces the relationships between religion in church and chapel and religion as manifest in non-institutional or 'folk' forms, arguing that both persist because they retain a legitimating function, investing meaning in the everyday experiences of local residents. Jenkins's *Religion in English Everyday Life* (1999) is more influenced by anthropological than sociological method.[13] This study of a village and its church in west Cambridgeshire and a Whit Walk in East Bristol is purely ethnographic in approach, seeks no statistical correlations, and proceeds from the author's long-term immersion in these communities. For Jenkins, the study of congregations and local communities is inseparable, for he defines religion as a form of collective self-imagining and self-worship which 'presents visions of social flourishing: of right social order and of what it is to be human' (p. 36). Jenkins therefore explores the meanings of congregations by moving outside the religious community itself and situating it within its socio-cultural locality, exploring local meanings and the place of religion within them. The distinction in the Cambridgeshire village of Comberton between 'villagers' and old and new 'incomers' causes tension, as the church finds itself caught between conflicting 'economies of fantasy' about the village, within each of which it has a different place. In Bristol, the organizing ideal is that of 'respectability' and part of the role of the church is to represent symbolically the virtues of control, sobriety, continence and thrift, which are both religious and social (see Jenkins, Chapter 8).[14]

---

[13] Jenkins's work also stands within the tradition of British community studies. His analysis of Comberton village, Cambridgeshire, for example, shows some similarities with Stacey's study of Banbury (1960), and Jenkins himself makes reference to this tradition in his reflections on method (1999, p. 91).

[14] Though it really belongs to the 'extrinsic' category, Allan's congregational study *The Face of My Parish* (1954) is an early insider (minister) account of a Church of Scotland parish in Glasgow which displays interesting similarities to 'situating' studies

Continuing the Scottish tradition, Dowie offers a contextualizing study of a single congregation in his ethnography of 'Riverstane' Church. In an early article, Dowie (1997) concentrates on this church as a centre of civic status, distinctive as an exclusivist institution resistant to change. While this resistance reinforces the boundaries which consolidate congregational identity, it also exacerbates processes of church decline. He develops his ethnography into a book-length congregational study (Dowie, 2002), which combines an intrinsic use of ethnographic methods, including the development of indigenous categories, and an extrinsic application of gathered insights to issues in pastoral theology. His work bridges the two kinds of approach, paying attention to local cultures, while retaining an understanding of congregational culture as the outcome of interaction among members of a group, their context, and the ethnographer himself (cf. Ward, Chapter 9).

Large-scale – wider social context   Small-scale contextualizing studies have been produced steadily in Britain since the 1970s. They take their place alongside a number of examples from the USA, including those by Williams (1974) and Eisland (1998). Though large-scale studies are rarer, here too there seems to be greater productivity in the UK than there is for many other types of congregational study.

The work of Bryan Wilson, David Martin, Grace Davie, Steve Bruce and Robin Gill may be mentioned in this context. Though few of these authors have devoted much time to formal empirical study of particular congregations, all of them make reference to congregations in their work, and all attempt to relate them to wider social trends. Their main concern is to establish links between congregational decline and aspects of modernization.[15] Though this is most often done in general terms, some of these sociologists of religion also attempt to relate variable rates of congregational (or denominational) decline to differences between types of congregation (or denomination). Thus Bruce relates the more rapid decline of liberal as compared to conservative congregations to the latter's greater ability to transmit clear and strict teachings to their own members as well as to potential converts (Bruce, 1989).

Bruce's argument is influenced by the work of Peter Berger and Dean Kelley in the USA, both of whom regard the move from 'strict' to 'liberal' Christianity (to use Kelley's typology) as a trend which leads inexorably to secularization, as Christianity loses its distinctness from the wider culture. Both Berger and Kelley paid attention to congregations as well as to individual belief in framing

---

such as Jenkins (1999) and Dowie (2002). Allan explains the failure of his church to assimilate new members with reference to the difference in culture between the church and its surrounding locality, finding a clash between two secular cultures: that of the local working classes, and that of the church's bourgeoisie, concerned with values like respectability, stability and security.

[15] Robin Gill has also devoted a great deal of time to establishing precise figures for church decline in Britain, sometimes looking at specific congregations in doing so. See, for example, Gill (2003).

this argument, though they did not themselves engage in formal empirical research. The connection between liberal congregations and decline has also been explored in a number of works of historical sociology, for example Wuthnow (1988) and Roof and McKinney (1987), both of which derive their evidence chiefly from large-scale survey data. In many ways Warner (1988) provides the best example of how this sort of argument can be grounded in congregational study, as he finds a direct correlation in the Mendocino Church between liberalization and decline and de-liberalization and growth.

At this point it is also worth mentioning Bellah *et al.*'s *Habits of the Heart* (1985), which generalizes about the state of contemporary American culture on the basis of empirical study which includes a number of studies of congregations, including those undertaken by Tipton. But given its central concern with the 'state of the [American] nation', and in particular with the dissolution of community and civic society by the acids of both 'expressive' and 'utilitarian' individualism, this study belongs to the extrinsic as much as the intrinsic category.

Here one might also note the work of Flory and Miller (2000), whose edited volume on *GenX Religion* includes a number of congregation-based studies which proceed from the assumption that religious identity in postmodern times is shaped by generational as well as cultural factors.[16] The wider context includes the deregulation of tradition in postmodernity, which has allowed local groups to reconfigure their presentation of the Gospel in line with the affinities of youth subcultures. As such, congregations become sites for the constitution of novel religious forms, which conflate and combine previously antagonistic spheres. For example, Jensen (2000) offers an illuminating picture of Committed Christian Fellowship, an evangelical, California-based congregation which affirms biblical literalism and moral conservatism while embracing punk-rock culture. Consideration of the deregulation of religion in post-modernity has also provoked reflection on cultural forms which may possibly take the place of congregations in offering an alternative sense of religious identity. In Britain Lynch (2002) has explored the possibility that a sense of spiritual community is forged within nightclubs, clubbers turning to youth culture for the sense of meaning they fail to find in traditional Christian congregations.

Multi-focused

The final category of congregational study is reserved for those that combine two or more of the approaches outlined above. Depending on the nature of the combination, a multi-focused study may be primarily extrinsic or intrinsic in orientation.

Some of the large-scale contextualizing studies mentioned above fall into this broad category, at least in so far as they combine a church-growth (or church-

---

[16] For a generational approach to congregational studies, see also Carroll and Roof (2002).

health) approach with a typologizing one. While studies like Kelley's *Why Conservative Churches are Growing* (1972) cross two types, however, truly multi-focused studies combine even more. Tipton's *Getting Saved from the Sixties* (1982) works with at least three of the approaches outlined above. Tipton studied three religious communities in California, including the Living Word Fellowship (LWF), a 'born-again, spirit-filled, revival church' of some three hundred members in a modest suburb of San Francisco (p. 31). As well as offering intrinsic, self-contained studies of these communities, Tipton both typologizes and contextualizes them by relating them to wider cultural trajectories. In addition, he considers reasons for their success, bound up with their appeal to baby-boomers disillusioned with the counter-culture of the 1960s. The richness of his descriptions and his concern to understand the moral economy of these different communities suggests an intrinsic approach, while his desire to throw light on contemporary American culture and, even more ambitiously, to 'help us clarify our moral commitments in the face of the hard realities ahead' (as Bellah puts it in the Foreword, p. xi), indicates an extrinsic concern.

Though somewhat less intensely multi-layered, Miller's study of Calvary Chapel, Vineyard Christian Fellowship and Hope Chapel in *Reinventing American Protestantism* (1997) and Tamney's study of four congregations in Indiana in *The Resilience of Conservative Religion* (2001) also fall into the 'multi-focused' category. Miller's starting point is self-consciously extrinsic. His interest in these churches arises from his own theological journey and a concern with wider issues of church growth and decline. Like Kelley, Miller is interested in why mainline liberalism has declined while conservative denominations have grown. But unlike Kelley, his focus falls on a new variation in this pattern, namely the exceptional success of churches which combine elements of conservative religion (such as supernaturalism and literalist Bible teaching) with more progressive elements (fostering individual empowerment and loose 'postmodern organisational structures' rather than paternalistic authority, p. 9). These churches are normally labelled 'charismatic' or 'Pentecostal', but Miller believes that such categorization is no longer adequate to the movements he is looking at – hence his claim that they represent a 'new paradigm' in Protestantism. His task is to describe them and what is new about them, to situate them in relation to wider cultural trends, to account for their success, and to spell out the lessons which can be learned by other forms of Christianity. Tamney does something very similar, though his work is based on the study of a range of separate, smaller local congregations, each of which is characterized by recent numerical growth. What they all have in common, he discovers – contra Bruce, Berger and Kelley – is not 'strictness' or a resistance to modernization, but the ability to accommodate it. Tamney finds that 'modernized tradition-alism' is what is doing well, chiefly because it has been able to accommodate such central elements of late modernity as structural differentiation, an affluence ethic and a therapeutic self-realization ethos.[17]

---

[17] For similar observations in relation to the Women's Aglow movement see Griffith (1997).

In the UK, the Kendal Project was influenced by multi-focused studies such as these, and shares something of their approach. It too was concerned to research and to categorize the different types of religion and spirituality on the ground in a single location (the town of Kendal in northwest Britain), and it too was partly concerned to assess and compare their relative rates of growth and decline and to offer an explanation. Its main finding was that it was those forms of religiosity which were able to attend to, heal and resource the subjective lives of individuals by bringing them into relation with the sacred that were proving most successful. By contrast, those that demanded that individuals conform to external sources of transcendent authority and live life in prescribed roles were doing least well. Congregational study in Kendal revealed that almost all the congregations still demanded a high degree of conformity and deference, and that the congregational domain had suffered massive decline since the 1970s. By contrast, holistic forms of spirituality in Kendal, which were almost uniformly devoted to resourcing subjective life, were found to have exploded since the late 1980s (Heelas and Woodhead, 2004).

Conclusion

Congregational studies in Britain have moved through two distinct phases. The first, through the 1950s and 1960s, was more extrinsic in orientation, while the second, since the 1970s, has been more intrinsic. In the former, studies displayed considerable concern about the breakdown of integrated community and the role – actual or potential – that the churches might play in relation to social cohesion and collapse. This reflected and was perhaps triggered by the post-war concern for the reclamation and reinvigoration of national identity and local community.[18]

Whilst American congregational studies have continued to be deeply engaged with these extrinsic concerns, the second phase of British studies displays a rather different orientation. Those who study congregations now come from a wide range of academic backgrounds, and their aim is generally to understand the socio-cultural characteristics of the group that is being studied for the sake of understanding. Of course the results of such study may be useful to those making decisions about the future of these groups, but such practical application is not the primary aim of the research.

---

[18] The fact that US studies have retained a consistently extrinsic focus throughout the twentieth century, while UK ones have not, may also relate to the different experiences of the Second World War on either side of the Atlantic. The war constituted a threat to a sense of national identity and community cohesion to a far greater degree in the UK, leading to a post-war quest for the reclamation of community. The North American tradition was driven by other factors, maintaining an extrinsic drive within congregational studies that suggests a continuity stretching from the Chicago School to Robert Putnam, characterized by the exercise of sociology in the service of a greater community.

There may be many explanations for this shift towards an intrinsic approach. One is simply that there appears to be a lower degree of anxiety about social cohesion and social capital in Britain than in America today (at least if one takes as an index the number of 'state of the nation' studies emerging from both countries). Another is simply that congregations in Britain, as in most of Europe, have now declined to such a point that it has become implausible to claim that they have great relevance to the formulation and exploration of wider questions about society. If social capital is under threat, it is unlikely that congregations will be turned to as the place where a solution will be found, either by policy-makers or the population at large. The UK is simply no longer a Christian country in the way the USA may still claim to be.

As the following chapter will make clear, congregational studies in the UK today suffer from severe disadvantages compared to their counterparts in the USA, not least a chronic shortage of funding. As the other studies in this book indicate, however, there are also rich opportunities in the contemporary situation. Those who study congregations in Britain today find themselves at a unique historical moment in which many congregations face collapse and extinction. This brings with it particular responsibilities: to study how congregations face this situation; to understand and explain why congregational decline has occurred; to illuminate the ways in which congregations maintain their distinctive life in the face of hostility or indifference; to explain why some congregations (and other forms of spiritual group) are managing to survive better than others. Only in twenty years or so, when the next chapter in the history of congregational studies in the UK comes to be written, will it become clear whether or not its practitioners have managed to rise to the challenge.

References

ACRA (1990), *Faith in the Countryside*, Worthing: Churchman Publishing.

Allan, T. (1954), *The Face of My Parish*, London: SCM Press.

Ammerman, N. T. (1987), *Bible Believers. Fundamentalists in the Modern World*, New Brunswick, NJ and London: Rutgers University Press.

Ammerman, N. T. *et al.* (1997a), *Congregation and Community*, New Brunswick, NJ: Rutgers University Press.

Ammerman, N. T. (1997b), 'Golden Rule Christianity: Lived Religion in the American Mainstream', in Hall, D. G. (ed.), *Lived Religion in America: Toward a Theory of Practice*, Princeton, NJ: Princeton University Press, pp. 196–216.

Ammerman, N. T. *et al.* (eds) (1998), *Studying Congregations: A New Handbook*, Nashville, TN: Abingdon Press.

Becker, P. E. (1999), *Congregations in Conflict: Cultural Models of Local Religious Life*, Cambridge: Cambridge University Press.

Belew, W. W. (1971), *Churches and How They Grow*, Nashville, TN: Broadman Press.

Bellah, R. N., Madsen, R., Sullivan, W. M., Swidler, A. and Tipton, S. M. (1985), *Habits of the Heart. Individualism and Commitment in American Life*, Berkeley, Los Angeles and London: University of California Press.

Briers, S. J. (1993), 'Negotiating with Babylon: responses to modernity within a Restorationist community', unpublished PhD thesis, University of Cambridge.

Brown, C. (2001), *The Death of Christian Britain: Understanding Secularisation 1800–2000*, London and New York: Routledge.

Browning, D. (1991), *A Fundamental Practical Theology*, Minneapolis: Fortress Press.

Bruce, S. (1989), *A House Divided: Protestantism, Schism and Secularisation*, London: Routledge.

Cameron, H. (1998), 'The social action of the local church: five congregations in an English city', unpublished PhD thesis, University of London.

Cameron, H. (1999), 'Are members volunteers? An exploration of the concept of membership drawing upon studies of the local church', *Voluntary Action*, 1 (2), pp. 53–65.

Cameron, H. (2000), 'Colleagues or Clients? The Relationship between Clergy and Church Members', in Malin, N. (ed.), *Professionalism, Boundaries and the Workplace*, London and New York: Routledge, pp. 106–119.

Capps, D. (1983), *Life Cycle Theory and Pastoral Care*, Philadelphia: Fortress Press.

Capps, D. (1990), 'The pursuit of unhappiness in American congregational life', *Pastoral Psychology*, 39, pp. 3–23.

Carroll, J. W. *et al.* (eds) (1987), *Handbook for Congregational Studies*, Nashville, TN: Abingdon Press.

Carroll, J. W. and Roof, W. C. (2002), *Bridging Divided Worlds: Generational Culture in Congregations*, San Francisco: Jossey-Bass.

Chalmers, T. (1821), *The Christian and Civic Economy of Large Towns*, Glasgow: Chalmers and Collins.

Clark, D. (1982), *Between Pulpit and Pew. Folk Religion in a North Yorkshire Fishing Village*, Cambridge: Cambridge University Press.

Clark-King, E. (2003), 'Sacred hearts. Feminist theology interrogated by the voices of working-class women', unpublished PhD thesis, Lancaster University.

Coleman, S. (2000), *The Globalisation of Charismatic Christianity: Spreading the Gospel of Prosperity*, Cambridge: Cambridge University Press.

Cotton, R. and Stevenson, K. (1996), *On the Receiving End. How People Experience What we Do in Church*, London: Mowbray.

Davies, D., Watkins, C. and Winter, M. (1991), *Church and Religion in Rural England*, Edinburgh: T. and T. Clark.

Dolan, J. P. (ed.) (1987), *The American Catholic Parish: A History from 1850 to the Present*, 2 vols, New York: Paulist.

Dolan, J. P. (1992), *The American Catholic Experience. A History – from Colonial Times to the Present*, Notre Dame, IN: University of Notre Dame Press.

Dowie, A. (1997), 'Resistance to change in a Scottish Christian congregation', *Scottish Journal of Religious Studies*, 18 (2), pp. 147–162.

Dowie, A. (2002), *Interpreting Culture in a Scottish Congregation*, New York: Lang.

Dudley, C. S. (ed.) (1983), *Building Effective Ministry: Theory and Practice in the Local Church*, San Francisco: Harper and Row.

Eisland, N. L. (1998), *A Particular Place: Exurbanisation and Religious Response in a Southern Town*, New Brunswick, NJ: Rutgers University Press.

Fichter, J. (1951), *Southern Parish vol. I: The Dynamics of a City Church*, Chicago: University of Chicago Press.

Fichter, J. (1954), *Social Relations in the Urban Parish*, Chicago: University of Chicago Press.

Flory, R. W. and Miller, D. E. (eds) (2000), *GenX Religion*, New York and London: Routledge.

Francis, L. (1996), *Church Watch: Christianity in the Countryside*, London: SPCK.

Fulkerson, M. M. (1994), *Changing the Subject: Women's Discourses and Feminist Theology*, Minneapolis: Augsburg Fortress.

Gibbs, E. (1981), *I Believe in Church Growth*, London: Hodder and Stoughton.

Gill, R. (2003), *The 'Empty' Church Revisited*, Aldershot: Ashgate.

Graham, E. (1996), *Transforming Practice: Pastoral Theology in an Age of Uncertainty*, London and New York: Mowbray.

Gray, D. (1986), *Earth and Altar. The Evolution of the Parish Communion in the Church of England to 1945*, Norwich: Canterbury Press.

Griffith, R. M. (1997), *God's Daughters. Evangelical Women and the Power of Submission*, California and London: University of California Press.

Guest, M. (2002a), ' "Alternative" Worship: Challenging the Boundaries of the Christian Faith', in Arweck, E. and Stringer, M. (eds), *Theorising Faith: The Insider/Outsider Problem in the Study of Ritual*, Birmingham: University of Birmingham Press, pp. 35–56.

Guest, M. (2002b), 'Negotiating community: an ethnographic study of an evangelical church', unpublished PhD thesis, Lancaster University.

Harris, M. (1995), 'Quiet care – welfare work and religious congregations', *Journal of Social Policy*, 24 (1), pp. 53–71.

Harris, M. (1998a), *Organising God's Work: Challenges for Churches and Synagogues*, London: Macmillan.

Harris, M. (1998b), 'A special case of voluntary associations? Towards a theory of congregational organisation', *British Journal of Sociology*, 49 (4), pp. 602–618.

Heelas, P. and Woodhead, L. (with Seel, B., Szerszynski, B. and Tusting, K.) (2004), *The Spiritual Revolution: Why Religion is Giving Way to Spirituality*, Oxford, UK and Malden, MA: Blackwell.

Hopewell, J. F. (1987), *Congregation: Stories and Structures*, London: SCM Press.

Hornsby-Smith, M. P. (1989), *The Changing Parish: A Study of Parishes, Priests and Parishioners after Vatican II*, London: Routledge.

Jenkins, T. (1999), *Religion in English Everyday Life*, New York and Oxford: Berghahn Books.

Jensen, L. (2000), 'When Two Worlds Collide: Generation X Culture and Conservative Evangelicalism', in Flory, R. W. and Miller, D. (eds), *GenX Religion*, New York and London: Routledge, pp. 139–162.

Kelley, D. A. (1972), *Why Conservative Churches are Growing*, New York: Harper and Row.

Lenski, G. (1963), *The Religious Factor*, New York: Doubleday.

Leslie, J. H. (1986), 'Resistance to change in a North Midlands parish', unpublished PhD thesis, University of Surrey.

Lovell, G. and Widdecombe, C. (1978), *Churches and Communities. An Approach to Development in the Local Church*, London: Search Press.

Lynch, G. (2002), *After Religion. Generation X and the Search for Meaning*, London: Darton, Longman and Todd.

Lynd, R. S. and Lynd, H. M. (1929), *Middletown. A Study in Modern American Culture*, San Diego, New York and London: Harcourt Brace.

Marty, M. E. (1970), *Righteous Empire. The Protestant Experience in America*, New York: The Dial Press.

McGavran, D. A. (1955), *Bridges of God*, New York: Friendship Press.

McGavran, D. A. (1959), *How Churches Grow*, New York: Friendship Press.

Miller, D. E. (1997), *Reinventing American Protestantism. Christianity in The New Millennium*, Berkeley and Los Angeles: University of California Press.

Mock, A. (1992), 'Congregational religious styles and orientations to society', *Review of Religious Research*, 34 (1), pp. 20–33.

Moore, M. E. M. (1998), 'Dynamics of religious culture: theological wisdom and ethical guidance from diverse urban communities', *International Journal of Practical Theology*, 2, pp. 240–262.

O'Sullivan, B. (1979), *Parish Alive*, London: Sheed and Ward.

Penhale, F. (1986), *The Anglican Church Today. Catholics in Crisis*. London and Oxford: Mowbray.

Percy, M. (1996), *Words, Wonders and Power: Understanding Contemporary Christian Fundamentalism and Revivalism*, London: SPCK.

Percy, M. (1998), 'The morphology of pilgrimage in the Toronto Blessing', *Religion*, 28 (3), pp. 281–289.

Percy, M. (2004), 'Adventure and atrophy in a charismatic movement: returning to the "Toronto Blessing"', *Journal of Contemporary Religion*, forthcoming.

Pickering, W. S. F. (1958), 'The place of religion in the social structure of two English industrial towns', unpublished PhD thesis, London University.

Reed, B. (1978), *The Dynamics of Religion: Process and Movement in Christian Churches*, London: Darton, Longman and Todd.

Roof, W. C. and McKinney, W. (1987), *American Mainline Religion. Its Changing Shape and Future*, New Brunswick, NJ: Rutgers University Press.

Roozen, D. A., McKinney, W. M. and Carroll, J. W. (1984), *Varieties of Religious Presence: Mission in Public Life*, New York: Pilgrim Press.

Ryan, D. (1996), *The Catholic Parish: Institutional Discipline, Tribal Identity and Religious Development in the English Church*, London: Sheed and Ward.

Sissons, P. L. (1973), *The Social Significance of Church Membership in the Burgh of Falkirk*, Edinburgh: Church of Scotland.

Southcott, E. W. (1956), *The Parish Comes Alive*, London: Mowbray.

Stacey, M. (1960), *Tradition and Change: A Study of Banbury*, London: Oxford University Press.

Stringer, M. (1999), *On the Perception of Worship*, Birmingham: University of Birmingham Press.

Stromberg, P. (1986), *Symbols of Community: The Cultural System of a Swedish Church*, Tucson: The University of Arizona Press.

Tamney, J. (2001), *The Resilience of Conservative Religion. The Case of Popular, Conservative Protestant Congregations*, Cambridge: Cambridge University Press.

Tipton, S. (1982), *Getting Saved from the Sixties. Moral Meaning in Conversion and Cultural Change*. Berkeley, Los Angeles and London: University of California Press.

Tonnies, F. (1955), *Community and Association, (Gemeinschaft und Gesellschaft)*, London: Routledge and Kegan Paul.

Tusting, K. (2000), 'Written intertextuality and the construction of Catholic identity in a parish community: an ethnographic study', unpublished PhD thesis, Lancaster University.

Wagner, C. P. (1976), *Your Church Can Grow*, Glendale, CA: Regal Books.

Ward, C. K. (1958), 'Some elements of the social structure of a Catholic parish', *Sociological Review* 6 (1), pp. 75–93.

Ward, C. K. (1961), *Priests and People: A Study in the Sociology of Religion*, Liverpool: Liverpool University Press.

Ward, F. (2000), 'Writing the body of Christ: a study in an Anglican congregation', unpublished PhD thesis, University of Manchester.

Warner, R. S. (1988), *New Wine in Old Wineskins. Evangelicals and Liberals in a Small-Town Church*, Berkeley, Los Angeles and London: University of California Press.

Watson, D. (1976), *I Believe in Evangelism*, London: Hodder and Stoughton.
Wickham, E. R. (1957), *Church and People in an Industrial City*, London: Lutterworth Press.
Williams, M. D. (1974), *Community in a Black Pentecostal Church*, Pittsburgh: University of Pittsburgh Press.
Williams, W. M. (1956), *The Sociology of an English Village: Gosforth*, London: Routledge.
Willmott, P. (1985), 'The Institute of Community Studies', in Bulmer, M. (ed.), *Essays on the History of British Sociological Research*, Cambridge: Cambridge University Press, pp. 137–150.
Wimber, J. (1985), *Power Evangelism: Signs and Wonders Today*, London, Sydney, Auckland and Toronto: Hodder and Stoughton.
Wind, J. P. (1993), *Constructing Your Congregation's Story*, Minneapolis: Augsburg Fortress.
Wind, J. P. and Lewis, J. W. (1994), *American Congregations. Vol 1: Portraits of Twelve Religious Communities*, Chicago and London: University of Chicago Press.
Wind, J. P. and Lewis, J. W. (1994), *American Congregations. Vol 2: New Perspectives in the Study of Congregations*, Chicago and London: University of Chicago Press.
Woodhead, L. and Heelas, P. (eds) (2000), *Religion in Modern Times: An Interpretive Anthology*, Oxford: Blackwell.
Wuthnow, R. (1988), *The Restructuring of American Religion*, Princeton: Princeton University Press.
Young, M. and Willmott, P. (1957), *Family and Kinship in East London*, London: Routledge and Kegan Paul.

Chapter 2

The Rise of Congregational Studies in the USA

Arthur Farnsley

Over the course of the past 25 years or so, the USA has witnessed a marked shift in the study of religion. Much of the attention that was once turned to broad theories of religion's influence on culture or on very large institutions such as denominations or ecumenical movements has now been directed towards relatively small, local and particular religious organizations, especially congregations.

Interest in congregations and the development of congregational studies as a subfield of both religious studies and sociology occurred at the confluence of three different streams. The first stream is a theoretical, intellectual movement away from grand theories and towards particular, empirical studies. A growing interest in organizational studies within sociology is just one part of that larger trend. The second stream carries concerns about the nature of community in a technological, post-industrial age, concerns that have led to greater practical, applied interest in what conservatives tend to call 'mediating institutions' and liberals term the 'institutions of civil society'. This preoccupation with organizational practice spawned everything from management consulting for congregations to faith-based welfare reform. The third is a funding stream, as money for research and the increased availability of certain kinds of academic jobs have drawn ever more intellectuals into the first two currents.

None of these developments could have changed the field so drastically by itself. The theoretical developments, even if they represent a true paradigm shift, would never have taken root if the applied interest and the funding had not been available. Proposed changes in practice would have foundered without the intellectual acceptance within the disciplines and the exploratory funding – essentially intellectual venture capitalism – from the foundations. And even large piles of money would not have created the field of congregational studies as a salient force unless it was perceived to have theoretical gravity and practical importance.

Rather than provide an exhaustive bibliography of American congregational studies, this chapter will sketch the three-pronged process by which the field developed. A better understanding of the conditions under which congregational studies flourished in the American setting may make it easier to compare the different conditions in the British setting in ways that offer at least a hope of predicting how developments in the UK might differ.

25

The Theoretical Stream

A New Paradigm

In 1988 R. Stephen Warner published *New Wine in Old Wineskins: Evangelicals and Liberals in a Small-Town Church*. This study of the triumphant rise of conservative evangelicals in Mendocino, California, made quite an impression, winning book-of-the-year in some sociology of religion circles.

Clearly Warner was on to something. In no sense had he created congregational studies or small-town ethnography. In fact, his approach was akin to Liston Pope's *Millhands and Preachers* (1942), written 46 years earlier. Neither had he suddenly uncovered a conservative, evangelical resurgence. Historians and sociologists had already written much about the rise of the Moral Majority and the success of Ronald Reagan's attempts to mobilize that constituency.

But Warner's narrative version – evocative, personal, even warm – struck a chord precisely because it showed how religion was experienced as particular, where people chose from a menu of possible, and often competing, experiences and organizations. He summed this up best himself in the paper, 'Work in progress toward a new paradigm for the sociological study of religion in the United States', published in 1993 in the *American Journal of Sociology*. The abstract for that paper reads:

> This article reviews recent literature on the U.S. religious institutions and argues that a new paradigm is emerging in that field, the crux of which is that organized religion thrives in the United States in an open market system, an observation anomalous to the older paradigm's monopoly concept. The article has six sections: first, a brief survey of the paradigm crisis; second, a development of the concept of an open market in the historiography and sociology of U.S. religion; third, fourth, and fifth, arguments that U.S. religious institutions are constitutively pluralistic, structurally adaptable, and empowering, sixth, a consideration of recent religious individualism in the light of the new paradigm.
>
> (Warner, 1993)

The new paradigm characterizes esteemed *Sacred Canopy*-ist Peter Berger as the bogeyman. Berger's 'old paradigm', associated also with Talcott Parsons, among others, is said to have developed to describe 'the European experience', whereas the new paradigm draws from the unique character of American history. The short version is that religion is not best described as a property that applies to society as a whole, at least not to highly pluralistic American society, but as particular practices and ideas belonging to specific subcultures.

Religion in America is thus, by nature, distinctly pluralistic and competitive. A number of scholars like Finke, Starke and Iannaccone have developed elaborate market descriptions of American religion but, as Warner says himself, that is not the crux of the matter. The axis on which the new paradigm turns is an understanding of *disestablishment* as the central feature of American religion, a realization that pluralism and competition and even marketing are the norm, not deviations from a given, dominant culture that require elaborate explanation. In Warner's new paradigm, the master function of religion is the provision of 'social space for cultural pluralism' (p. 1058). Religion is infinitely structurally adaptive as it empowers both groups and the individuals within them.

Working within the new paradigm, 'students of religious communities and subcultures would focus more on the building of religious institutions and the role of religion in social mobilization, less on the erection and maintenance of plausibility structures'. They 'would focus as much on the rise of new religious organizations as on the decline of old ones'. Finally, they 'would investigate the ways in which religion alternatively facilitates and inhibits collective action, but would extend their time horizon for these processes to the span of a generation and complicate their models to include indirect effects of group solidarity' (Warner, 1993, p. 1081).

Warner's paper is by no means the last word on the subject, but it is a coherent discussion of the theoretical shift at work in the field and the bibliography is extensive. Although there is no call for 'congregational studies' per se, the injunction is to think locally, to recognize adaptability in organizations, and to forget older notions of 'norm' and 'deviancy'. Together these trends push towards a level of analysis where specific groups of people engaged in specific religious activities – congregations are the prime example – assume more importance and overarching structures receive relatively less. Books such as Nancy Ammerman *et al.*'s *Congregation and Community* (1997), Penny Becker's *Congregations in Conflict* (2000), and Nancy Eiesland's *A Particular Place* (2000) are all congregational studies that fall under the rubric of the new paradigm.

Organizational Ecology

A second theoretical trend in sociology – the study of organizational behaviour – also fuelled sociology of religion's interest in congregations. It would be unfair to say that organizational studies paced congregational studies. More likely that scholars with a developing interest in congregations saw advantages in borrowing arrows from the organizational studies quiver. As interest in congregations as organizations narrowed, terms like 'institutional isomorphism' and 'resource mobilization' began making their way over into the vocabulary of those whose primary interest was religion.

Perhaps most importantly, the emerging field of 'non-profit studies' began to blur over into the sociology of religion, and vice versa. Congregations were considered alongside those other institutions of civil society such as charities, social service groups and service fraternities. Congregations began, at least in some circles, to be seen as 'neighbourhood-based groups'.

Some of the most important names in this field are Paul Dimaggio, Carl Milofsky and Walter Powell. Powell edited *The Non-Profit Sector: A Research Handbook* (1987), which included Milofsky's 'Neighborhood-Based Organizations: A Market Analogy'. Here the idea took hold that a place – a neighbourhood – could be understood as an ecology of organizations. Congregations played an important role, but one that was dependent on other factors in the environment. Powell and Dimaggio's *The New Institutionalism in Organizational Analysis* (1991) was also influential.

One of the strongest links between the developing field of non-profit organizational analysis and the sociology of religion was through the Program on Non-Profit Organizations (PONPO) at Yale University. Dimaggio's paper 'The relevance of organization theory to the study of religion' (1992), written as a working paper for that group, provided a very direct link, as the title suggests. That linkage gelled in the publication of *Sacred Companies: Organizational Aspects of Religion and Religious Aspects of Organizations* (1998). In that book, Demerath *et al.* bring together organizational theorists like Dimaggio to challenge the notion that religious organizations and religious expression needed to be treated as unique:

> A common theme throughout this literature involves the singularity of the religious experience and the organizations that serve it. Rarely are other societal spheres or sectors invoked for congenial or instructive comparisons. For some, even admitting the presence of a secular dimension to the sacred experience is akin to profanation. Rather than treat religious organizations as sharing some basic characteristics with all organizations, there is a tendency to treat them more as the exception than as the rule . . .
>
> (p. vii)

While it is clear that congregational studies scholars such as Ammerman, Becker and Eiesland work in the new paradigm, in so far as they eschew the old paradigm juxtaposition of normative and deviant religious culture, is it equally clear that they are influenced by these developments in organizational studies. Ammerman's conclusion to *Congregation and Community* makes clear her debt to the field.

> The metaphor of ecology has been helpful here. . . . We can think about the community in which a congregation is lodged as an ecology of resources and organizations in which people seek out social support for everything from the most basic survival needs to sociability, aesthetic pleasure, meaning making, and community improvement. . . . We should pay attention, then, not so much to the decline of any given social organization but to the whole inventory of organizations and the available social capital that may lie dormant outside officially organized structures.
>
> (pp. 346–347)

Here one can see the competitive, interactive, particular notions embodied in the new paradigm and the importance of organizational analysis drawn together. The merger of these intellectual trends has helped to create the foundation on which the framework of congregational studies is built.

The Applied Stream

Congregational Management

America came to be defined by religious pluralism. As religion lost some of its institutional force vis-à-vis government and a dominant culture with the waning of the religious establishment, it looked to its roots in specific communities that shared ethnic, racial and other socio-demographic characteristics that strengthened their religious coherence.

Congregations, the truly local religious organizations where members shared all of those characteristics in the context of a common history, became central to 'lived' religion in America. These were the places where people actually worshipped. This was where they made friends or enemies, celebrated births and deaths.

Given the strength of pluralism's pull, Protestants were especially likely to switch denominational affiliations to find a congregation that suited them. (Catholics and Jews switched too, though were still somewhat more tied to parish boundaries or theological traditions.) If religion really was competitive, then congregations were the organizations that needed to market themselves in order to keep members and pay the bills.

Not to spoil the story, but such marketing to religious consumers is precisely what happened. Protestant congregations, both liberal and conservative, began to look to American business for models that would help them promote their strengths and appeal to the consumers most likely to constitute their target audience. Denominations still mattered because they offered some assurance by way of 'branding'. Episcopalians were most likely to be liberal, to be inclusive (including gays and lesbians), and to attend to ritual. Assemblies of God were likely to be biblically conservative but still to offer emotive charismatic experiences such as faith healing and speaking in tongues. Any particular congregation might not fit the mould, but they had reason to stay within accepted parameters or risk having their members switch brands.

Because supply nearly always rises to satisfy demand, there arose a great company of consultants to congregations. Conservative churches were most likely to judge their success or failure in terms of membership growth, since that was the most direct measurement of the degree to which they were spreading a true message and being rewarded by God for it. An entire field of evangelical consulting developed in the 1970s as the Church Growth Movement.

One of the central features of the Church Growth Movement was the Homogeneous Unit Principle (HUP). Conservatives had always been critics of ecumenical movements like the National and World Councils of Churches because those had been linked, for better or worse, both to biblical liberalism and to political liberalism, if not outright socialism, which the conservative churches demonized. Despite those concerns about liberal ecumenism, however, there was a nagging concern that the Gospel message called for inclusion, including racial inclusion, in an environment of universal brotherhood. At the very least, Christ's love extended to everyone.

HUP made clear that the most important thing was that people be led to an individual relationship with Christ. The most important thing was to get them there, even if that required catering to their imperfect predispositions. Men and women could be led to Christ, but in ways that were most comfortable for them, which is to say, with other people most like themselves. So the homogeneity of churches – by race, class, education and other measures – was portrayed as beneficial towards the end of individual salvation, even if such prejudice was ultimately a necessary evil measured against God's ideal. Better that we be separate now that we might be together one day in God's eternal kingdom.

As American society became ever more multicultural, HUP became an evangelical relic. The Church Growth Movement, however, continued apace. It is worth noting that today such movements are led by international figures such as Paul Cho of Korea as well as by American gurus such as Peter Wagner of Fuller Seminary.

Liberals, needless to say, did not ever embrace HUP, but they did engage in full-scale management consulting of their own kind. Members of these churches were, after all, the management classes of American life. Nothing made better sense to them than defining a mission statement, choosing direct, cooperative action – missions in the traditional sense – to carry out that mission statement, and research to identify and then to market to target audiences. They might not always have used such commerce-driven language, but they often came pretty close.

Two names closely associated with the rise of congregational consulting are Carl Dudley and Loren Mead. Dudley is an ordained minister and Alinsky-trained neighbourhood organizer dedicated to helping congregations find their appropriate social ministry. Mead is the Episcopal priest whose interest in applying business practices to ministry led to his founding of The Alban Institute, the USA's foremost consulting house for congregations, in 1974.

Dudley is perhaps best known for his attempts to make congregational studies relevant to social ministry. In the 1980s he spearheaded the Church and Community programme at Chicago's McCormick Theological Seminary, an ambitious attempt to stimulate church-based community organizing in several cities around the country. Among Dudley's many books are *Basic Steps Toward Community Ministry* (1991), *Energizing the Congregation* (with Sally Johnson, 1993) and *Where Have All Your People Gone?*, a Protestant wake-up call published at the forefront of the congregational studies boom in 1979.

Dudley was also a co-author of the original *Handbook for Congregational Studies* (1986). The co-authors of that volume, including Jackson Carroll and William McKinney, are congregational studies leaders who either work at or have passed through Hartford Seminary. The updated version, *Studying Congregations* (1998), involved many of the same authors, with Ammerman as the new lead editor.

Loren Mead's bibliography reads like something from an MBA course: *New Hope for Congregations* (1972), *The Once and Future Church* (1991), *Transforming Congregations for the Future* (1994a) and *More than Numbers* (1994b). He even produced a sequel, *Five Challenges for the Once and Future Church* (1996).

The books themselves, however, are less important than The Alban Institute, the large consulting organization Mead founded in 1974. Alban is the leading provider of congregational consulting, keeping a stable of experts on matters from church budgets and hiring pastors to dealing with crises. Seminary professors and church management experts like Speed Leas, another contributor to the *Congregational Studies Handbook*, are components of the Alban enterprise.

In the mid-1990s Mead stepped down from the presidency of Alban to pursue retirement as a consultant and author. He was replaced by James Wind, a programme officer at the Lilly Endowment whose area of specialization was helping congregations. Wind is co-author, with Jackson Carroll and Carl Dudley, of *Carriers of Faith: Lessons from Congregational Studies* (1991). He is also co-editor, with James Lewis of the Louisville Institute, of the two-volume collection *American Congregations* (1994), in many ways the best summary of congregational history and contemporary sociological interest in congregational studies.

In the late 1990s, the Alban Institute opened a branch office in Indianapolis, Indiana: The Indianapolis Center for Congregations. For the first time, a concerted effort was under way to bring all the benefits of years of congregational study and consulting to the churches of one mid-sized city. The grant made to start the Indianapolis Center was for more than the entire $3.5 million annual budget the Alban Institute had when Mead stepped down just a few years earlier.

Social Capital and Welfare Reform

Virtually everyone is now familiar with Robert Putnam's use of James Coleman's term 'social capital'. In America, where so much analysis begins, and occasionally ends, with de Tocqueville's observations concerning voluntary organizations, debating the community-building capacity of different organizations has become something of an obsession. Everyone wants to know where community comes from and how we can get some more. There seems to be widespread agreement that community is generated in small groups containing people who share common interests linked to race, social class, education, and so on. Their geographic proximity to one another still matters, but there is a widespread sense that it matters less than it once did.

It may seem artificial to label this interest in social capital 'applied' in a way that separates it from the organizational analysis labelled above as 'theoretical'. Much has been written about mediating institutions or about civil society that means to use theory to develop practice. Putnam himself stands in that breach. Peter Berger and Richard John Neuhaus have, in an earlier period, tried to bridge that same theoretical/applied divide (1977) from a more conservative angle, with their book on mediating institutions.

What is crucial about social capital from the point of view of congregational studies, however, is the degree to which congregations are now assumed to be places where community is created and nurtured. Not least because congregational studies scholars have touted the organizations' many benefits, others in American society now look to congregations as organizations capable of transforming lives and perhaps even transforming distressed communities.

A renewed interest in congregations helped fuel the turn towards 'faith-based organizations' that first arose in the Charitable Choice legislation of 1996 and is now embodied in President Bush's charge to the 'Armies of Compassion'. Many see in congregations the chance to deliver services or spur community economic development with the least complex bureaucracy. Moreover, some see a chance to instil positive values of moral character in those who need the most help conquering addictions, meeting familial obligations, and learning to assume responsibility for their lives.

This is not the place to debate the relative costs and benefits of such policies, but the place to see that faith-based reforms, as a style of thinking, are grounded in the intellectual impulse towards devolution. American government already had substantial and relatively successful partnerships with large religious organizations such as Catholic Charities and Jewish Federations. These new proposals are grounded in the recognition that Protestant churches, especially evangelical Protestant churches, and very especially black evangelical Protestant churches, no longer functioned well at that higher level of organization, if indeed they ever did. This is an acknowledgement that religious vitality and the ability to mobilize resources exist at the congregational level, and it is this strength that welfare reformers are trying to exploit.

The Funding Stream

Readers paying close attention may have already noticed that certain names seem to reappear regularly. While this may be a symptom of the author's limited bibliographic range, it doubtless also stems from the interconnected, if not exactly inbred, nature of the field in the USA. And nothing unified the field quite so much as the funding of Lilly Endowment, Inc., the most prominent funder of congregational research in American history.

Carl Dudley benefited from Endowment support from an early stage. The Church and Community project was paced by Endowment support and several of its initiatives were in Indianapolis, the Endowment's home. Hartford Seminary and the Hartford Institute for Religious Research, at one time home to both Dudley and Ammerman, was also a prime beneficiary of Endowment funds.

The project that produced Ammerman *et al.*'s book, *Congregation and Community*, was the brainchild of Peter Berger. It was fully funded by Lilly Endowment. Becker, Eiesland and I were supported by the Endowment as we worked on that project, which led to both of their dissertations being published as the books named above. The Endowment also supported the Yale Program on Non-Profit Organizations that produced *Sacred Companies*. The *Congregational Studies Handbook* received Lilly Endowment support as well.

Though the academic links are strong, and virtually every author or researcher named herein has received Lilly Endowment support at one time or another, Endowment funding for applied, practical work with congregations is stronger still. It was no surprise that when Loren Mead left Alban Institute, James Wind went from his job as a programme officer at Lilly Endowment to Alban as the new president. The new Alban initiative in Indianapolis, the Indianapolis Center for Congregations, has received several million dollars from Lilly Endowment, its sole sponsor. Wind's co-author on the *American Congregations* volumes, James Lewis, heads the Louisville Institute, a subsidiary organization wholly funded by Lilly Endowment for the purpose of making smaller grants to researchers working in applied fields surrounding religion. Many graduate students now benefit from one-year thesis-writing fellowships from Louisville Institute.

In 1999, the Religion Division of Lilly Endowment spent $104 million on the study of religion in America. It approved a further $88 million during that period. In 1998 it approved $89 million and spent $101 million. In 1997 it paid $66 million and approved $50 million. (Money approved in any given year may be paid out over the multiple years of any programme's life, making a direct year-to-year correlation impossible.)

These are very large sums, and although they are not all earmarked for the study of congregations or even the sociology of religion, they have shaped the field. Most of the research cited here has been either totally or substantially supported by the Lilly Endowment. Organizations like Alban Institute are now largely dependent on the Endowment, as are graduate students looking for dissertation-year stipends in the field.

But Lilly Endowment is clear – clearer just now than they have been for several years – that they do not fund research for its own sake. They spend their money in the interest of improving religious life in America and of building better organizations and institutions, especially in the churches of the old liberal establishment. Catholics came to be included in the past two decades, but the liberal, Protestant mainline still dominates Endowment thinking and its staff and board members are frequently drawn from those groups.

There is no need to imply that any other scholar's findings or judgement – including my own – is swayed by the Endowment's influence. But it would be folly to think that the research subjects chosen and the methods employed were not shaped by the Endowment's pragmatic approach, oriented as it is towards the goal of enhancing and improving American congregational life. Scholars and dissertation students are often keen to make sure that their research results in something that will be useful and beneficial for people of faith and their congregations.

Lilly Endowment is by any measure the largest funder of congregational studies, but there are other major funders as well. The Ford Foundation continues to pay for research into religion and society, though their goals generally lean towards more broadly public interests such as religion and social services or religion and politics. Pew Charitable Trust, however, spends several million dollars each year supporting direct study of religious groups themselves, with some of those funds directed into congregational studies. Understandably, however, most funders consider congregational studies 'covered' in the USA and look for specific niches where their funding can make a difference.

Of course, all of this money poured into understanding applied religious practice has had a knock-on effect for the whole academic marketplace. Most importantly, a number of PhD students found jobs in research centres doing this kind of work. Seminaries created jobs around the field of Religion and Society in ways that combine the older fields of social ethics and sociology of religion with more practical concerns about congregational management. The point is not that academics are 'selling out', because virtually everyone in the academy needs to make a living on terms they do not set unilaterally. The point is that young scholars with an interest in sociology of religion may take a longer second or third glance at the field of congregational studies, recognizing a market for applied skills that might buffer the consequences of a soft market for academic jobs.

Comparing the Environment for Congregational Studies in the United Kingdom

If the three streams suggested here correctly describe the US scene, it makes sense to compare the situation in the UK in order to predict whether congregational studies will develop in a similar fashion or to note where differences are likely to arise. The field is much smaller in the UK at present and current practitioners of the craft, including the authors of the present volume, are helping to determine where it is headed. Comparing developments in the theoretical stream is a little tricky because proponents of the new paradigm in America view older models as Eurocentric and see Britain as precisely the kind of place where they better apply. There can be little argument that Britain has an historical religious *establishment* and that America developed very consciously along an axis of religious *disestablishment*, despite the ad hoc formation of a mainline Protestant core there.

There is considerable religious pluralism in Britain today, along with relatively unfettered access to religious 'markets' and some competition. But the model of church and sect is roughly accurate, historically speaking, as are Wilson's theories of secularization. Many people may be 'spiritual', and that spirituality may be the thing most worth studying, but there is no way to ignore the decline of institutional religious authority. In so far as congregational studies in the USA has been spurred by the realization that pluralism and competition define the religious landscape, and have always done so, the cases are substantially dissimilar. In America, it would be short-sighted to look only at the decline of the mainline Protestant establishment. In Britain, it would be myopic not to see the decline of the Anglican communion as a central feature.

This is not to say that some conditions are not similar. British religious experience today, though a smaller part of the culture than in the USA, is pluralistic. There are good reasons to focus at least as much on the advent of new religious movements, and indeed on spiritualities that do not consider themselves religious at all, as on the decline of the established church. To the degree that the Anglican Church can simply be written off as bad debt, and opinions vary, it makes sense to focus on the pluralism of other religious experiences. And yet those stone churches dot every countryside panorama and anchor every tiny village.

It is clear that advancing organizational theory, including some application to religious organizations and other non-profits, is a transatlantic phenomenon. Margaret Harris's research, such as *Organising God's Work* (1998), is a good example, as it is of a piece with the work done by Dimaggio, Powell or Milofsky.

The question is not, then, whether the same kind of work being done on congregations in America can be done in the UK, because it can be and it is. The question is whether such work will matter as much because congregations simply matter less in the UK. There is a lively debate in the USA about what percentage of people attend worship weekly in America, with the two ends of the spectrum being about 25 per cent and 40 per cent. Religious adherence, membership in some faith community, steadily held just above 50 per cent for all of the twentieth century. Reasonable people can disagree about the rough percentages in the UK, but membership rates are well below 50 per cent and weekly attendance rates nearer to 10–15 per cent, when all faith traditions are combined.

Britain is home to many forms of individual spirituality that are not always expressed organizationally, but that is precisely the point. Studying religious expression – from Tai Chi to Quaker Buddhism to New Age phenomena – may matter a great deal. But studying religious *organizations*, even congregations, is a somewhat more esoteric interest in Britain than in the USA. One notable exception, and a place where congregational study may well advance social understanding in Britain, is the study of the congregations formed by recent immigrants and what that may teach us about multiculturalism in British society.

Such a discussion pushes rapidly towards a comparison of the applied stream. The debates about civil society occur in the UK too, but few are arguing that mediating institutions could or should play anywhere near the large role here that many see for them in the USA. The relationship between the state and civil society is always under negotiation, but the role of the state in the UK is much larger and the role of those other institutions, including religious ones, proportionally smaller. In America, these conversations always come back to de Tocqueville's fascination with the prominence of voluntary organizations, and the role of the state remains a hanging question. In the UK, the state is at the heart of the social story and the rest must be told in that context.

As for the management culture that institutionalized congregational consulting in the USA, there is nothing on anywhere near the same scale in the UK. Clearly the denominations do some of their own institutional research and do offer some organizational help, though this is relatively limited. There are a few evangelical programmes, often associated with very large, successful churches like Kensington Temple, designed to spur church growth and solidarity. But it is hard to imagine where the interest or money for sustained efforts in these fields might come from.

And money, as is so often the case, speaks loudly here as well. There is no Lilly Endowment pouring tens of millions of dollars into studying congregations for the sake of revitalizing them. There are not ten or a dozen dissertation fellowships offered each year to encourage young sociologists of religion to think specifically about the church's relationship to its social environment with an eye towards improving that relationship. There may be concerted, cooperative efforts to study religion and cultural interplay in cities, as there is in Birmingham, but they operate without multi-million-pound budgets.

The point is not, of course, that projects like the one in Birmingham may not prove more intellectually sound or fruitful than work done with millions of dollars in Indianapolis. Money does not guarantee intellectual quality by any stretch. But money does have an effect on the direction of future research and on the topics chosen both by established scholars and by their graduate students. In Britain, will congregational studies be a cottage industry of interest to a handful of theologians, sociologists, anthropologists, and perhaps students of non-profit management, or will it be a full-blown institution with research centres, dissertation fellowships and named professorships?

Conclusion

These comparative remarks are meant primarily to spark conversation. It may well be that a new kind of congregational studies field will evolve in the UK, fed by very different streams. Multicultural comparisons among congregations from different world religions have not driven the field in the USA, for instance, but could well do so in Britain.

But three overriding factors, two of which are beyond debate, make the contexts very different in ways we must remember. First, the USA has a much higher level of organizational religious participation and congregational membership. Congregations simply matter more to more people. Second, proportionately much greater resources have been poured into the study of congregations as religious organizations in the USA. Both the data and the incentive to exploit them are present. These two differences cannot be gainsaid.

The third difference is more open to discussion and debate, and may therefore prove the most crucial. It seems clear enough, though the deduction is not exactly seminal, that voluntary organizations in the UK play a much less important role in social life than in the USA precisely because the state plays a much larger role. A much higher proportion of social bonds, from welfare services to family life to education, are mitigated by the state rather than by other kinds of social organization.

If this is so, and especially if the social trajectory is inclined in this direction, then it seems unlikely that interest in congregations will ever be as strong in the UK because religious life is essentially peripheral to political or economic life, despite the more direct linkage between church and state. The role of the national state in the social organization of the USA has grown tremendously in the past several decades, but there is always a strong political current seeking to limit that growth and to emphasize other forms of social organization. Current debates about the role of congregations and other religious groups in welfare reform demonstrate that many Americans, probably most, are looking for ways to limit the state's reach and to promote other institutions of civil society, or at least to create mediating institutions that mitigate the state's power.

Many of those who study religion in the UK are critical of secularization theories like those advanced by Bryan Wilson or Steve Bruce. These critics of Wilson or Bruce, much like Steve Warner criticizing Peter Berger in the USA, see plenty of religious activity and much spirituality that has not been erased by the rise of rationalism or science. They cannot understand why Wilson and Bruce continue to focus on the church's decline when there is so much other spirituality to be studied in abundance.

Those spiritualities are interesting, to be sure, and the groups that cluster or congregate around them are worth describing and analysing. But the nagging question remains whether many of these are not still very individualistic pursuits, even if practised in clusters, with only limited and particular consequences. If, in the bigger picture, these spiritual activities are wholly incidental to the polity, to the marketplace, or even to the development of strong social bonds that create organizational social capital, then the impetus for studying them is more personal and the case for social utility is much weaker.

Intellectual pursuit need not be utilitarian and we are all free to study what we will to the extent that we can still find food and shelter. But the future of congregational studies as an academic field in Britain is likely to be determined not by whether it matters to those who practise it, but by whether it matters to anyone else.

References

Ammerman, N. T., with A. E. Farnsley *et al.* (1997), *Congregation and Community*, Rutgers, NJ: Rutgers University Press.

Ammerman, N. T. *et al.* (eds) (1998), *Studying Congregations: A New Handbook*, Nashville, TN: Abingdon Press.

Becker, P. E. (2000), *Congregations in Conflict: Cultural Models of Local Religious Life*, Cambridge and New York: Cambridge University Press.

Bellah, R., Madsen, R., Sullivan, W., Swidler, A. and Tipton, S. (1985), *Habits of the Heart: Individualism and Commitment in American Life*, Berkeley, CA: University of California Press.

Berger, P. and Neuhaus, R. J. (1977), *To Empower People: The Role of Mediating Structures in Public Policy*, Washington, DC: The American Enterprise Institute.

Chaves, M. (1994), 'Secularization as declining religious authority', *Social Forces*, 72 (3), 749–774.

Demerath, N. J., Hall, P. D., Schmitt, T. and Williams, R. (1998), *Sacred Companies: Organizational Aspects of Religion and Religious Aspects of Organizations*, New York and Oxford: Oxford University Press.

Dimaggio, P. (1992), 'The relevance of organization theory to the study of religion', Working Paper #174, Program on Non-Profit Organizations, Yale University.

Dudley, C. (1978), *Making the Small Church Effective*, Nashville, TN: Abingdon Press.

Dudley, C. (1979), *Where Have All Your People Gone?*, Cleveland, OH: Pilgrim Press.

Dudley, C. (1991), *Basic Steps Toward Community Ministry*, Bethesda, MD: The Alban Institute.

Dudley, C. *et al.* (1986), *Handbook for Congregational Studies*, Nashville, TN: Abingdon Press.

Dudley, C. and Johnson, S. (1993), *Energizing the Congregation: Images that Shape Your Church's Ministry*, Louisville, KY: Westminster/John Knox.

Eiesland, N. (2000), *A Particular Place: Urban Restructuring and Religious Ecology in a Southern Exurb*, New Brunswick, NJ: Rutgers University Press.

Harris, M. (1998), *Organising God's Work: Challenges for Churches and Synagogues*, London: Macmillan.

Mead, L. (1972) *New Hope for Congregations: A Project Test Patten Book in Parish Development*, New York: Seabury Press.

Mead, L. (1987), *Critical Moment of Ministry: The Change of Pastors*, Bethesda, MD: The Alban Institute.

Mead, L. (1991), *The Once and Future Church*, Bethesda, MD: The Alban Institute.

Mead, L. (1994a), *Transforming Congregations for the Future*, Bethesda, MD: The Alban Institute.

Mead, L. (1994b) *More than Numbers: The Ways Church Grow*, Washington, DC: The Alban Institute.

Mead, L. (1996), *Five Challenges for the Once and Future Church*, Bethesda, MD: The Alban Institute.

Mead, L. (1998), *Financial Meltdown in the Mainline*, Bethesda, MD: The Alban Institute.

Milofsky, C. (1995), 'Reinforcing social capital in small towns: a role for religious non-profits', prepared for Lilly Endowment Working Conference on Small Religious Non-Profits.

Pope, L. (1942), *Millhands and Preachers*, New Haven, CT: Yale University Press.

Powell, W. (ed.) (1987), *The Non-Profit Sector: A Research Handbook*, New Haven, CT: Yale University Press.

Powell, W. W. and Dimaggio, P. (eds) (1991), *The New Institutionalism in Organizational Analysis*, Chicago, IL: University of Chicago Press.

Putnam, R. (1995), 'Bowling alone: America's declining social capital', *Journal of Democracy*, 6, 65–78.

Warner, R. S. (1988), *New Wine in Old Wineskins: Evangelicals and Liberals in a Small-Town Church*, Berkeley: University of California Press.

Warner, R. S. (1993), 'Work in progress toward a new paradigm for the sociological study of religion in the United States', *American Journal of Sociology*, 98 (5), 1044–1093.

Wind, J. P. and Lewis, J. W. (1994), *American Congregations* (2 vols), Chicago, IL and London: University of Chicago Press.

Wind, J. P., Carroll, J. and Dudley, C. (1991), *Carriers of Faith: Lessons from Congregational Studies*, Louisville, KY: Westminster/John Knox Press.

Chapter 3

'Conference People': Congregational Studies in a Globalizing World

Simon Coleman

When I originally located the fieldwork for my PhD in two congregations in Sweden, the decision was informed by my training as an anthropologist. As I later came to realize, I was implicitly assuming that these congregations would be my 'tribes': self-contained units that I would somehow come to understand in the round. On entering 'the field' (otherwise known as Uppsala) in 1986, my intention was to examine the interrelations between two groups that appeared to be rivals: a long-standing Filadelfia (Pentecostal) congregation that had become part of the inner-city landscape; and a new, controversial Faith (Prosperity) ministry called the Word of Life (*Livets Ord*). Eventually, however, I wrote a different kind of PhD, one that mostly focused on the new ministry and its congregation as representing a 'deviant' organization in the context of supposedly secular, tolerant Sweden. Then, by the time I wrote the research up as a book (Coleman, 2000), my focus had again shifted, towards examining the ministry – increasingly a transnational missionizing force – in the context of social-scientific theories of globalization.

I mention these intellectual moves because of the admittedly crude trajectory they trace, from the 'tribal' to the global, from a well-defined field (bounded congregations) to a much more ambiguous set of reference points. In the preceding chapter, Arthur Farnsley notes that the rise of congregational studies, at least in the USA, can partly be attributed to a theoretical and intellectual movement away from grand theories and towards empirical studies. Thus, if the sociological trend he describes is towards examining the local and the small, the anthropological journey I have traced has moved in the other direction, using an initial study of 'the local' as a catalyst for reflections on wider theoretical and substantive concerns. I suspect that, in certain respects, Farnsley and I do indeed meet in the middle, but it is a centre-ground the ambiguous location of which reveals something of the dilemmas currently facing both congregations and congregational studies. Farnsley argues that recent interest in congregations relates in part to their potential role as creators – or measures – of levels of community organization. If such a role is evident, however, it usually depends upon the ability of such groups to adapt to contexts marked by voluntarism, pluralism, mobility and post-industrialization.

In this chapter, I shall be juxtaposing general reflections on congregations as organizational forms with specific accounts of particular churches and ministries. As an anthropologist, my initial instincts are 'situationist' and small-scale, to adapt phrases from Woodhead, Guest and Tusting's introduction, in other words to attempt to understand congregations by looking at how they interact with their local contexts (cf. Jenkins, 1999). However, part of my argument is going to be that, at least for some of the groupings I discuss, it is very difficult to assess what the primary context of reference actually is. Thus one of my interests is in what locality and community, and indeed mobility and globality, might mean to members of different congregations. An associated question asks how a globalizing world might shape the project of congregational studies.

To be sure, these are questions that resonate with social-scientific literature on religious organizations, but they have also emerged inductively from the fieldwork that I have carried out in the two Swedish congregations referred to above. They can be traced, for instance, in my own shift from studying the Word of Life largely in the context of its deviancy from Swedish society (or 'The Social Order' as the title of my PhD put it), towards understanding it as further connected with social imaginaries and networks that extend far beyond Sweden. They also lead me to the title of my chapter, 'Conference People'. This phrase was used in an interview by a Swedish Pentecostalist woman to characterize many of those people (some of them ostensibly Pentecostalist) who had 'gone over' to the Word of Life. It encapsulated a number of meanings (and much feeling) within just two words. It was intended to describe those believers who had abandoned their regular church and gone looking for powerful experiences in the mass contexts and transnational workshops regularly organized by the new charismatic ministry. On one level, the term 'conference' was implicitly contrasted with 'congregation' or 'church'. It was meant to be critical of people who were seemingly addicted to the excitement of one-off events that usually involved foreign, especially American, preachers. For a Pentecostalist to be criticizing the in-gathering of Christians for an apparently spontaneous experience of worship is rather remarkable, but the woman – and many others like her in her congregation – not only doubted the spontaneity displayed at Word of Life conferences, but also mistrusted its lack of rootedness in a local congregation. As we shall see, 'conference' in these terms can be seen as a metonym for ideological conflicts over the nature of religious belonging, and therefore not only a comment on the dynamics between two Swedish congregations but also a summary, in lay terms, of ambiguities over the meanings of affiliation and community that are equally evident in social-scientific studies of the contemporary role of congregations in the West. We shall reflect further on such ambiguities towards the end of this chapter, but in the next section I wish to preface my case studies by sketching some broad background to the recent study of conservative Protestant congregations.

Shifting Boundaries of Belonging and Believing

The social drama that was played out between the two Swedish congregations in the 1980s, and which to some extent has continued since then, can be seen as a deeply local matter, but it is also one that has wider resonances for the social-scientific study of 'conservative Protestant' congregations in other parts of the world. Scholars as well as nonconformist practitioners (and some who combine these two roles) have debated the significance of the constantly shifting boundaries among the various theological camps of fundamentalists, evangelicals, Pentecostalists and charismatics. Most writers are agreed on the continuing importance of the USA as an epicentre of much that has, and will, take place. For instance, in a recent survey of Pentecostals in Britain, Kay (2000, p. 88) traces the influence of American healing evangelists (Osborn, Roberts, and so on) in Britain in the early post-war period, and notes how such missionizing was given further impetus in the 1980s and 1990s by the easy movement of videos and tapes featuring Kenneth Hagin Sr, Kenneth Copeland and Morris Cerullo across national boundaries. Indeed, Hunter (1987, p. 8) argues, with some hyperbole but also a certain amount of plausibility, that trends within an increasingly diverse American evangelical constituency have important implications for like-minded believers on a global level.

Conservative Protestantism can also be seen as responding to broader sociological processes, such as secularization, privatization, individualization, pluralization and detraditionalization (cf. Becker, 1999, p. 7; for a survey, see Woodhead and Heelas, 2000). So-called 'conservatives' or proponents of 'old-time religion' appear to be surprisingly good at changing their theological spots and orientations to the world, and as a result they are certainly not going to fade away in the near future; indeed, new markets are being cultivated all the time. Furthermore, an important factor in the vitality of the 'movement' is its ability to 'globalize', to take advantage of modern technologies to spread the Word (Poewe, 1994; Coleman, 2000).

For my purposes, the important point is that conservative congregations can be shown to display many of the trends evident in wider social, cultural and technological realms. Thus, Carpenter (1997, p. 239) notes of the religious scene in the USA since the Second World War: 'Large Protestant denominations have been losing members, income, and influence while special-purpose, nondenominational religious agencies have grown, multiplied, and taken on increasing importance in shaping and carrying people's religious identity.' Personal mobility and the growth of the consumerist ethic have weakened ties to single denominations. Meanwhile, for Miller (1997, p. 129), in some churches personal conviction is increasingly valued over doctrine, an attitude that reflects new forms of voluntarism (Wuthnow, 1993; Hunt et al., 1997, p. 10).

One expression of these processes has been the growth of megachurches and parachurches in the USA and beyond. Literature, tapes and videos are circulated by larger ministries, which act like international corporations (Poewe, 1994, pp. 5–6). Numerous fellowships and networks have been set up as impermanent, flexible structures that can maintain a sense of constant flow and movement. For Carpenter (1997, p. 236), these trends reflect the kinetic popular culture and mobile lifestyles of the post-war era. More broadly, the emergence of megachurches can be seen as asking new questions about the relationship between 'community' and 'place', alongside offering multiple potential modes of attachment (Becker, 1999, p. 223; cf. Eiesland, 1997; Coleman, 2000).

Yet such developments, in themselves often intensifying rather than radically transforming activities of the past, have not necessarily expressed unfettered cosmopolitanism or a kind of spiritual Brownian motion on the part of religious consumers. Woodhead and Heelas (2000, p. 56) draw significant parallels between the work of Warner (1990), Roof (1978) and Ammerman (1997) in the sense that these authors stress the importance of strong local communities in American Christians' search for spiritual fulfilment. Warner (1990, pp. 292–296) refers to the 'elective parochialism' of many US churches, the affinities that appear to exist between, on the one hand, a religious affiliation that is chosen rather than given, and, on the other, a search for organic connections with locality. Thus a sense of belonging can be created that is adapted to mobile people seeking (temporary) roots (cf. Ammerman, 1997; Woodhead *et al.*, this volume). For Warner, 'localism' is not a matter of particular geographical attachments per se; it is more a state of mind. In the migratory contexts of the USA, congregations must not appear to constrain their members too much in social or cultural terms, but they need simultaneously to convey a sense of community. (Even megachurches maintain numerous smaller churches as their affiliates.)

These remarks about the significance of localism within the subcultural world of (at least American) evangelicals have some parallels with more theoretically wide-ranging analyses of the construction of place and community in contexts of globalization. Appadurai (1996), for instance, presents 'locality' in contexts of global cultural flow as 'constituted by a series of links between the sense of social immediacy, the technologies of interactivity, and the relativity of contexts' (1996, p. 178). Locality is both a matter of embodied sensibility and an appreciation that any single place must always be understood as relating to 'elsewhere'. Similarly, Lovell (1998, pp. 10–11) points to the performative aspects of religious activities in anchoring a sense of belonging and making it tangible through social practice, but adds that 'the local' is never quite what it seems, since transcendence of territory and mythologies of belonging can be maintained in dialectical relationship. And Poppi (1997, p. 285) stresses the links between localizing *strategies* and global concerns, with both 'locality' and 'difference' themselves becoming globalized as representations and social practices.

How might these arguments about attitudes to modernity, voluntarism and the ambiguous construction of locality play out in specific congregations? One way into this problem is to consider the similarities and differences between Sweden (my initial focus) and the USA as contexts for the articulation of conservative Protestantism. The USA is generally 'religious' if measured in terms of levels of practice as well as belief; in crude terms, Sweden is much more 'secular'. The USA is ethnically and religiously pluralist, with no established faith; Sweden encourages freedom of religion but its history of ethnic and religious pluralism is much shorter than that of the USA, and the former state church has only been disestablished for a few years. Perhaps the most interesting comparison is in terms of attitudes to mobility. Contemporary Sweden can hardly be said to be a country lacking either in internal migration to the larger cities or in emigration to other parts of the world. However, while American mobility within and beyond the country has regularly been linked to a sense of divine calling and global mission, the meanings of movement (and therefore also locality, with its concomitant ideology of localism) may be rather different for people living in a politically still relatively centralized, geographical periphery of Europe.

In the Uppsala congregations to which I have referred and to which I shall return in the next section, the idea of the local is certainly discussed by members. Within Swedish free church (nonconformist) circles, the notion of the 'local congregation' takes part of its meaning from the fact that it is a code word for the condition of autonomy and therefore lack of administrative or theological interference from a central organization. The idea of the independent fellowship has been a key point of principle for Pentecostalists in their attempts to maintain that, despite growing cultural respectability and increasingly ecumenical relations with other Christians, they are still a democratic and spirit-led movement rather than a bureaucratically driven and static organization. Meanwhile, despite growing evidence of ties between Scandinavian Health and Wealth groups (with the Word of Life at the centre of these networks), the independence of Faith congregations is still asserted, for the most part. I want to argue, however, that the Filadelfia and Faith congregations articulate distinct senses of locality in significant if often implicit ways. Just as the two groups present variations on Pentecostal themes of worship, so they give literal and metaphorical space to significantly different notions of belonging, community, temporality and place. We see played out within both congregations, but also and crucially in their ambivalent interrelations, minor versions of some of the major shifts that have occurred in Western conservative Protestant groups in recent decades. The lessons that we learn from them can be applied, with some modifications, to congregational debates in the UK and indeed beyond.

My approach has some parallels with that of Collins's piece in this volume (Chapter 7), since I trace the connections between locality and congregational narrative, with the latter understood not only as text but also as material form. What is fascinating about the Filadelfia and Faith cases, however, is not just their differences but also the fact of their uneasy affinities. Furthermore, we shall see how the embodied 'debates' between the groups resonate with political and cultural concerns that in Sweden have extended far beyond the micro-worlds of nonconformist congregations. Through commenting on the believer's body, the body of the congregation and indeed the body of Christ, believers from both groups present contrasting Christian perspectives on the tensions between movement and rootedness, event and locality, that are at the heart of their ambivalent affinities and oppositions.[1]

---

[1] Warner, in *New Wine in Old Wineskins* (1990), explores the tensions between congregational models by examining change over time (cf. Woodhead, Guest and Tusting, this volume), whereas I am contrasting two congregations in part by looking at how they conceptualize and deal with memory itself.

Between Filadelfia and Faith

Introduction

By the mid- to late 1980s, during the time of my first fieldwork, a number of long-standing members of the Filadelfia congregation had left to join the Word of Life Church; others were making open or sometimes clandestine visits to its services. Debates over the character of 'them over there' certainly occupied informal conversations, which would frequently be hushed or abruptly halted as members entered the precincts of the Pentecostal church. Some of the issues raised included questions about identity, local culture and belonging: were 'Word of Lifers' really Pentecostalist?; why were they so Americanized?; which members of the Pentecostal church were 'pro' the Word of Life and therefore might 'go over'?

Similar questions were occupying the minds of other Christians in Uppsala at the time, but they were particularly salient for members of Filadelfia. For one thing, services at the two groups looked relatively similar: both deployed a Pentecostal repertoire of simple praise songs, sermons, glossolalia and an attempt to capture spontaneity in worship. Although the Word of Life was clearly affiliated to the Faith/Health and Wealth Movement, its members spoke a language of revival and mission that was relatively familiar to Pentecostal ears. The very existence and success of the new group could therefore be seen as a form of self-rebuke: was God sending a new revival to Sweden because older revivalist forms had become too institutionalized and moribund? As one active member of the Pentecostal congregation put it to me: 'In our congregation we have had to discuss many of the difficult areas, which one can almost call splits. Quite a few of our members have gone over to . . . [silent pause] . . . and one wonders why. There must be something lacking in our congregation since people are going elsewhere.'

These losses often caused much pain to Pentecostal members (note the apparent unwillingness to name the Word of Life directly), since they indicated not a 'going home' to God at the end of one's life but rather an active decision to leave the older fellowship. References to the new group and its prosperity theology were sometimes presented in veiled language by Filadelfia's pastors during sermons, so that such semi-concealed allusions to it became part of a congregational restricted code that was decipherable by most members. Finally, at the end of a service in the late 1980s, the head pastor felt forced to make his position clear. With evident reluctance, he urged sympathizers of the new group to leave the Pentecostal congregation. However, even this act of boundary maintenance (compare Guest, this volume) could not produce the impression of a clean break: after the pastor spoke, an elder came to the pulpit to apologize for the fact that, speaking personally, he could not support the exclusion of his brothers and sisters in Christ.

In one sense, the tensions between these organizations can be explained quite simply. They were competing for the same market of Christians while deploying rather different variations on Pentecostalist and charismatic themes. However, I want to argue that the divisions went deeper than considerations of theology and size of membership. They revolved around different conceptions of place, movement and the very nature of belonging.[2] To explore such themes, we start by examining the buildings themselves.

Buildings in Place and Space

Uppsala is not the most obvious place in Sweden to found a Pentecostal or charismatic congregation. It is located far from the relative Pentecostal strongholds in the west of the country, and is a little removed from the concentration of population in Stockholm. However, the city is large by Swedish standards, with some 150,000 inhabitants, and has a mobile and influential population in the form of the students who attend its famous university. The centre of the city is dominated by the medieval castle and cathedral that indicate the past political significance of the city. On the other side of the river lie the commercial buildings, as well as most of the free congregations.

The Pentecostal church, which replaced an older one in the 1960s, is located in the hub of the city. It blends in quite well with the commercial and residential buildings surrounding it, with its grey-white walls and dark glass doors leading directly on to a busy street. Apart from a plain sanctuary, sufficient to hold hundreds of congregants at a time if necessary, there is a smaller side hall, a dining area and some offices. After the building had been constructed, a congregation newsletter noted that its excellent position in Uppsala should help it to become a refuge for people in spiritual need.[3] A couple of months later, another newsletter article stated that while the new church was larger than its predecessor, the congregation did not want it to be too large as it would therefore become uncomfortable for its users: the continued commitments to mission were balanced with the social needs of the fellowship.[4] These newsletters describing the church also made some symbolic play with its replacement of an older, crumbling edifice: now, a firm ground had been found for the congregation, reflecting the need for the church 'to be built on a rock'. In general, these sentiments about the building still seem to hold among present users. Although many of the members I spoke to saw the function of the building primarily as a 'spiritual home' and facilitator of *gemenskap* ('fellowship') alongside worship, they also appreciated its central location and potential ability to attract people through its doors in a low-key manner, often through the café or perhaps the bookshop attached to the side of the church. The church appeared to provide a measure of visibility within the city, but was also well integrated into the spaces and activities of daily life.

The Word of Life building, completed in 1987, shares the Filadelfia church's quality of plainness. Yet its location within Uppsala could hardly be more different (Coleman, 2000; Coleman and Collins, 2001). It is situated far from

---

[2] For a discussion of the connections between worship and congregational memory, see Stringer (1999).
[3] March–April 1967, vol. 6, p. 3.
[4] May–June 1964, vol. 3, p. 2.

the centre of Uppsala in an industrial park, and its massive size and glass and concrete surfaces fit in well with the surrounding warehouses. If the Pentecostal church was built within an urban context that clearly integrated the commercial, civic and leisure activities of Uppsala inhabitants, the Word of Life construction is placed firmly within a sector of the city that is dedicated to the temporal and spatial disciplines of industry. Alongside a sanctuary that can hold up to 5,000 people, there are offices, lecture halls, a television studio, a café and a shop. Adjacent are buildings to house the Word of Life schools and university. The ministry as a whole is thus peripheral to Uppsala but forms a kind of city in itself, providing the potential for virtually full-time engagement with fellow charismatics. However, to characterize its locale as constituting an introversionist or purely sectarian orientation to the world would be misleading. What is striking about the Word of Life complex is not just its size and multi-functionality but also its ability to accommodate flows of people through its numerous doors. The schools and Bible school are provided for international as well as Swedish users; the services are translated into various languages; whereas in its early days the group needed to hire sports halls to stage its international conferences featuring visiting star preachers on the faith circuit, it can now cope with these in its own premises. The 'centrality' of the site in Faith terms is constituted not by proximity to the centre of Uppsala's old town but by its orientation towards a much more consciously transnational realm of operations and influence. The places constructed by the group aid in the construction of a neo-Pentecostalist form of symbolic capital because they both facilitate and illustrate the presence of movement to and from the ministry, a constant flow that is taken to signify a revivalist mission which is expanding and therefore, in charismatic terms, 'living'.

The arrangement of the Word of Life's premises is highly relevant for an understanding of the group's congregational life. The group has some 2,000 active members in its congregation and is therefore perhaps twice the size of Filadelfia. However, any given service may well be attended by hundreds of 'outsiders', members of other churches in Uppsala or visitors from outside the city. Furthermore, the 'local' congregation is just one part of a wider set of operations that are oriented to the development of the ministry elsewhere in Sweden and, in particular, abroad. To provide a sense of how the congregation is depicted in these terms, here is a quotation from a review of the ministry's previous eight years of existence, published in 1991:[5]

> The Word of Life congregation is a 'mission congregation', like an airport, where planes fly off and land constantly. Very many people who experience a calling to journey out and preach or who are preparing themselves to go out to the mission field are present in the congregation.

Appropriately, the group (as is pointed out frequently in its literature) is indeed situated relatively close to Arlanda, Sweden's main international airport. In a

---

[5] *Word of Life Newsletter* 9, p. 2.

sense, the congregation is described here as being in a process of constant self-deconstruction, with its members supposedly not content to stay in one place. In practice, by far the majority of the congregation stay in Uppsala, but the point is that the symbology and the actuality of surrounding movement leach into representations of its functions. Certain parallels between Word of Life constructions of place and those surrounding the Toronto Blessing are also evident. As Richter (1997, p. 111) notes, the Canadian epicentre of the Blessing occupied a rather dismal industrial estate at the end of a runway of Pearson International Airport; yet the time–space compression of global mobility was apparently facilitated through a location that valorized flows of people and images, leading to a (rhetorical) disembedding of place that also, ironically, highlighted those spatial contexts which facilitated and attracted spiritual travellers.

The Word of Life complex gains significance because of the way it contests and transforms the locations of Swedish institutional life. For instance, the presence of the nursery and other schools on the site is something of a triumph for the group, since in the 1980s it had to fight long and hard with local and national inspectorates to be able to keep the nursery school open. In this sense, the ministry embodies an appropriation of the power to socialize its members' children, an act that takes on considerable significance in a country where almost all schooling is still state-run. More subtly, the numerous courses and indeed the university run by the group both parallel and compete with an educational institution that has long been a popular feature of Swedish civic life: participation in study circles (Stromberg, 1986, p. 30). Indeed, in its explicit affiliation with Oral Roberts University in the USA, the university points not to Swedish tradition but to a transnational alliance with charismatic forms of self-development. Difference from local context is marked out at the same time as similarity with 'elsewhere' is asserted, using the same symbolic means.

Pentecostalists whom I asked about the Word of Life ministry expressed a variety of opinions about its buildings, ranging from scorn for their apparent pretentiousness to admiration of the ambition they represented. The implicit contrast was with the homely fellowship of a Pentecostalist community.[6] However, from a Faith point of view a conference held in Uppsala derives power not only because of the opportunities it provides for healing, material prosperity and Bible study, but also because it involves the in-gathering of believers from many other places, building mobility and the transcendence of distance into the experience of worship. As Guest argues (this volume), an evangelizing church may be faced with the task of reconciling conservative ideology with the need to maintain a perpetual focus on outsiders, and on the promotion of flow from the outside. However, a charismatic or evangelical conference can mediate between the inside and outside because it brings in new

---

[6] And perhaps also with the idea of mission, as spreading salvation but also charity to others, often specifically through indigenous networks.

people, often from other parts of the world, who are nonetheless already saved and therefore 'safe' in terms of their support of the faith.

Bodies in Motion

The mobility and energy expressed by the physical landscape of the Word of Life is also evident in Faith uses of the body. Services at the ministry invoke the sense that explicit revival is happening all the time, rather than corresponding to the more annual pattern evident in classic Pentecostal churches in Sweden. The embodied performance of ritual expresses the urgency of the group's mission: tongues, for instance, are spoken not just occasionally (as is the case in the Pentecostalist congregation) but are employed in every service, by virtually all who are present, and are often enunciated in a very fast, almost gabbled tone. The contrast between Filadelfia and Faith bodily styles is most evident when members or supporters of the latter come to Pentecostal services, and signify through dancing, glossolalia or arm movements both their commitment to God and their support of the new group. When performed consciously, this is a semi-public declaration of affiliation, 'spoken' through a Pentecostal language of the body.

Mobility of worship is complemented by literal mobility of people. Pentecostal as well as Faith groups support missionary work, but in the latter group an office coordinates numerous opportunities to travel abroad not only for professional missionaries, but also for Bible students and even congregation members if they wish. Faith pastors are frequently depicted – in newsletters, sermons, even ordinary conversations – as on the move, travelling throughout and beyond Sweden in order to evangelize. Pastors and ordinary believers sometimes go together on semi-touristic journeys. Regular trips to the Holy Land are put on by a Word of Life travel agency specializing in what is, in effect, a Pentecostal form of pilgrimage (cf. Bowman, 1991).

A sense of movement is also cultivated through Faith uses of metaphor. If Faith worship is 'living', that of other groups – including at times the Pentecostalists – belongs to a 'graveyard'. Thus, a discourse of death is introduced as a means of criticizing others as arthritic and even immobile in their spirituality. The search for spiritual 'life' is of course shared rhetorically by Pentecostalists. Here, a middle-aged member of Filadelfia reflects on the emergence of the new group:

> And then came the Word of Life and you thought 'Oh great, now here comes a *living* group'. And then, there was . . . good in it in the beginning. But after some time and the years have gone by one has felt that it has not been entirely authentic [*äkta*] at times.

Thus, in this person's view, the signs of spiritual life are betrayed, rather than confirmed, by Faith means of embodying mobility. The suggestion that the Word of Life was not entirely genuine, indeed was too theatrical, was common in interviews and conversations with Pentecostalists. Part of the problem seemed to come from the specific characteristics of Prosperity thinking, which tends to emphasize the need to present a positive face in light of all circumstances. In addition, however, aggressive Faith styles of self-presentation were seen as too foreign, too Americanized. Explicitly local cultural characteristics were therefore perceived by Pentecostalists as relevant to genuine expressions of spirituality.

This is not to say that contemporary Pentecostal and Faith presentations of self and notions of body maintenance do not share some characteristics. Both, for instance, promote a general relaxation of the physical forms of self-control that had characterized earlier forms of nonconformity: coffee drinking, wearing make-up, even seeing the occasional James Bond film are permissible activities. Yet, even here, some differences prevail. The following remark comes from a middle-aged woman who is a prominent figure in the Pentecostal church: 'When I grew up one placed great weight on outer things; it was very important how one looked. You were meant to have long hair, a hat on your head.... Now...we look like normal people...and [can] witness through our *inner* characteristics.' This shift in congregational *habitus* presents in microcosm a more historical movement in Swedish Pentecostalism. The original emphasis on 'outer things' mentioned by the woman implied not a conventional form of materialism, but the unambiguous signification of a kind of anti-worldliness. In contrast, her description of contemporary styles of bodily presentation recalls transformed Pentecostalist attitudes to their church: a sense of 'witness' is always present, but need not be made overt in one's interactions with 'normal' life. Thus a blending into the bodily styles of the local community is (within reason) achieved. Faith discourse also stresses that 'witness' need not always come initially through explicit verbal challenge, but along with the emphasis on positive self-regard comes the notion that the body must be presented as neatly as possible. Faith adherents are not meant to wear a distinctive garb in the sense that a Hare Krishna devotee would; however, smartness is to be achieved at all times, often drawing on the classic Western indicators of mobility and conventional success: business suits, jackets and ties.

Charisma in the UK

In juxtaposing two Swedish congregations, I have tried to bring out their mutual differences but also the ways in which their strategies for constructing locality and movement take on particular meanings within the religious and political environment of Sweden (including, at times, *denying* the relevance of national context). However, my argument is also meant to have a comparative dimension, and my assumption is that the congregational narratives that I have been recounting have resonances elsewhere. Filadelfia is hardly the first well-established Pentecostal church to have had the spiritual ground taken from under its feet by more aggressive newcomers. Various waves of charismatic renewal have been felt in supposedly secularized Europe over the last few decades, and there is no reason to assume that they will ebb away in the near future. McBain and Hunt (1997, p. 46) note that, in the UK at least, there has been a certain amount of picking and choosing among believers and congregations, as they decide which aspects of a particular charismatic package most appeal to them at any given time, and the point made by these authors echoes the attitude of some Swedish Christians, who display an interest in being 'topped up' by the lively worship and media products available at the Word of Life, but do not see the need to commit themselves to joining it as members.

Space does not allow me to provide a full-scale comparison of my Swedish case study with the whole of the Pentecostalist and charismatic scene in the UK. I therefore focus instead on two recently published studies of Faith activity in England, and my basic question is the following: do these studies raise similar questions regarding transformations of locality and belonging to the ones that have been invoked in Uppsala?

Stephen Hunt's (2002) study of the Logos Church in 'Bordertown', a sprawling urban area of some 200,000 people located in the southern part of the country, displays certain very clear parallels with my own depiction of the Word of Life. The English congregation is one of the fastest-growing exponents of the Prosperity Gospel on a national level, with a membership that has grown to some 1,200 over a space of seven years. Its premises exhibit the bleakness but also some of the aspirational qualities of those of the Swedish group, since they have been converted from a former ice-rink in the central part of town and are situated in an urban area clearly in need of regeneration. The Logos Church's lack of social connection with its (relatively deserted) immediate environment is balanced by its participation in religious networks made up of comparable churches throughout the UK, while members may travel to the Sunday morning meetings in Bordertown from a radius of fifty miles or more.

Forms of mobility appear, therefore, to be built into the Logos *habitus* of expressing faith. The economic self-advancement implied by the valorization of a business ethic (in the context of a white, young, working-class and lower-middle-class membership)[7] is complemented not only by church-growth strategies, but also by other practices that avoid stasis at the level of individual commitment. Every six months, the church invites its members to sign up for an exclusively Christian Mediterranean cruise (there are echoes here of the Word of Life visits to the Holy Land). Its minister may attend conferences organized to showcase the visits of leading North American preachers. In addition, the trajectory of participation is flexible, with those attending the church often having just come from, or apparently being on their way to, affiliation with more mainstream congregations.

As in Sweden, such mobility is carried out against the background of a church and a movement that face scepticism and cultural resistance. In fact, Hunt argues that the Prosperity message cannot ultimately flourish in its 'pure' forms within a wider Christian population in the UK that patently dislikes the seeming vulgarity of certain forms of American worship styles. Middle-class

---

[7] Comprehensive data on the class make-up of the Word of Life congregation are not available, but seem likely to be close to lower-middle-class levels.

churches may be influenced by broader aspects of the enterprise culture, but are less likely to buy wholesale into the specific *subculture* of Health and Wealth. As a consequence, the Logos Church in Hunt's view remains rather parochial, aiming for expansion but accepting that it cannot cater for an international demand.

In this last observation, we have a clear contrast with the orientation displayed by Word of Life leaders and supporters. If anything, the Swedish religio-political context is less promising for the expression of Faith ideology than that of the UK: low levels of weekly religious practice, opposition from relatively centralized media, medical and political forces, and ambivalence towards perceived Americanization are evident to even greater extents (Coleman, 2000). Yet the ministry in Uppsala maintains an unabashed, self-consciously globalizing attitude in its internal worship styles as well as its missionizing practices. What is the reason for the differences in attitude between the congregations in Uppsala and Bordertown? One answer to this question may lie in the way the Word of Life congregation cannot be seen as entire unto itself. In other words, its activities are complemented, even at times permeated, by powerful influences from the group's Bible school and university, both of which bring in a temporary and inherently flowing population from Scandinavia and beyond. The mobility that is built into the spiritual and material landscape constructed by the Swedish group has explicit connections with a moving world beyond Sweden and even Europe; and such movement is inserted socially and metaphorically into the congregation. The latter is not only (or sometimes even explicitly) seen as a place of 'local community' in the conventional sense; rather, it ideally provides the means for those believers who happen to live in Uppsala to engage in projects that reach out into the world beyond. Indeed, since February 2002 the founder of the ministry and head pastor of the group, Ulf Ekman, has himself passed on the 'local' leadership of the congregation to his deputy, in order to focus on international work that is aimed at establishing fifteen new centres in strategic places around the world.

Thus Logos and the Word of Life construct locality in partially different ways, despite their common commitment to Faith ideology. Yet Hunt does more than focus on one church in his paper. He notes that the Health and Wealth Gospel has often been adopted by a growing, translocal movement of what he terms the 'New' black churches. Here, a powerful element of ethnicity is introduced into Faith expressions of religion that is almost entirely absent from the Swedish examples. Purely American-style Prosperity thinking is again eschewed, in favour of a self-help ethos that contributes to a kind of localized but also pan-West African diasporic identity. Those who participate in such churches almost seem to represent a new variety of Warner's elective parochials, since they are educated, middle-class Nigerians who have temporarily settled in the West in order to gain educational and professional qualifications. Here, the resources of globalization are used to reinvent and foster ethnic identity through congregational life.

While Hunt focuses on congregations, Nancy Schaefer's (2002) work has looked at specific aspects of the Faith-oriented conference culture evident among black immigrant churches of African Caribbean and African Pentecostalists. Her argument is that Morris Cerullo's 'Mission to London' revival meetings in the 1990s – supported predominantly by black congregations – created 'domestic space' for collective ethnic identity articulations at the same time as they incorporated a self-consciously transnational Prosperity ideology and practices. It seems that Cerullo was able to tailor his approach to a specific niche in the UK religious marketplace because of his own awareness and experience (as a well-travelled preacher) of worship in the places of 'origin' of many of the participants, especially the Caribbean. The free space thus created for ethnic identity articulations led to a celebration of 'community' not only at the level of the local congregation, but also in terms of a wider, diasporic celebration of black immigrant experience.

Hunt's and Schaefer's work illustrates some significant variations on the themes raised by the Word of Life. However, common to all is the desire to articulate a sense of religious affiliation – however loosely held – that can be justified in the face of mainstream scepticism, alongside an associated need to express congregational identities that acknowledge but also transcend immediate locality. 'Conference' and 'congregational' culture exist in an ambivalent alliance in these cases. The promotion of mobility on ritual and rhetorical levels allows (potentially transnational) flows to give 'life' back to 'locality' precisely by implying that, in the global economy of Faith, a 'here' always implies an 'elsewhere'.

Concluding Remarks

Clearly, all congregations are likely to become 'sites of memory' as they persist in place over time. However, we see how the Word of Life currently combats the implications of being ideologically bound by the past through deploying varieties of mobility – practices that rage against the dying of the revivalist light through ensuring, among other things, that a large number of those who are present in Uppsala at any given point are not likely to be there very long. Such an approach provides a particular variation on the church-growth rhetorics summarized by Woodhead, Guest and Tusting (this volume). Numbers of believers touched by the group remain important, as does the self-perception of constant increase in influence, but there is less of an emphasis on retaining such people within the official membership of the ministry and its congregation. Movement of people to new environments increases the ministry's global networks, reduces the risk of developing institutional arthritis and creates a sense of plugging into a constantly living revival. In contrast, other nonconformist congregations in Sweden have learned explicitly to accommodate themselves to their social and cultural surroundings, and such accommodations have been expressed in certain understandings of mortality. In Stromberg's (1986) study of the SMF (*Svenska Missionsförbundet*) Immanuel Church in Stockholm, death is exposed as a metaphor for a breakdown in local connectedness. By contrast, for the Word of Life, death is associated with the inability to transcend locality, so that images of mortality reflect broader developments in understandings of community and mobility.

The contrasts I have been exploring clearly have resonances with other social-scientific ways of describing congregational life. Becker's (1999) discussion of cultural models of local religious life contrasts a number of congregational means of emphasizing locality and community with so-called 'leader' orientations that emphasize activism at the expense of intimacy. While the Word of Life undoubtedly resembles the latter model, it is worth remembering that many of those who participate in its services explore other aspects of their spiritual lives in congregations where very different forms of sociality are valorized. A ministry such as the Word of Life gives the impression – to itself and to others – of converting huge masses of people 'for Christ', at home and abroad. In practice, and in common with much other apparent conservative Protestant expansion in the West, the ministry is profiting from 'transfer growth' (Kay, 2000, p. 38). Yet such growth need not necessarily even depend on people taking the active decision to join the group. At any given time, the services and products of the group are likely to be patronized by believers who come from elsewhere – from other congregations or even countries. In the Faith scheme of things, such lack of apparent commitment is actually a sign of spiritual health, an indication that it is attracting and promoting the global flow of people and products through transnational realms of faith. The result is a congregation that is located in Uppsala and yet gains much of its meaning from other contexts: either from the Bible school, media business and missionary organization that are also part of the Word of Life ministry, or from the connections set up with apparently similar Faith organizations abroad. In this sense, the Word of Life is setting up a subculture, the 'environment' of which reflects its national context (cf. Farnsley, this volume) but is not entirely confined by it.

If the Pentecostal and SMF congregations have established 'localities' of operation that reach into and therefore attempt to constitute local communities, this function is more muted in the Faith Church. Yet the logic of the Uppsala ministry, which encourages numerous forms of semi-detached participation, is that Christians can, if they wish, seek community in a more traditional church while they look for mobility in its services. Thus the concern for the breakdown of community that Woodhead, Guest and Tusting associate most closely with Bellah *et al.*'s *Habits of the Heart* (1985) is problematized here by the very lack of a perceived need to stick with one religious organization. Voluntarism and increased reflexivity in choice of spiritual experience (cf. Aldridge, 2000, p. 91) can allow for the creation of a spiritual division of labour in a believer's life. 'Conference' and 'community' can be balanced in some cases, possibly co-existing in uneasy tension. While the expression of translocalism is important in many Faith contexts, it can also ironically take on particular flavours according to context. In Sweden, situated on the periphery not of modernity but of global revival, the clear connections the Word of Life has established with global charismatic flows is an attraction for many Christians. Indeed, we should not assume that health and wealth are the only selling points for any given Prosperity ministry.

According to Woodhead and Heelas (2000, p. 485), those religious expressions that are likely to do well in the contemporary West are those that make room for senses of belonging alongside individual participation and self-expression. They are very probably correct. We must also remember that participation and belonging can refer to a range of contexts: some expressions of agency and engagement can be extended beyond geographical proximity into spheres of action that demonstrate difference from one's immediate culture, even as they assert 'close' connections with communities of believers whose value resides precisely in their distance from the self. As a result – whether we like it or not – Conference People are probably 'here' to stay.

References

Aldridge, A. (2000), *Religion in the Contemporary World: A Sociological Introduction*, Cambridge: Polity Press.

Ammerman, N. (1997), *Congregation and Community*, New Brunswick, NJ: Rutgers University Press.

Appadurai, A. (1996), *Modernity at Large: Cultural Dimensions of Globalization*, Minneapolis: University of Minnesota Press.

Becker, P. E. (1999), *Congregations in Conflict: Cultural Models of Local Religious Life*, Cambridge: Cambridge University Press.

Bellah, R. *et al.* (1985), *Habits of the Heart. Individualism and Commitment in American Life*, Berkeley, Los Angeles and London: University of California Press.

Bowman, G. (1991), 'Christian Ideology and the Image of a Holy Land: The Place of Jerusalem Pilgrimage in the Various Christianities', in Eade, J. and Sallnow, M. (eds), *Contesting the Sacred: The Anthropology of Christian Pilgrimage*, London: Routledge, pp. 98–121.

Carpenter, J. (1997), *Revive Us Again: The Reawakening of American Fundamentalism*, New York: Oxford University Press.

Coleman, S. (2000), *The Globalisation of Charismatic Christianity: Spreading the Gospel of Prosperity*, Cambridge: Cambridge University Press.

Coleman, S. and Collins, P. (2001), 'The Shape of Faith (Or, The Architectural Forms of the Religious Life)', paper presented at the BSA Sociology of Religion Study Group Conference, Plater College, Oxford.

Eiesland, N. (1997), 'Contending with a Giant: The Impact of a Megachurch on Exurban Religious Institutions', in Becker, P. E. and Eiesland, N. (eds), *Contemporary American Religion: An Ethnographic Reader*, Walnut Creek, CA: Alta Mira, pp. 191–219.

Hunt, S. (2002), 'The "Health and Wealth" Gospel in the UK: Variations on a Theme', *Culture and Religion* 3 (1), 89–104.

Hunt, S., Hamilton, M. and Walker, T. (eds) (1997), *Charismatic Christianity: Sociological Perspectives*, London: Macmillan.

Hunter, J. D. (1987), *Evangelicalism: The Coming Generation*, Chicago: University of Chicago Press.

Jenkins, T. (1999), *Religion in English Everyday Life*, Oxford: Berghahn.

Kay, W. (2000), *Pentecostals in Britain*, Carlisle: Paternoster Press.

Lovell, N. (ed.) (1998), *Locality and Belonging*, London: Routledge.

McBain, D. with Hunt, S. (1997), 'Mainstream Charismatics: Some Observations of Baptist Renewal', in Hunt, S., Hamilton, M. and Walter, T. (eds), *Charismatic Christianity: Sociological Perspectives*, London: Macmillan, pp. 43–59.

McDannell, C. (1995), *Material Christianity: Religion and Popular Culture in America*, New Haven: Yale University Press.

Miller, D. (1997), *Reinventing American Protestantism: Christianity in the New Millennium*, Berkeley: University of California Press.

Poewe, K. (ed.) (1994), *Charismatic Christianity as a Global Culture*, Columbia, SC: University of South Carolina Press.

Poppi, C. (1997) 'Wider Horizons with Larger Details: Subjectivity, Ethnicity and Globalization', in Scott, A. (ed.), *The Limits of Globalization: Cases and Arguments*, London: Routledge, pp. 284–305.

Richter, P. (1997), 'The Toronto Blessing: Charismatic Evangelical Global Warming', in Hunt, S., Hamilton, M. and Walter, T. (eds), *Charismatic Christianity*, London: Macmillan, pp. 97–119.

Roof, W. C. (1978), *Community and Commitment: Religious Plausibility in a Liberal Protestant Church*, New York: Elsevier.

Schaefer, N. (2002), 'Morris Cerullo's London Revivals as "Glocal" (neo-)Pentecostal Movement Events', *Culture and Religion*, 3 (1), 105–123.

Stringer, M. (1999), *On the Perception of Worship*, Birmingham: University of Birmingham.

Stromberg, P. (1986), *Symbols of Community: The Cultural System of a Swedish Church*, Tucson: University of Arizona Press.

Walker, A. (1997), 'Thoroughly Modern: Sociological Reflections on the Charismatic Movement from the End of the Twentieth Century', in Hunt, S., Hamilton, M. and Walter, T. (eds), *Charismatic Christianity: Sociological Perspectives*, London: Macmillan, pp. 17–42.

Warner, R. (1990), *New Wine in Old Wineskins: Evangelicals and Liberals in a Small-Town Church*, Berkeley: University of California Press.

Woodhead, L. and Heelas, P. (2000), *Religion in Modern Times: An Interpretive Anthology*, Oxford: Blackwell.

Wuthnow, R. (1993), *Christianity in the Twenty-First Century: Reflections on the Challenge Ahead*, Oxford: Oxford University Press.

PART TWO
CONGREGATIONS
IN THE UK

Chapter 4

The Effects of Evangelical Renewal on Mainstream Congregational Identities: A Welsh Case Study

Paul Chambers

Introduction

If the story of mainstream religion in England and Wales in the last century has generally been one of falling congregational numbers and declining member-ship, evangelicalism, it has been widely suggested, constitutes a significant (and successful) site of social and cultural resistance to the currents of seculariza-tion. The global explosion of evangelical Christianity is seen as proof positive of its power to generate new converts (Edwards, 1987; Martin, 2001). Nearer to home, the apparent success of the Alpha Course has received widespread publicity and captured the imagination of many religious professionals (Hunt, 2001). Statisticians of UK church growth and decline regularly suggest that evangelical churches constitute a success story in a receding sea of faith (Bible Society, 1997; Brierley, 2000), while some sociologists also see in evangelicalism the most likely future for organized religion in the UK (Bruce, 1995; 2002). In a nutshell, evangelical belief and practice appear to have become synonymous with effective recruitment and church-growth strategies.

There is no shortage of literature relating to church growth (McGraven and Wagner, 1990; Gill, 1994; Bible Society, 1997) or to the activities of evangelical congregations (Hunt *et al.*, 1997), but there is little or nothing written in a critical vein about the introduction of evangelical ideas and practices into mainstream congregations. For example, underlying much of the current widespread publicity and high-profile endorsements surrounding the Alpha Course is the uncritical assumption that 'one size fits all', even if the evidence on the ground suggests otherwise (Hunt, 2001). Empirical studies of congregational life remain thin on the ground, despite the fact that they offer the best means through which to critically approach these questions. This chapter seeks to redress this situation through a case study of a traditional working-class Anglican parish where, over a period of thirteen years, two successive evangelical incumbents sought to impose an evangelical ethos, with what might be considered less than positive outcomes for the congregations in question. The material is drawn from a three-year research project which examined diverse strategies for church growth in a Welsh city (Chambers, 2000) and builds theoretically on ideas developed in a previous set of congregational studies (Chambers, 1997). Particular emphasis will be placed on the social character of religion, including congregational identity, social networks and the surrounding social, economic and cultural conditions within which congregations operate.

Evangelicalism and Anglicanism in Wales

Historically, evangelicalism has been strong in Wales, and this was reflected in the series of popular religious revivals that characterized the development of Welsh Nonconformity in the eighteenth and nineteenth centuries (Jenkins, 1988; Lambert, 1988; Bebbington, 1999). However, the 1904 to 1905 Revival associated with Evan Roberts proved to be the high point of evangelicalism as a pervasive force in Welsh society (Morgan, 2001). In the conditions of secularization that progressively developed throughout the twentieth century, evangelicalism became something of a marginalized force within the Welsh religious economy as the main Nonconformist denominations liberalized and the Church of England in Wales underwent disestablishment, emerging as the Church in Wales in 1922 (Morgan, 2001). In particular, the profile of Anglican evangelicalism declined within a church that increasingly identified itself as Catholic, emphasizing the centrality of worship over the Word and an inclusive ministry oriented towards meeting the needs of the surrounding population. In a recent major survey of the Church in Wales (Harris and Startup, 1999), evangelicals were largely conspicuous by their absence, a situation markedly at variance with that of the Church of England. Elsewhere, contemporary evangelicalism in Wales presents a fragmented profile, with many competing indigenous and imported evangelical organizations claiming to represent the evangelical community (Chambers and Thompson, 2001). Despite this fragmentation and weakness, continuing decline within mainstream Non-conformity has led to a situation in which evangelical congregations now constitute a far more visible overall presence, not least because their rates of decline are much lower than their mainstream counterparts. The historic Nonconformist denominations are undoubtedly in a state of crisis. With a few isolated exceptions, Wesleyans and Congregationalists are staring at a total collapse of membership and attendance, and the situation is not much better among Presbyterians (Bible Society, 1997). As liberal Nonconformity withers, the profile of evangelicalism has become raised to the extent that 29 per cent of congregations in Wales now describe themselves as 'evangelical' (Bible Society, 1997, p. 24).

In the light of this, the authors of a recent nationwide report into the condition of religion in Wales unanimously concur with the view that evangelical churches represent the best defence against the creeping tide of secularization (Bible Society, 1997). While the data marshalled reveal impressive growth among certain evangelical congregations, it is also evident that not all are immune from the general numerical decline that characterizes most congregations in Wales. Furthermore, among the denominations it was the Church in Wales, liberal and inclusive in character, that actually recorded the highest levels of growth, something the authors have little to say about in constructive terms. Anglican congregations represent 30 per cent of Christian congregations in Wales and, out of a total of 1,521 Anglican congregations, 360 (24 per cent) were described as 'growing' (Bible Society, 1997, p. 41). In conditions of secularization this is no mean feat, and what is particularly interesting with church growth in the Anglican sector is that it is not, with a few isolated exceptions, informed by evangelical belief and practice.

This raises a number of interesting questions concerning strategies for the successful recruitment and retention of adherents. In terms of relations with surrounding communities, evangelical congregations can be said to operate with hard boundaries, exemplified by their insistence on personal conversion and separation from the world (Chambers, 1997). The centre of focus is the gathered congregation and, in a social and cultural environment characterized by widespread indifference towards organized religion, these groups potentially offer some defence against the tidal ebbing of faith. As Steve Bruce (2002) notes, the strongly bounded sectarian nature of these groups and an emphasis on religious socialization aids them in retaining the children of members, something with which their liberal counterparts have had rather less success. On the other hand, Bruce also notes that in terms of growth through the recruitment of those outside the congregation, this is primarily through transfers from other evangelical congregations rather than the unchurched, a process that has been described elsewhere by myself in some detail (Chambers, 2000). While both strategies undoubtedly lead to congregational growth, this hardly resonates with the current rhetoric of evangelicalism, which presents itself as somehow more relevant to the general population than its non-evangelical counterparts.

Conversely, the inclusive nature of traditional Anglicanism raises some interesting possibilities in terms of outreach into surrounding communities. Despite disestablishment, the Church in Wales continues to operate on the ground in much the same way that it always has (Harris and Startup, 1999). Based on a system of territorial organization into parishes, Anglicanism is necessarily inclusive, a moral community ministering to all, regardless of whether they are regular churchgoers or simply resident within the parish. The rationale underlying Anglican parish ministry is significantly different from that informing their Christian counterparts. Unlike the Free Churches, where a minister serves a congregation or congregations, Anglican clergy have a pastoral remit which covers both their congregation or congregations and the religiously unaligned general population who live in the parish. As such, Anglican congregations have what we might term 'soft boundaries'. Structured as they are along parish lines, they both operate as denominations for their members and, in a wider sense and particularly through the occasional offices – baptisms, weddings and funerals – as a religious resource for their relatively uncommitted surrounding populations. Both roles are exemplified by the parish priest, resident in the community and offering their services to anyone who desires them. Furthermore, in contrast to the evangelical model, stress is not laid on a dramatic personal conversion as a criterion for belonging, which makes it relatively easy for people to affiliate if they so desire (Gill, 1994).

While these soft boundaries operate to differentiate Anglican congregations from their surrounding human environments, by their very permeable nature, they create very few barriers between the people in the pews and the surrounding population. Bernice Martin (1992) develops this theme in both theological and sociological terms, suggesting that, sociologically, a distinctive aspect of Anglican congregational life is the way that it manifests itself in the mundane local networks of social relations and associational activities that constitute the interface between congregations and their local communities. For writers such as Gill and Martin, the genesis of religious sympathies and their subsequent realization are to be found in the networks of face-to-face relations as exemplified in the local life of a parish.

This then constitutes the ideal of parish-based associational life. The realities of parish life are often something else. While it is clear how parishes *should* operate in principle, what happens in practice may be rather different. Harris and Startup note that, in practice, many of the congregations they surveyed operated primarily in the interests of the regular congregation, with 'the effect of closing parishes in on themselves' (1999, p. 11). In part, this is due to the effects of secularization where surrounding populations make less use of the occasional offices. It also reflects the growing atomization and privatization of community life and the decline in public associational life, a factor that also effects evangelical congregations, who increasingly find themselves in the situation of preaching to the converted (Chambers, 2000). Nevertheless, despite markedly different ideologies and recruitment strategies, and notwithstanding the difficulties of operating in a highly secularized society, it is clear from the evidence contained in the 1995 Welsh Churches Survey that evangelicalism and Anglicanism constitute the most vibrant sectors of the Welsh religious economy. What is less clear is how these two ideologies, stripped of their rhetoric, work in practice and why evangelicalism should be privileged over other expressions of Christianity in terms of expectations of growth. Furthermore, in the light of the largely uncritical reception that has accompanied the Alpha phenomenon, it is also unclear what negative outcomes might result for non-evangelical congregations which adopt evangelical strategies for growth.

Religion in an Urban Environment

The parish of 'St John'[1] is situated in the dockside area of a major Welsh seaport. Historically, this was an area of heavy industry, although the city has struggled in the past thirty years to accommodate the economic, social and cultural changes which have accompanied the decline of local industries. To the east and north of the city centre lie the traditional areas of residence, characterized by nineteenth-century housing and predominately working-class

---

[1] The identity of both the parish and the individual churches within it have all been disguised in this chapter through the use of pseudonyms.

communities. To the west lie the suburbs, predominately post-war in provenance, middle class in character, and noticeably more prosperous. The post-war years were marked by a westward drift of the socially and geographically mobile to these western suburbs, creating a split along class lines between the expanding affluent west and the declining industrial areas (Rosser and Harris, 1965), a situation that persists today. Historically, religious belief and practice was central to the social, cultural and even economic life of Welsh working-class communities where chapel and church were important institutions (Lambert, 1988). This is reflected in the impressive numbers of places of worship (many now abandoned and derelict) to be found in the streets of these locales, mute witnesses to the effects of secularization. Archival and anecdotal evidence from the oldest inhabitants (see Chambers, 2000) paints a picture of communities where people worked together in traditional labour-intensive industries, lived together in the same warrens of streets surrounding the workplace and worshipped together in the local chapels and churches. Economic and structural changes have done much to undermine the solidarity of these communities, although the attitudes and values which underpinned community life are kept alive by the oldest inhabitants and their families.

These changes have left the local chapels and churches in a seriously weakened condition. This is particularly noticeable among the Free Churches, where congregations of a dozen (or fewer) elderly worshippers are not untypical. Anecdotal evidence from chapel leaders and long-term members suggests that post-war prosperity and the opening up of educational opportunities led to a westward drift to the suburbs of younger individuals and their families seeking to 'get out and get on'. This left congregations seriously depleted in numbers, struggling financially to pay their ministers, bereft of future lay leadership and ill equipped to face the future. Evangelical congregations were subjected to the same forces and, despite their best efforts, many have experienced the same outcomes, haemorrhaging members to the more fashionable congregations situated in the suburbs. Working-class Anglicans, in contrast to their Free Church counterparts who placed great store on education and individualism, were more likely to stay put in their communities of origin. Nevertheless, Anglican congregations were not immune from the effects of numerical decline, and this is reflected in the average age of congregations, which continued to creep upwards. The crucial difference is the continued presence of paid leadership. Funded centrally, this continued source of congregational leadership appears both to give direction to congregations and to help maintain local confidence in the future of their parish church.

Parish Life in a Working-class Locality

The parish of St John is not a prosperous area. The community numbers approximately 7,000 persons and census data suggest that on all indices – housing, health, environment, employment, crime and car ownership – local people are relatively disadvantaged compared to their counterparts elsewhere in the city. The demographic profile of the population indicates a higher than average number of retired persons and lone-parent families, while ethnically the population is predominately white. There are still many long-established families living in the area and these constitute a core of interconnecting and cross-cutting social networks which continue to underpin what remains of the area's community life. However, these 'local' people tend to emphasize the changes that have taken place in the last twenty years and point to the presence of a substantial proportion of incomers as being corrosive of community structures and 'neighbourliness'. The area now has many of the social issues – drugs, vandalism, theft, single-parent families – associated with any inner-city location.

There are ten active congregations in the area: three Anglican (all grouped in the one parish), one Roman Catholic, one Congregational, one United Reformed, one Baptist, one Presbyterian and a small independent evangelical mission. The high number of churches, in what is quite a small geographic area, is more a reflection of the past religious history of the region than an accurate indicator of current religious adherence. With the exception of the main Anglican congregation and the Roman Catholics, congregations are small, elderly and overwhelmingly female, with little short-term future. In what can only be described as an environment of general religious decline, the three Anglican churches in the area have maintained a continuing, visible presence in the community. The Anglican presence comprises the main parish church of St John, a congregation which has experienced significant numerical growth in recent years, and the smaller congregations of 'St James' and 'All Souls'. The first two lie in the heart of the community, while All Souls, originally forming part of a separate parish now defunct, looks down on the community from its vantage point on a large hill which overshadows the area. Two clergy, a vicar and curate, serve the parish. The overwhelming majority of the three congregations are working class, and 93 per cent of church members, many of whom are related, live locally.

All three congregations were established to meet the needs of new communities that had sprung up in the wake of industrial development. All Souls was established in 1842 to serve the surrounding community of copper workers. The closure of the works fifty years later, and the destruction of the houses surrounding the church, left All Souls without a role until the construction of a nearby private housing estate during the inter-war years. By this time, the original parish had ceased to exist and the remaining congregation has since been served by clergy from St John's, although numerically the congregation has been small. The original foundation of St John's was medieval, although the building was destroyed by coastal erosion. The present building was opened in 1888 at the same time as the nearby docks were established. The parish itself was incorporated in the same year, and St James was built and opened in 1920 as the local population expanded further. In the early years these churches were well attended and they contributed fully to the vibrant religious life of the community. However, the post-war decline of industry and the running down of the docks all put strains on the local churches and chapels, as local community life began to be eroded and families began to leave the area for the western suburbs.

While the Anglican congregations were not immune from these changes, this pattern of migration appears to have affected them less than their Free Church counterparts. Where families did move out, this tended to be to nearby local authority housing and was more an attempt to escape the very high levels of air pollution emanating from the docks and the very poor quality of local rented housing, rather than due to aspirations towards upward social mobility. Many families found life on the new estate unsettling, particularly the lack of those tight community structures that they had grown up with. The introduction of tighter environmental controls and the running down of the docks improved the air quality locally, and changes in the laws relating to rented housing, notably the 1965 Housing Act, saw many local landlords seeking to sell their houses. These three factors contributed to something of a return of local families, a process made easier by the numerous links through social networks. These links run along extended social networks, which also serve to connect congregation and church to the local community. With very few exceptions, members of the congregation are also members of local social networks based on kin, friends and neighbours. These networks intersect and cross-cut each other in turn. Older members, particularly, appear to know every detail of the family histories and current circumstances of all the long-established residents in the area. While the character of the area is changing, with many incomers not part of these networks, they remain important for those individuals whose family connections go back more than one generation. The ethos of family life is pervasive. Most mothers in the congregation still see their married children on a daily basis, not least because they often provide pre- or after-school care for their grandchildren. Even where grown-up children no longer attend church on a regular basis, grandmothers try to ensure that their grandchildren attend church and Sunday school weekly, and this often extends to taking the children of neighbours also. Their own children tend to attend on a very occasional basis and it is more likely to be daughters than sons who make the effort. Invariably, they do not appear on the electoral roll but still regard themselves as attached to the church.

In an area characterized by a low incidence of car ownership, much of the life of the community takes place on the streets, further facilitating contact with family, friends and neighbours. Front doors are always open and people visit each other's houses on a regular basis with little or no standing on ceremony. There is still much local community use of the occasional offices of weddings and funerals. These are always big events, and even where the participants concerned are ostensibly 'unchurched', there is usually a family connection to the church, often through current members of the congregation. There is a thriving mother and toddler group, and educational and recreational activities centred on the parish hall are popular locally; again, this creates opportunities for interaction, lessening the distance between members and the local population.

In terms of a distinctive congregational identity, the two most striking elements are conservatism and continuity. The values and attitudes of the overwhelming majority of the congregation are both socially and theologically conservative, with a dislike of innovation for innovation's sake. Members identify with what might be termed a 'low Catholic' or 'middle of the road' position and great emphasis is placed on the right order of things, particularly with respect to the consecration of the elements and strict adherence to prayer book worship and conventional Anglican theology. The high proportion of congregational members living locally and with long-standing intra-genera-tional family connections is also reflected in a strong sense of local tradition and a staunch loyalty to their parish church and to each other. In particular, these long-standing family connections (many stretching back to the very early twentieth century and beyond) have led to a strong sense of 'ownership' of the church on the part of its members. There is also the factor of a more universal Anglican identity underpinning and running like a thread through the life of the church. The parish, through activities such as the Mothers' Union, has regular contact with other parishes in the city. This allows people both to identify with and tap into wider Anglican networks and to affirm a broader, more abstract identity based upon the inclusive principles of Anglicanism.

All these values, attitudes and qualities were to be tested to the limit during the period 1980 to 1993, a period of innovation when evangelical incomers came to control the life of the congregation, challenging the traditional foundations on which congregational life and identity had been based. This period was not a happy one for most long-term members and, in the light of the current high profile of innovations such as Alpha, it raises significant questions about the wisdom of imposing 'quick-fix' church-growth strategies on traditional congregations.

An Evangelical Sea Change

By 1980, although the local Anglican churches were significantly outperform-ing their local Free Church counterparts in terms of numbers, the number of Easter communicants had fallen to 117 persons, a figure half that of those who had been present in 1966. In the same year, in a departure from tradition, the parish gained the first of two successive evangelical incumbents, in an experiment which was to split the congregation, alienate the church from its local population and seriously test the traditional foundations of congrega-tional identity. By 1993, and largely as a result of this experiment, the number of Easter communicants had fallen to 61 persons. During the following three years of interregnum and the eventual appointment of a new priest, returning members and new recruits accounted for a 77 per cent rise in Easter communicants, who numbered 108 persons in 1996. Clearly, given the trajectory of these figures, something had gone amiss in the intervening years of the evangelical ascendancy.

Initially, in terms of church growth, there were new recruits, as word got out on the evangelical grapevine. A handful of disaffected Anglican evangelicals from other non-evangelical parishes in the city began to attend services at St John's, with eight individuals eventually settling into membership. At the same time, attendances by local people began to fall as the character of the church changed. Individuals within the congregation found themselves increasingly alienated both by liturgical innovation along evangelical lines and what they perceived to be a shift away from a traditional, inclusive Anglican ethos.

Among both those who returned in 1993 and those who stayed despite their reservations, a number of common concerns relating to the 1980s emerged. The state of buildings in the parish was seriously neglected by the incumbent clergy as they adopted what they termed a 'people first' policy. In practice, this eventually led to the parish hall becoming semi-derelict and a danger to users. Consequently, local community groups were forced to use other premises, while members perceived this as part and parcel of a clergy-led attempt to separate the congregation from the local community. While it was highly unlikely that this was the motivation behind this neglect, the clergy certainly appeared to fail to realize the central place that the parish hall had in local community life and the attachment that the community had to these buildings. By neglecting the buildings, local feeling was that the Church was both neglecting the people of the local community and undermining what had formerly been an inclusive congregational identity. For the parishioners, despite the rhetoric of 'people first', it appeared that the then clergy had little or no insight into the local working-class culture and the importance of family and friendship networks in and outside of the Church. The clergy began to scale down their pastoral activities as their energies were directed elsewhere towards parish renewal strategies, and the small but deeply committed congregation of St James, which had vigorously resisted liturgical change, began to see the neglect of their own building as a group metaphor for the neglect of their congregation.

Disquiet about liturgical change was widespread in all three congregations. Members were deeply unhappy about the often ad hoc nature of worship and deviations from established Anglican liturgical practices, particularly the use of unlicensed preachers. The introduction of charismatically orientated healing services and the sight of individuals being 'slain in the spirit' and speaking in tongues were profoundly disquieting to long-term members. Local women also complained that Sunday services were overlong, with no fixed closing time. One long-term member, echoing the comments of many others, remarked 'You would be sitting there thinking about the joint in the oven burning, and just *praying* for him to finish. He didn't *care*, he used to laugh about it when we said!' This observation, while apparently trivial, emphasized the deep cultural divide between the then clergy and the local community. Sunday lunch is seen locally as an important time when all the family get together. Married children bring their families to see 'Mam' and 'Dad' and the occasion is seen as more than a shared meal. What might have seemed a very trivial point, housewives worried about the condition of their joint in the oven, was, in the climate of increasing mistrust, seen as an attack on the family values that underpin the traditional social life of the area.

The unsettling effect of middle-class incomers within the congregation was further exacerbated as they were quickly given key roles within the administration of the parish. Suddenly, local members and church officers (and even the organist), who had faithfully served the congregation for years, found themselves replaced by evangelical 'outsiders', further eroding the sense of local ownership of the churches and further raising internal tensions. People progressively voted with their feet, and eventually only the most committed members remained. One long-term member who chose to stay at the time said, 'You just had to tough it out sometimes, the important thing was to remain faithful in your attendance.' Another couple commented that they 'had seen vicars come and go', the important thing from their perspective being that the congregation needed to 'remain constant' in their traditional faith and practice. Some did choose to 'tough it out', and one positive outcome of this period of uncertainty was the reinforcement of a strong sense of solidarity and corporate identity among the remaining local members.

Eventually, while the main parish church would be packed with visiting evangelicals for regular series of renewal days, the local members of the congregation were conspicuous by their total absence at these services. Although innovations like these renewal days were putting the parish on the map alongside other evangelical churches, they were looking increasingly threadbare as a strategy for local evangelism. Towards the end of this period the frustrations felt by the then clergy, about what they saw as lack of local support for them and their endeavours, came through clearly in the editorials in the parish magazine. In these, the blame for the failure to recruit and the decline of the congregation is laid squarely with the remaining congregation. Inevitably, there was a parting of the ways, and under a new incumbent the life of the parish re-emerged.

This incumbent, working class and not an evangelical, summarized his immediate efforts as 'giving confidence back to the people'. Traditional liturgical forms were reintroduced with the wholehearted support of the congregation. The ruinous state of buildings was successfully addressed. Links with the local population were re-established, and not only did the people return but there was even a modest number of new recruits, all living locally. Most importantly, local people could again re-appropriate ownership of their church, reconstituting groups and activities that had fallen into abeyance in previous years, and this is reflected in an active social life which reaches out into the community. As far as the evangelical incomers were concerned, most left the congregation immediately, although three remained, and they continue to contribute in various low-key ways to the life of the congregation. Remarkably, given the past upheavals, there is little residual rancour among locals and the remaining evangelicals have been fully accepted into the life of the congregation. In part this is because their decision to stay has been interpreted as a vote of confidence in the congregation and the local community. Furthermore, now that outsiders no longer control all aspects of church government, their current contributions to the life of the congregation can be better appreciated by all members. This has resulted in a growing mutual respect, although in one sense clearly demarcated boundaries remain.

Conclusions

In retrospect, it is clear that in this case, the project to renew the life of a parish through the imposition of an evangelical identity on a traditional mainstream congregation must be adjudged a failure in terms of church growth. This failure was informed by a number of factors. The evangelical emphasis on individualism failed to resonate with a long-standing communitarian congregational identity. Incumbents failed either to understand or empathize with the surrounding working-class population and its culture, or the place of the parish church and its buildings in the life of the community. In terms of recruitment strategies, there was little or no attempt to evangelize the local population, despite the presence of a complex cross-cutting net of localized social relations, ideally suited for this purpose. This failure to recognize the potential of social networks for church growth, what is now known as 'friendship evangelism', is particularly telling, given that this has been proven as an effective recruitment strategy (Bible Society, 1997, p. 30; Chambers, 1997, p. 149).

From the perspective of the congregation, their church was in danger of being taken away from them, while at the same time the clergy were distancing the church from the local community. In these circumstances, the congregation found it increasingly difficult to reconcile what was happening within their parish with their own understandings of Anglican identity and the inclusive ethos of parish life. Furthermore, they felt that the clergy and their supporters viewed them as 'second-class' Christians and that this was reflected in a lack of consultation over the direction the three congregations were being taken in. While the parish church was being packed with occasional visitors, most of the regular congregation were allowed to drift away, while at the same time the distance between the clergy and their supporters and the remaining congregation was allowed to grow. As far as local people were concerned, parish 'renewal', if it meant anything, appeared to be synonymous with running down the parish and not building it up. Given that it is unlikely that this was the intention of either incumbent, it is ironic that the policies that they set in motion had precisely the opposite effect to the one they intended.

Martin Percy invites us to view evangelicalism as an ideology that is primarily concerned with power and certainty. Dialogue is discouraged if it threatens to lead to compromise, different viewpoints are rarely tolerated and a commitment to orthodoxy is seen as more important than a commitment to unity (Percy, 1996, pp. 162–164). Within the context of this case study, one could be forgiven for coming to the conclusion that its leaders saw the established congregation as expendable if it continued to fail to take on board an evangelical vision for the future. Whatever the motives of the then leadership, it is also clear that local people had their own expectations of what their church should be. In this case study, the innate conservatism of the congregation, coupled with a strong identity forged over a long period of time, frustrated clergy attempts to bring innovation into the life of the church. In the same way, this strong sense of identity, solidaristic but inclusive and quintessentially Anglican, held the congregation together during a difficult period and contributed to the subsequent return of local people to the congregation.

Carr *et al.* (1992) suggest that 'ownership' is not a question of ideology, but a matter of the heart, informed by history and tradition and, above all, a sense of belonging. Traditionally, the style of Anglican ministry is 'interpretative'; that is, it should 'seek to interpret people's experiences of life in relation to God' as realized within a parochial context (Carr *et al.*, 1992, pp. 16–17). In a highly secularized environment where clergy vocations are falling and new ordinands are increasingly also evangelicals, this understanding of parochial ministry is being challenged by very different ministerial models. While these under-standings are perfectly appropriate within other contexts, traditionally, parish ministry is necessarily predicated upon a degree of openness towards the expectations of congregations, and a recognition that it remains for many people in the surrounding population 'an institution towards which they look' (Carr *et al.*, 1992, pp. 50–51). This case study graphically illustrates the negative consequences for one traditional parish when this vision was lost.

References

Bebbington, D. W. (1999), *Evangelicalism in Modern Britain: A History from the 1730s to the 1980s*, London: Routledge.

Bible Society (1997), *Challenge to Change: Results of the 1995 Welsh Churches Survey*, Swindon: Bible Society.

Brierley, P. (2000), *The Tide is Running Out: What the English Church Attendance Survey Reveals*, London: Christian Research.

Bruce, S. (1995), *Religion in Modern Britain*, Oxford: Oxford University Press.

Bruce, S. (2002), *God is Dead: Secularization in the West*, Oxford: Blackwell.

Carr, W. *et al.* (1992), *Say One for Me: The Church of England in the Next Decade*, London: SPCK.

Chambers, P. (1997), ' "On or Off the Bus": Identity, Belonging and Schism. A Case Study of a Neo-Pentecostal House Church', in Hunt, S., Hamilton, M. and Walter, T. (eds), *Charismatic Christianity: Sociological Perspectives*, Basingstoke: Macmillan, pp. 140–159.

Chambers, P. (2000), 'Factors in Church Growth and Decline', unpublished PhD thesis, University of Wales.

Chambers, P. and Thompson, A. (2001), 'Public Religion and Political Change in Wales', paper presented at University of Wales, Bangor, 20 December.

Edwards, D. L. (1987), *The Futures of Christianity*, London: Hodder and Stoughton.

Gill, R. (1994), *A Vision For Growth*, London: SPCK.

Harris, C. and Startup, R. (1999), *The Church in Wales: The Sociology of a Traditional Institution*, Cardiff: University of Wales Press.

Hunt, S. (2001), *Anyone For Alpha? Evangelism in a Post Christian Society*, London: Darton, Longman and Todd.

Hunt, S., Hamilton, M. and Walter, T. (eds) (1997), *Charismatic Christianity: Sociological Perspectives*, Basingstoke: Macmillan.

Jenkins, G. H. (1988), 'The New Enthusiasts', in Herbert, T. and Jones, G. E. (eds), *The Remaking of Wales in the Eighteenth Century*, Cardiff: University of Wales Press.

Lambert, W. R. (1988), 'Some Working-Class Attitudes Towards Organised Religion in Nineteenth-Century Wales', in Parsons, G. (ed.), *Religion in Victorian Britain: Interpretations*, Manchester: Manchester University Press.

Martin, B. (1992), 'Church and Culture', in Carr, W. (ed.), *Say One For Me: The Church of England in the Next Decade*, London: SPCK.

Martin, D. (2001), *Pentecostalism: The World Their Parish*, Oxford: Blackwell.

McGraven, D. A. and Wagner, C. P. (1990), *Understanding Church Growth*, Grand Rapids, MI Eerdmans.

Morgan, D. D. (2001), *The Span of the Cross*, Cardiff: University of Wales Press.

Percy, M. (1996), *Words, Wonders and Power: Understanding Contemporary Christian Fundamentalism and Revivalism*, London: SPCK.

Rosser, C. and Harris, C. (1965), *The Family and Social Change: A Study of Family and Kinship in a South Wales Town*, London: Routledge.

Chapter 5

'Friendship, Fellowship and Acceptance': The Public Discourse of a Thriving Evangelical Congregation

Mathew Guest

Introduction

According to the 'welcome cards' distributed to newcomers, the Anglican church of St Michael-le-Belfrey, York[1] is

> ... a fellowship of Christian believers who believe seriously in the life-changing power of God's mercy and truth. We are a church where you can experience friendship, fellowship and acceptance as we grow together in our love and commitment to Jesus Christ.

The language used here is telling: it reflects the church's location in the evangelical tradition, while affirming a place for the relational and for power typical of the charismatic renewal movement. The fact that the church prints 'welcome cards' which are freely and deliberately distributed among interested visitors at Sunday services is also indicative of its passion for evangelism. A shared hope is that newcomers will convert and make their own commitment to Jesus. A further key emphasis is the notion of community – expressed here in the idea of 'fellowship'. Members of the church enjoy a sense of collective unity and mutual care, which they invite newcomers to share upon entering into fellowship with the congregation.

The text of the 'welcome card' raises another issue. Aside from enjoying a common experience of friendship, acceptance and spiritual growth, what does it mean to be a member of St Michael's? What do the congregants share that they see as legitimizing their place in the fellowship? Recent studies of evangelical churches have re-affirmed a long-standing emphasis upon theological correctness, usually grounded in scriptural authority and moral precept. Evangelical Christians express their identity and, in turn, recognize the

---

[1] This chapter is a development of research conducted as part of a doctoral thesis (Guest, 2002). As the identity of the church in question was given in that thesis – with the permission of the church leadership – and is therefore in the public realm, it is also given here.

identity of others, in terms of clear and exacting demands (Kelley, 1972). While 'commitment to Jesus' is mentioned on the welcome card, the leadership of St Michael's has chosen not to set alongside this a related set of expectations usually seen as central to a confession of faith by contemporary evangelical believers. There is no mention of judgement, for example, of scripture, of 'sound teaching' or even of salvation.

Commentators may dismiss this as a sign of astute marketing. Being ever more aware of their minority stake in a secular context, evangelical churches have become sensitive to the features of their message which are most offensive or off-putting to outsiders (Hunter, 1987). They 'soften' evangelism so as to stress positive affirmation and evade negative judgement. But if this is indicative of how the expression of belief is negotiated in relation to context and audience, this is a process that extends beyond Sunday welcome cards, and beyond the particulars of mission strategy. Indeed, the life of this congregation is shaped by a sensitivity to both the prejudices of outsiders *and* the tensions and diversity of its internal membership. While driven by the demands of evangelism, St Michael's has taken on these demands as requisite strategies for coping with its distinctive congregation. In this respect I proceed from the assumption that congregational identity is forged out of a negotiation of community boundaries (Cohen, 1985; Dowie, 2002). In the terms used in Chapter 1 of this volume, my approach is that of an 'intrinsic' study with contextualizing concerns, seeking to understand this congregation as a site for the negotiation of historical and cultural pressures (Briers, 1993; Stromberg, 1986).

This chapter draws from an extensive period of ethnographic fieldwork among the congregation of St Michael-le-Belfrey, conducted over twelve months during 1999–2000. Immersed participant observation over seven months was augmented by a series of semi-structured interviews with leaders and congregants. Shortly afterwards, I administered a detailed questionnaire survey of the congregation, charting attitudinal trends and patterns in participation. My initial aim was to explore degrees and patterns of accommodation to secular modernity within a shared evangelical worldview, as expressed in public meetings and group discourse. Research eventually exposed complex processes of negotiation, whereby shared values were forged and expressed in light of changing contexts and in dialogue with shared histories. This chapter explores these processes, focusing on how the distinctive history and constituency of the St Michael's congregation has generated a particular set of tensions, and on how the congregation has developed particular ways of dealing with them, notably through its public discourse. As a preface to this, it will be useful to trace the recent history of St Michael's in order to show how the pressures the congregation currently faces emerge from its achieved status as a centre of evangelical success.

Thriving on the Margins: The Case of St Michael-le-Belfrey

According to Al Dowie, '[Congregations] do not exist apart from their particularity, which in certain respects is like that of all others, like some others, and like no other congregation' (Dowie, 2002, p. 65). While it exists firmly within the English evangelical Anglican tradition, and follows patterns of development seen elsewhere, it is often difficult not to treat St Michael-le-Belfrey as a unique case. It is tempting to regard the church as an epicentre of evangelical activity, the axial point from which innovations emanate – like ripples in a pond – into other churches across the country, churches which are keen to imitate their successful cousin. After all, St Michael's is known for having achieved what most English evangelical churches only dream of: exponential growth, a thriving tradition of worship, Christian drama and creative outreach, and a lasting fame that attracts evangelical pilgrims from across the nation and beyond, either as doting visitors or as newly committed members. Its pedigree status is also bound up in the figure of the late David Watson, who led the church as its minister from the mid-1960s until 1982. His numerous books and missions – which attracted a global audience – secure his place on the map of evangelical history. In turn, and by association, St Michael's has gained celebrity status, becoming well known as the site on which Watson put his radical teachings on discipleship, community and evangelism into concrete practice (see Saunders and Sansom, 1992; Watson, 1981, 1983).

While a part of the Church of England, St Michael's has been a thoroughgoing evangelical concern since David Watson's arrival. Since then it has followed a particular course of development, generally characterized by an increasing willingness to engage more positively with things outside of the evangelical world. This trend, driven by a passion for evangelism, has caused the shared outlook of the church to become gradually more inclusive, and in some respects more liberal. In this respect, it is worth citing H. Richard Niebuhr's famous argument that, as religious groups grow, they experience a transition from sect into denomination, the latter characterized by a greater accommodation to external forces. Niebuhr (1962) isolates three main pressures which drive this process: younger generations become less committed as they inherit rather than choose religious identity; increasing wealth and status makes worldly accommodation more likely; and the necessary development of a more formal leadership and organizational structure 'subverts the initial radical impetus' (Bruce, 2002, p. 24).

This pattern of development may, with some qualification, be mapped onto the history of St Michael-le-Belfrey. A moribund church was revitalized by a charismatic leader who attracted many new members. He introduced a charismatic evangelical model of faith and encouraged strong community ties which may be characterized as quasi-sectarian. (In the 1970s, for example, a number of church members committed to living communally, in what were known as 'households', and were supported by a common purse in order to free individuals for their ministry in the church.) Teaching was conservative and stressed the absolute authority of scripture. Participation was regular and extended outside Sunday worship, and the congregation was close-knit and interdependent. Subsequent years have seen a greater influx of middle-class congregants, a high turnover of members and several changes in leadership. St Michael's has increasingly engaged in dialogue with external agencies:

ecumenical initiatives, university links, local social aid projects and creative evangelism. The 1980s marked a peak in what members refer to as a great spiritual diversity, described by one former leader as a 'cord made of many strands': charismatic spirituality, the contemplative tradition, evangelical Bible teaching and social justice. Invoking a conception well entrenched among the congregation, she went on to comment that alone, each strand is weak, but bound together as a cord, they provide the elements necessary for a healthy church. Moreover, this eclectic vision of evangelical mission was complemented by an ethic of delegation which recognized and fostered the diverse gifts of the fellowship. The deep-seated entrenchment of this 'broad' vision – centred on eclecticism and lay empowerment – was made apparent when a more narrowly defined agenda was championed by new leadership in the early 1990s. When a fresh incumbent introduced reforms which prioritized the performance of charismatic gifts, re-centralized leadership structures, and marginalized women, this provoked dissonance throughout the congregation. However, recent developments suggest something of a return to a 'broad' agenda comparable to that which was dominant in the 1980s. This set the tone of congregational life around the time of my fieldwork; the affable presence of the recently appointed vicar was interpreted in terms of a return to things lost. The new incumbent was returning, according to one member, 'to a much more open approach to different spiritualities . . . while being very strongly in the evangelical charismatic [tradition] . . . '.

At the time of fieldwork, there was evidence that this 'broad' vision of evangelical spirituality was both embraced and understood by many within the fellowship. According to one of the lay preachers, one could explain the persistent popularity of St Michael's with reference to four factors: the sense of love and acceptance in the place, the contemporaneousness of its worship, good teaching, and its inclusivity, expressed most vividly in its attempts to be culturally relevant. However, while many favoured this 'open', inclusive vision, some criticized it as a capitulation to liberal trends in wider British culture, lamenting a loss of focus and yearning for a more directive leadership. One member even suggested that St Michael's is no longer a truly evangelical church, preferring to see it as 'liberal charismatic'. While internal views may be placed along a spectrum in between these two extremes, both are premised on an observation of the same trends in current congregational life: a pervasive return to a vision of Christianity characterized as broad, open and inclusive. And while the use of these words may be ambiguous, their positive invocation in an evangelical context signals both significant change and intentional accommodation.

The peculiar history of St Michael's has, in part, shaped its present congregational constituency. For example, David Watson was apparently attracted to St Michael's because its location within the York city centre – busy and popular with tourists – has obvious advantages for evangelism. However, because of this geographical peculiarity, it has no parish as such, at least not one that is home to its committed membership. In the year 2000, there were 365 people on the church electoral roll, but only 6 of them lived within the parish boundaries. In this sense the congregation is a 'gathered' one, embodying a distinction between 'membership' and locality.

The fact of geographical dispersion is also reflected in survey data, which suggested that only 21 per cent of the present congregation live in the city centre, with nearly 18 per cent living more than five miles away. One of the clergy claimed that regular congregants travel from within a 20-mile radius of the church building, and the address list reflects this, listing residents of Malton, Selby and Harrogate. Moreover, geographical dispersion is matched by a high turnover. Over 10 per cent of the congregation have been regularly attending for less than twelve months, and another 24 per cent have attended for less than five years. Many congregants are newcomers to the area, whose jobs may also take them on to new locations in the not so distant future. Effective university links also ensure a constant flow of undergraduate attendees, who make up 30 per cent of the regular congregational body. Unsurprisingly, geographical mobility is matched and driven by economic advantage, the current congregation being disproportionately middle class. Many of the 700 or so listed on the church address list work in the service professions as managers, teachers or civil servants, and, according to survey data, a massive 70 per cent have either passed through or are currently engaged in higher education.

St Michael's appears to incorporate a high proportion (perhaps 40 or 50 per cent if one includes students) of what some sociologists have called 'elective parochials', those who forge temporary community attachments by affiliating themselves to local institutions, such as the church. American sociologists have argued that this mode of affiliation is a consequence of social uprootedness and increased social and geographical mobility (Tipton, 1982; Warner, 1988). In the UK, it has emerged alongside the growth of the 'megachurches', which are popular among middle-class evangelicals who are mobile and whose local allegiance is often a temporary one (Hunt, 1997). The most significant consequence of this arrangement within St Michael's concerns an attenuation of commitment. Many congregants are unable or unwilling to engage in church involvement that makes demands on time outside of Sunday worship. Others restrict their membership to a part-time, partial or occasional basis (for example, 24 per cent of the congregation claim regularly to attend another church in addition to St Michael's). The entire picture is one of a church which continues to affirm the importance of radical Christian commitment – of the practically demanding nature of Christian living – but which only appears to elicit such high levels of commitment within its own structures among a limited segment of its membership. The problem was identified by one of the St Michael's clergy interviewed during my fieldwork:

St Michael's is a great place. There is a lot going for it. But, it isn't what you might call a real...church...because we have an eclectic congregation. It comes in, it listens to what it wants to listen [to], it puts into practice what it wants to put into practice, and the rest is thrown out. Because, we don't see one another from week to week. We meet on a Sunday, have a great time, and then we go into our worlds, and we meet again on Sunday. Don't we have community?

If a sense of unity within St Michael's is compromised because of its scale and because of the demography of its congregation, this is also not helped by a significant diversity of belief among congregants themselves. The 'diversity of spirituality' celebrated in the 1980s has persisted in a diversity of faith perspectives among its membership. For example, while many would identify themselves as 'evangelical', there is no clear consensus on what this term might mean. For some it signifies a style of Christianity that is thoroughly Bible-centred, obedient to the truth of scripture and uncompromising on biblical moral precepts. Others affirm a passion for the texts, but a more creative approach to their interpretation, some emphasizing inclusivism over more traditionalist ethics, mirrored in a focus upon Jesus over Paul. Some more cynical parishioners latch onto these as negative features, 'evangelical' being used as a pejorative label for a pushy or unreasonably narrow kind of Christianity. There is also a disparity between members who embrace a charismatic worldview, and those who view such things with suspicion, preferring to rely on scripture rather than on what they see as personal sentiment. In this way the notion of being 'evangelical' incorporates personal and collective meanings, positive and negative associations, all shaped by past experiences and present concerns. It is very much a 'contested' term (Baumann, 1996), its meanings open to question and challenge from within the congregation itself. Put another way, while the congregation is united by a common set of symbolic boundaries, members relate differentially to the symbolic resources available to them (Cohen, 1985).

To summarize thus far, we may shed light on the accommodating strategy expressed on the church welcome cards by referring to two related factors. First, an inclusive vision of evangelical identity is built into the history of the church itself, and has been recently revived as a focus of celebration in popular memory. Second, the current demography of the congregation suggests a lack of stability, causing leaders to maintain a persistent focus upon flow from the outside, upon levels of attendance and comparative levels of enthusiasm. The first instance points to an accommodation to established internal expectations, the second to an acclimatization to predicted tensions at the margins of the church fellowship. But if this accommodating strategy is a shaping feature of congregational life, how does it feed back into expressions of congregational identity? Insights into this process can be gained by examining the public discourse of the congregation: its identity as expressed in communal and public gatherings.

The Negotiation of Boundaries Through Public Discourse

Partly inspired by Michel Foucault's (1977, 1984) seminal work on power, some recent studies of evangelicalism have focused on 'discourse' as a shaping constituent of the evangelical worldview (Boone, 1989; Brown, 2001). My own concern is more specific, and the discourse I am referring to approximates to what Penny Becker has called the identity of a community publicly symbolized (Becker, 1999, p. 90). Expressed each week in the St Michael's Sunday services, the public discourse of the congregation amounts to the entirety of its public self-presentation. It serves as a kind of mirror in which the congregation also sees itself and through which it forges a collective self-image. Echoing Peter Collins's chapter in this volume (Chapter 7), I am in this sense interested in the narratives which the congregation both produces and tells itself. This is an especially important source of identity here because of the scale of St Michael's; while organizationally complex, Sunday services are the only context in which large segments of the congregation gather for a common experience. While discernible in prayer, prophecy and other forms of public address, this discourse is most clearly expressed in Sunday sermons, which I take as an illustrative example. My key observation may be summarized in the claim that *St Michael's is held together by a discourse which accommodates its various schools of belief while also controlling public utterance so that conflict is avoided.*

During fieldwork, I listened to forty-nine sermons at St Michael's, delivered by various preachers at the morning, family and evening services each Sunday. I took detailed notes on each of them, either during or after the event, and many were also made available to me as cassette recordings. Although they purported to focus on numerous topics – sometimes dictated by the readings suggested in the Church of England's *Common Lectionary* – subsequent analysis has revealed a tendency to focus on certain issues on a regular basis, and with the same key emphases. Central to the majority of sermons were three main areas of concern: universal sin, conversionism and the reformed Christian life. I take these in turn.

First, there was a continual emphasis upon a vision of humankind that was both uniform and thoroughly negative. As the vicar preached on one occasion, humans are basically all the same and are typified by misery and a tendency to fail. Attending Sunday services, I was repeatedly struck by the emphasis upon the inevitability of sin and wretchedness, which was stressed in in-house versions of the liturgical confession as well as by preachers and in prayer. This stress on the negativity of mankind is a natural accompaniment to substitutionary atonement, which is its theological resolution. It is because we are fallen that we need to be saved. But the stress on sin and confession extended beyond the logic of shared theologies. It also fostered what Stephen Warner has called a 'culture of public humbling', that is, a readiness to express a mutual neediness which opens the way for religious exchange and mutual support within the fellowship (Warner, 1988, pp. 293–294). This sense of humility was repeatedly stressed by the vicar, whose claims to being a normal 'sinner' were an effective levelling device, his parishioners often remarking on how reassured they felt that he was as imperfect as they were.

Second, sermons were ridden with a repeated call to faith and to repentance, emphasizing the need for parishioners to base their lives 'entirely on Jesus' and to accept and embrace the Holy Spirit. In David Bebbington's terms, there was an overwhelming focus upon conversionism (Bebbington, 1989). This was rather curious in one respect, as sermons often evoked the style of a revivalist altar call rather than an ongoing body of teaching, steered towards the nurturing of an established parish community. However, it may be the case that preachers were responding to the demography of the congregation, outlined in the previous section. It is possible that 'elective parochials' and visitors were kept firmly in mind, so that preaching retained an evangelistic urgency. If this is the case, then it is significant that the needs of one cohort were clearly prioritized and used to frame the public discourse as a whole. Moreover, this appeared to be a norm which was accepted without protest by the congregation. Congregants seemed perfectly happy to hear the same message of faith and repentance each week, and while this may be explained with reference to the emotive draw of sung worship and charismatic gifts, many attendees also shared a common commitment to the importance of foregrounding conversionist motifs on a weekly basis, for the benefit of passing visitors.

Invoking a call to convert and turn to Christ, sermons also addressed the practical consequences of identity change: the reformed Christian life. This formed a large part of public teaching, and preachers always found room to emphasize the importance of prayer, financial giving, reaching out to the needy, embracing charismatic gifts and developing our God-given gifts. What was striking about their presentation was the imprecise way in which they were dealt with. For example, one morning sermon was concluded with a call for us all to embrace the Holy Spirit in our lives. The preacher then went on to say that he was not going to define what this meant, but that we should put this idea into practice ourselves and find out that way. The common teaching on financial giving was that, although important, it was not a 'Gospel issue' and should be left up to the conscience of the individual. In the words of Peter Stromberg, who encountered a similar phenomenon at Immanuel Church in Stockholm, teaching was characterized by 'an impassioned plea to act without saying what to do' (Stromberg, 1986, p. 47). In sum, while congregants were implored to follow a devoted, Spirit-filled life of prayer, sacrifice and neighbourly love, preachers left these ideas in such a vague and malleable form that they could easily be moulded to fit the existing everyday lives of the average member. From this angle, a radical challenge can amount to mild accommodation.

Foucault makes the claim that discourses are interesting not only for their content, but also for what they exclude from public utterance (Foucault, 1984). Similarly, sermons in St Michael's may be analysed not only in terms of what they cover but also in terms of what they avoid or fail to comment upon. One notable omission from sermons – and from all public discourse in fact – was moral teaching. This was especially striking, considering the usual emphasis that evangelical churches place upon correct Christian living and ethical integrity. Of all forty-nine sermons analysed, I found only three clear references to moral issues that also offered a clear judgement upon them. Other references were largely incorporated into narratives communicating a different message, so that, for example, issues such as abortion were mentioned but left without moral comment. On other occasions, a sense of moral prescription was implied, but not concretized, as in one preacher's comment that the Bible is a good source of reproof and correction, as well as guidance. What he failed to point out were the actions identified in the Bible as worthy of reproof. More emphasis was placed throughout on positive qualities like love, care and responsibility. On the rare occasions when a preacher isolated particular qualities as morally wrong, the solution suggested was not behavioural reform as such, but an openness to the Holy Spirit in the same vague vein discussed earlier. In short, sermons were characterized by both an evasion of moral issues and by a tendency to avoid offering specific moral prescriptions and sanctions. As with teachings on the 'Christian life', advice was more often than not vague, malleable and open to interpretation.

The lack of clear moral instruction within the public discourse of St Michael's is especially curious as, according to survey data, individual members express highly conservative views on personal moral conduct, especially on sexual morality. According to questionnaire returns, 81 per cent think that homosexual relations between consenting adults are 'always wrong', while the figures are 90 per cent for adultery and 73 per cent for premarital sex. Sixty-seven per cent feel the same about drinking to excess, and 64 per cent about the use of profanity. Moreover, the overwhelming majority also feel that the church *should* speak out on moral issues, ranging from issues of personal conduct to national politics. What we are faced with is a separation of public and private discourses, the first characterized by a general tolerance and the second by a rather strict moral economy. Furthermore, the fact that 76 per cent of the congregation also claim that St Michael's Sunday sermons adequately cover moral teaching suggests that parishioners are, on the whole, satisfied with this arrangement. One explanation of this would be that such moral teaching is so well entrenched among the congregation that there is no perceived need for it to be taught. However, the fact that preachers clearly cater to 'elective parochials' (most clearly evident in the 'altar call' style of preaching, described earlier) suggests that they feel a need to repeatedly address core aspects of the faith life.

I would rather argue that the reason moral judgement and prescription are avoided relates to the need to accommodate the liberal diversity that is recognized as existing within the congregation. Public discourses have been shaped around the perceived attitudes and composition of the St Michael's membership. This is a sustainable arrangement because of the long-standing set of preachers who are well acquainted with church members. For example, while the church has had four incumbents and numerous attached ministers over the last thirty years, all of the lay preachers are long-standing members, some appointed as elders during the late 1960s and 1970s. It could be argued that they very much steer the style and tone of public teaching, in response to congregational needs and, for the most part, informed by a broad vision of evangelicalism associated with the heyday of the late 1970s and early 1980s.

There appears to be a collective requirement for a shared public discourse which underplays issues likely to provoke conflict or divide the congregation. In practice, of course, this means that certain concerns are effectively privatized, as there is no room for their expression in the public realm. Indeed, in some respects the very subject of personal belief is ushered into the private realm, something at least suggested by the church's reluctance to issue a collective statement of belief. Any public statements of the church's identity –

such as the welcome card 'blurb' quoted at the beginning of this chapter – are notable for their inclusive and affirmative tone. While ethnographic study revealed areas of conservatism, such convictions were notable for their expression within private or small group contexts, such as questionnaire returns or closed conversations among friends.

But if a privatization trend is evident, then it is a selective one, forcing some issues into the private sphere while locating others in public discourse. Investigation of the shared values of the congregation, drawing from a variety of sources, revealed a curious pattern. Public teaching presents itself as a mixture of hard, traditionalist doctrine and soft, ambiguous or non-judgemental commentary that hints at a more tolerant outlook. Public discourse avoids moral issues, affirms a generalized, undefined picture of the faith life, and retains an emphasis on accommodating to diversity within the group. But it also stresses sin, the moral depravity of secular modernity, and the radical difference between those inside and those outside of the faith. Conversely, privately expressed convictions downplay notions of hell and punishment for non-Christians, and suggest unease with strong boundaries between the saved and unsaved. At the same time, they reflect a thoroughly conservative take on moral issues, especially on sexual matters (see Figure 5.1).

SCRIPTURE AS FOUNDATIONAL AUTHORITY
(Drawn from according to context)

Private Discourses	**Public Discourses**
Ambiguous anthropology	Conservative anthropology
Conservative morality	Inclusive, affirmative morality

Figure 5.1 Selective privatization among the St Michael's congregation.

In summary, while aspects of the shared evangelical worldview held within St Michael's are to some degree liberalized, this process has become subject to a certain selectivity, by topic as well as by context. Divergent emphases can be found in public and in private discourses. Of course, expressions of belief are inevitably shaped by contextual factors, and changing contextual needs generate significant variations in the kind of claims individuals make (Stringer, 1996). But these variations are not random, and the patterns described above suggest an ordered system, whereby certain issues are privatized and others dominate public exchange. I would argue that this system has become infused into the shared culture of St Michael's as a method for the avoidance of in-group conflict and maintenance of a sense of united community. Moreover, this is conveyed and sustained through public discourse.

Put another way, the boundaries of the group have come to coalesce around a set of ideas which encompasses both liberal (open, broad and tolerant) and conservative (narrow, exclusivist) camps, holding each in a delicate balance while attempting to compromise neither. Fracture or conflict occurs, not when members disagree with this general discourse as such, but when they *openly* endorse one pole of the tension at the expense of the other, and in so doing dissolve the delicate separation of public and private discourses. Hence it is a kind of tension – and its propensity to hold conflict at bay – that generates unity, and which consolidates the boundaries of congregational identity.

A glance at the history of St Michael's suggests that this pattern may have been entrenched within congregational culture for some time, as key moments of fracture have occurred only when it has been challenged. In the early 1980s, under the influence of American Restorationists, a splinter group broke away from the church because of disagreements over women's leadership and the authority of charismatic prophecy. In the mid-1990s, a new incumbent introduced a similarly narrow vision of Christianity, based around a supernaturalist theology, a conservative take on ethics and gender roles, and a paternalistic approach to leadership. On both occasions, a narrow, directive – almost exclusively charismatic – theology was rejected by the congregational majority, protest becoming mobilized in significant disinvolvement. Extremes of the liberal kind are unsurprisingly less common, although the *Visions* group may be seen as an example. *Visions* are a progressive, 'alternative' worship group attached to St Michael's. They have established themselves as a separate initiative with their own services and home group meetings, and advocate an understanding of evangelical faith based on environmental and social justice, and the need to retain authenticity in a postmodern world. Some of the St Michael's members cannot relate to their multi-media worship as church, and see its experimentalism as objectionable and misplaced. In this sense, *Visions* endorse an openness to change and diversity that is seen by some parishioners as excessively liberal. While they are not openly denounced and have not been ejected from the fellowship, they are certainly distanced and treated with some caution. It is developments such as these, which challenge the dominant tension of conservative and liberal convictions, that render the boundaries of the congregation most clearly visible (Douglas, 1966). Moreover, it is by engaging in an ongoing conversation with its rich past that the congregation is continually reminded of the propensity of such moments to cause conflict and threaten the cohesion of the church (Wuthnow, 1998, p. 12).

Concluding Remarks

The dominance of the secularization thesis has caused sociological interest to gravitate towards things marginal, exceptional and novel (Gill, 1992, p. 90). If comment is passed upon mainstream churches, it is most often that they are depressed and in decline, or else about to become so. And while exceptions to this dubious 'rule' are acknowledged, they are rarely taken as exemplars from which we can learn about wider trends. But to what extent is St Michael's a part of broader movements? In terms of scale and the richness of its congregational culture, there are certainly few churches like it. Astute insiders may cite the examples of St Aldates, Oxford, or Holy Trinity, Brompton – the famous home of the Alpha Course – charismatic evangelical churches which have enjoyed large and committed congregations since the 1960s (Hastings, 1991, p. 615). We might add the Pentecostalist 'megachurches', centres of piety in the urban metropolis such as Kensington Temple or centres of the Vineyard Church (Hunt, 1997), which have gained ground in subsequent years. Often either theologically infused or financially sponsored by American evangelical groups, these signify an emerging trend, though the globalizing forces which fuel them enjoy only limited currency in the UK context (see Chapter 3).

While this case study appears particularistic, it does generate insights which may shed light on the construction of congregational cultures in other contexts, not least those 'thriving' centres mentioned above. Indeed, the return to a 'broad' agenda within St Michael's may be seen as reflecting a more general shift among evangelicals towards cultural accommodation and ecclesiological innovation, emergent partly as a backlash against the Toronto Blessing and the emotionally intensive 'third wave' of charismatic renewal (Hall, 1994; Tomlinson, 1995). But what may be learned from this case study for the broader field of congregational studies? First, the case of St Michael's reminds us that beliefs and values are often heterogeneous, even within so-called 'evangelical' congregations. It is tempting to assume that churches identified as 'strict' or 'conservative' elicit an equally strong commitment to public teaching across the congregation. The public face of evangelicalism has a complex relationship to its expression in private spheres, which often suggests a diversity and individualism that sit uncomfortably with neat presuppositions about evangelical understandings of truth and knowledge. A similar point can be made about power. Even within congregations that align themselves with conservative traditions such as evangelicalism, power is negotiated rather than simply imposed. Congregations are characterized by a 'negotiated order' (Fine, 1984), and congregational studies need to adopt multi-focused methods in order to explore patterns in the construction and distribution of religious authority.

Second, the teaching imparted and learned within congregations may be understood in part as a response to the specific circumstances of that community. Penny Becker has warned against idiosyncratic readings of congregations, favouring the use of the institutional lens as a reminder of the factors that bind congregations of the same denomination (Becker, 1999). But an equally serious mistake is to infer creedal uniformity on the basis of church style or churchmanship, an error often inflicted upon evangelical churches because they are an easy target for popular stereotypes and cynical parody. While institutional forms are important, local histories cannot be overlooked. Indeed, an examination of inherited traditions can – as in this case – provide the essential key to understanding the peculiarities of congregational life.

Finally, St Michael's is testament to what might be called 'the myth of evangelical success' as a pressurizing factor that shapes the shared expectations of those who choose to remain within such churches. To be a 'successful' church in popular evangelical terms is to be numerous, active and to elicit practical commitment, and this is essential to the identity of the congregation as conceived by its members. When the appearance of these indicators is compromised, the legitimacy of the church is on one level called into question. Hence measures arise that seek to suppress forces which have previously provoked disinvolvement and curbed enthusiasm. For example, while a 'hard' conservative public discourse may be an emblem of evangelical identity for some, it is a threat to existing unity and cohesion for others, and thus also a threat to those indicators which are such an important signal of the evangelical legitimacy of the church, that is, a populace and active congregation. Moreover, unity is an especially poignant issue for those 'elective parochials' who perhaps depend upon the church for a sense of belonging, intimacy and collective support. With a premium placed on the role of the congregation as a close-knit support network, albeit a temporary one for some participants, it is of no surprise that interpersonal conflict is avoided and that measures are taken to minimize its occurrence. 'Friendship, fellowship and acceptance' are not merely bywords for evangelical community; they are emblems of cohesion and tools for securing a shared image of harmony and success.

References

Baumann, G. (1996), *Contesting Culture. Discourses of Identity in Multi-Ethnic London*, Cambridge, New York and Melbourne: Cambridge University Press.

Bebbington, D. W. (1989), *Evangelicalism in Modern Britain – A History from the 1730s to the 1980s*, London: Unwin Hyman.

Becker, P. E. (1999), *Congregations in Conflict. Cultural Models of Local Religious Life*, Cambridge: Cambridge University Press.

Boone, K. C. (1989), *The Bible Tells Them So: The Discourse of Protestant Fundamentalism*, Albany: State University of New York Press.

Briers, S. J. (1993), 'Negotiating with Babylon: responses to modernity within a Restorationist community', unpublished PhD thesis, University of Cambridge.

Brown, C. G. (2001), *The Death of Christian Britain*, London and New York: Routledge.

Bruce, S. (2002), *God is Dead: Secularization in the West*, Oxford: Blackwell.

Cohen, A. P. (1985), *The Symbolic Construction of Community*, Chichester: Ellis Horwood Ltd.

Douglas, M. (1966), *Purity and Danger. An Analysis of the Concepts of Pollution and Taboo*, London: Routledge.

Dowie, A. (2002), *Interpreting Culture in a Scottish Congregation*, New York: Lang.

Fine, G. A. (1984), 'Negotiated orders and organizational cultures', *Annual Review of Sociology*, 10, 239–262.

Foucault, M. (1977), *Discipline and Punish*, London: Penguin.

Foucault, M. (1984), *The History of Sexuality*, London: Penguin.

Gill, R. (1992), 'Secularization and Census Data', in Bruce, S. (ed.), *Religion and Modernization: Sociologists and Historians Debate the Secularization Thesis*, Oxford: Clarendon Press, pp. 90–117.

Gill, R. (1993), *The Myth of the Empty Church*, London: SPCK.

Guest, M. J. (2002), 'Negotiating community: an ethnographic study of an evangelical church', unpublished PhD thesis, Lancaster University.

Hall, I. R. (1994), 'The current evangelical resurgence: an analysis and evaluation of the growth of contemporary evangelicalism in Britain and the USA', unpublished PhD thesis, University of Leeds.

Hastings, A. (1991), *A History of English Christianity, 1920–1990*, London: SCM Press; Philadelphia: Trinity Press International.

Hunt, S. (1997), ' "Doing the Stuff": The Vineyard Connection', in Hunt, S., Hamilton, M. and Walter, T. (eds), *Charismatic Christianity. Sociological Perspectives*, Basingstoke and London: Macmillan, pp. 77–96.

Hunter, J. D. (1987), *Evangelicalism: The Coming Generation*, Chicago and London: University of Chicago Press.

Kelley, D. M. (1972), *Why Conservative Churches Are Growing*, New York: Harper and Row.

Niebuhr, H. R. (1962), *The Social Sources of Denominationalism*, New York: Meridian.

Saunders, T. and Sansom, H. (1992), *David Watson: A Biography*, London, Sydney and Auckland: Hodder and Stoughton.

Stringer, M. D. (1996), 'Towards a situational theory of belief', *Journal of the Anthropological Society of Oxford*, 27 (3), 217–234.

Stromberg, P. (1986), *Symbols of Community: The Cultural System of a Swedish Church*, Tucson: The University of Arizona Press.

Tipton, S. M. (1982), *Getting Saved from the Sixties: Moral Meaning in Conversion and Cultural Change*, Berkeley and Los Angeles: University of California Press.

Tomlinson, D. (1995), *The Post-Evangelical*, London: SPCK.

Warner, R. S. (1988), *New Wine in Old Wine Skins: Evangelicals and Liberals in a Small-Town Church*, Berkeley, Los Angeles and London: University of California Press.

Watson, D. (1981), *Discipleship*, London, Sydney and Auckland: Hodder and Stoughton.

Watson, D. (1983), *You Are My God. An Autobiography*, Sevenoaks: Hodder and Stoughton.

Wuthnow, R. (1998), *After Heaven: Spirituality in America since the 1950s*, Berkeley: University of California Press.

Chapter 6

Display and Division: Congregational Conflict among Roman Catholics

Peter McGrail

Introduction

During the second half of the twentieth century the Roman Catholic (hereafter just Catholic) community in England and Wales has been engulfed by a process of change that has been tracked by a number of sociological studies (see, for example, Ward, 1961; Brothers, 1964; Archer, 1986; Ryan, 1986; Hornsby-Smith, 1987, 1991, 1999; Timms, 2001). The picture emerging from such studies is of a progressive breakdown in those communal structures and patterns of behaviour that had rendered Catholics distinct within British society. The cultural shift has been accompanied by a marked reduction in the numbers of its active members – both of lay people regularly participating in the church's liturgy or contributing to its costs and of priests available to staff parishes. The latter fall in particular has catalysed an accelerating programme of parish amalgamations and closures, resulting in a sense of insecurity on the part of many lay Catholics for the future of their parish (see Archdiocese of Liverpool, 2000[1]). The comprehensive network of truly local cells of the Catholic community is under threat. To those changes must also be added the effect upon the Catholic community of two largely externally driven administrative changes that in different ways have altered both structures and practice at local level. These are the development of laws governing the charitable status of each of the Catholic dioceses in England and Wales, and the need for the community to review its procedures for child protection and the prevention of abuse.[2] Two impacts of these developments have been to increase the central role of the archdiocese over local Catholic institutions – thereby tilting power balances within the community – and to call into question traditional customs and practices.

My own focus of attention is the manner in which such changes impact on the local unit of the parish. I ask how all these changes are lived out in concrete

---

[1] For a sense of the popular response to this document, see the *Liverpool Echo*, 16 March 2001 and 11 September 2001; the *Daily Post*, 16 March 2001 and 8 December 2001.

[2] An independent Review on Child Protection was established under Lord Nolan in 2000, and produced two reports during the following year (Nolan Review 2001a, 2001b).

situations, and how they bear upon relationships between individuals and groups and thereby influence local power structures. My special concern is to explore the manner in which all this finds expression in ritual processes at local level, so that those rituals themselves may serve as lenses to view a rapidly changing scene. In 1999 and again in 2002 I observed one such ritual in which the impact of the above-mentioned fiscal and protective changes was clearly played out against the background of the uncertainties introduced into the community by the general process of change in Catholic England.

The ritual in question was the annual Field Day of a working-class Catholic parish located just outside the centre of St Helens, a large south Lancashire industrial town. The event in 1999 was made up of two distinct elements: a procession through the streets of one section of the parish and the Field Day proper (essentially an outdoor bazaar with games and stalls). Linking the two was the crowning of the parish Rose Queen, who was accompanied throughout by the year's first communicants. By 2002 the procession, Rose Queen and first communicants had all disappeared from the event. This chapter seeks to understand why and how this happened. After clarifying my methodological stance, I shall briefly locate the event in its historical setting, focusing in particular upon the described previous experience of participants. I shall then describe the event as staged in 1999, and go on discuss the differences between 1999 and 2002. In the second part of the chapter I shall analyse the differences, and what I perceive to be the deeper underlying issues.

Methodology

My research stance was necessarily that of participant observer as not only am I myself a Catholic priest, but also in 1999 I was resident within the parish, though without any pastoral responsibilities there. By 2002 I had moved elsewhere. The reality of my participant status was crystallized by the anxiety that was expressed on both occasions with regard to my use of a tape-recorder. In 1999 one woman refused to continue a conversation until I switched it off (I have not quoted from what she said off tape). In 2002 another insisted that I outline my questions off tape before she would agree to my recording her responses. Such reticence was never explained, but it is not impossible that it reflected the internal conflict within the parish that formed a background to the event in both years. This was a divided community, and people were unwilling to risk declaring themselves publicly. Even though I was not, in fact, directly part of any power structure within the parish, there would have been a general assumption that I was allied to the parish priest. This did not, however, prevent some subtle criticism of him being expressed.

Background: The Local Tradition of Catholic Processions

From conversations carried out during the procession, it became evident that the event was regarded as traditional within the parish. One woman stated:

And it's been going for about, well, I used to walk with the procession years ago. So it's a tradition here, and there's not many have the Walking Days like they used to. We call it a Field Day, but it's an old-fashioned Walking Day.

A male respondent, asked the same question, replied:

Erm, thirty odd years, easy. Because I was in the Field Day when I was in the infant school over there. I used to go on it then, yeah.

In addition to parish-based processions, the town's Catholic community had in the past come together to process through its streets. The local history library holds photographs of a Catholic Walking Day on Whit Monday 1914, in which a number of parishes – including the subject of this chapter – took part.[3] The single photograph relating to the subject parish reveals certain features that also emerged in 1999, and which will be considered in my discussion of the 1999 event. Nor was the subject parish unique in associating processions with 'Field Days'; the town collection contains a photograph of one such event in another parish dating from 1954.[4] Several participants in 1999 spoke of their own memories of taking part in processions in other parishes:

Yes, we always walked. It was good, because all my aunties and that used to come out and run into the road and give you twenty p's as you were walking down. Yeah, they used to run out and slip you ten pences or, you know – sixpences I suppose they were then as well. They'd slip you some money and say [whispers] 'Here you are. Spend that when you get to the end.'

There was no evidence of such practice during the 1999 procession, but the first communicants were the centre of attention, as bystanders identified their young relatives and waved and shouted to them. Yet while such events had once been widespread, they had now largely died out in the town. In 1999 the only other Catholic procession was a 'Rosary Rally' through the town centre streets one Sunday afternoon, which attracted a very small following.

The Event in 1999

The Procession

The procession left the church grounds just after 1 p.m., and took forty minutes to make its way back. The route lay through a small section of a council estate and then briefly back along the main road. Five police officers were detailed to patrol the event, halting the traffic when necessary. Earlier in the day the parish priest had explained to me that every group in the parish would take part in the procession. In the event, however, the procession was

---

[3] Catalogue no. PH/5/100/1–14.
[4] Catalogue no. M/SE/1/3.

primarily made up of parish children and of adults who worked with them. There was a sense among participants that numbers were down. One woman noted, 'There's not many walking with them this year – we usually have a lot more than that.' Another said, 'There's usually both schools walk, but they're not here today. We've had more in the past.' I estimated the total number of participants to be a little more than two hundred.

An adult altar server, carrying a processional crucifix, headed the procession. He was immediately followed by four servers of junior school age (three girls, one boy) all vested as for Mass. This echoes the 1914 photograph, though in that case the crucifer was flanked by two other adult servers, and led a party of eighteen vested altar boys. In 1999 the parish priest followed the servers, wearing clerical dress but not vested. The invited guest of honour – one of the players from the town's professional rugby club – walked alongside the priest. The player's task was to crown the Rose Queen and formally open the Field Day when the procession had returned to the church premises. Then followed the first of two large banners, carrying the image of Christ and the words, 'Sacred Heart of Jesus have mercy on us'. A similar banner was carried in 1914, its streaming ribbons held by young girls dressed in white. In 1999 a mixture of boys and girls performed this task. A second banner was carried in the 1999 procession, depicting the Virgin Mary and bearing the words, 'Mother of God, pray for us'. While the 1914 photograph does not feature a Marian banner, the traditional use of the two banners in Catholic processions in the town was noted by one of the women taking part:

> I used to love walking days – we had them regular when I was little. I loved – I always liked the banners – and they had red ribbons for the Sacred Heart and blue for Our Lady's banner. It depended which banner you was dragging along. Because it was only, like, practising Catholics of the parish that was allowed to hold the banner, you know. And seeing we was kids from an Irish family, we was like first in the line, you know.

In this procession, too, the question of who carried the banners was significant – though, as will be noted in the analytical section below, for very different reasons.

The main body of the procession moved on behind the Sacred Heart banner. A local brass band, hired for the occasion, led a group of children in fancy dress. Then followed the largest single group in the procession: the 'Little Church', with its own banner. The background, meaning and significance of 'Little Church' will be considered in the analytical section below. A party of school-children behind their own banner, the above-mentioned Marian banner, and a troupe of girl morris dancers followed them. A small number of parishioners came next, and then the band of the local Sea Scouts, whose repertoire included the anthem of the town rugby club. Another small cluster of seventeen parishioners (two men, the rest women and children) and the uniformed associations followed, and finally a lorry drawing a flatbed trailer decorated with red and white paper rosettes brought up the rear of the procession. The first communicants, who faced outwards, occupied two rows of benches arranged along its length. At the head of the trailer, with their backs to the driver's cab, sat the new and retiring Rose Queens and a pageboy, himself one of the first communicants, holding the Rose Queen's crown.

The Rose Queen was always chosen from the girls in the final year of the junior school, and parishioners used a tear-off slip printed on the parish bulletin to nominate candidates. This manner of selection favoured nominations from among church-going families as the bulletin was only distributed in church during Sunday. Unfortunately, it was impossible to establish the criteria used by the committee to choose between the nominated girls; two members of the committee who were interviewed did not volunteer the information, and were generally unwilling to respond to follow-up questions. It is difficult to judge whether their reticence related to this particular issue, as both women were exceedingly cautious in talking to me; one was the person already noted who had asked me to switch off the tape-recorder. The committee provided the Rose Queen with a red cloak trimmed in white, worn on this occasion over the girl's mother's wedding dress, while the retiring Rose Queen was given a blue cloak. One of the women explained to me that both cloaks and the crown had been used by the parish for 'twenty to thirty years'.

The first communicants were effectively identical with an academic cohort: that is, those Catholic children currently in year three of the parish schools. The chief forum for their preparation for first communion had been their classroom, though their school lessons were supplemented by a brief series of sessions led by a group of parish catechists. Weekly participation in the Sunday assembly – though encouraged – had not been a necessary element in the build-up to the event. These children were dressed in the clothes they had worn for their first communion. For the twelve girls the outfit consisted of white dresses, headdresses and short veils; all the girls wore white shoes and socks, and two wore white lace gloves. The boys wore long dark trousers and white shirts, generally complemented with red bow ties. Four boys wore matching red cummerbunds, while six others struck a different note with matching waistcoats and bow ties (chiefly silver-grey). The dress worn by both genders was consistent with first communion dress that I have observed in other parts of the Liverpool archdiocese, although the clothes were generally less elaborate than those being worn that same year by children in the inner city. This was particularly true of the boys, none of whom wore the full morning suit (frequently completed by top hat) that was becoming increasingly common in the city. Four women accompanied the children on the float, and four men – fathers of children on the float – walked alongside it during the procession.

The Field Event

The field event was held on a large playing field adjacent to the parish school. Admission was by programme, sold at the back of the church and in the school over the preceding weeks, and also available at the gate. The procession broke up upon returning to the church property, and people entered the field informally as Gounod's 'Ave Maria' was played across the public address system. Along one side of the field a number of simple stalls had been laid out, staffed by regular Sunday worshippers. Another flatbed trailer had been parked opposite the stalls, a row of seats arranged along its length. The parish priest and guest of honour made their way to the trailer, as did the Rose Queens and their pageboy – still carrying the crown – and the first communicants. The girls were seated on the chairs while the boys sat on the deck. In the three central seats sat the new and retiring Rose Queens with the pageboy. While the children were still taking their seats, the priest introduced the guest of honour, whom he asked to 'just say a few words' before crowning the Rose Queen. The player responded:

> I'd like to welcome you all this afternoon to the Field Day. I hope you're all enjoying yourselves. And I'd like to crown this year's queen. Okay.

He then took the crown from the pageboy and gingerly placed it upon the head of the new Rose Queen. As the priest invited applause, one verse of an instrumental version of 'Congratulations' was played over the public address system. The guest of honour, again prompted, then announced, 'I officially open the Field Day'. With that, the first communicants moved quickly off the trailer, and her predecessor led the new Rose Queen around the various stalls.

The Event in 2002

When in July 2002 I attended the parish Field Day again, it was immediately evident that three elements that had been of major significance in 1999 – the procession, the Rose Queen and the prominent participation of the first communicants – were all missing. I shall briefly consider each one of these in turn.

The procession was last held in 2000. Several parishioners explained that it was omitted in 2001 for reasons beyond the control of the parish authorities:

> Erm, you see, the problem is, erm, last year when we talked to the police about having a float, erm, the police didn't want us to walk – we always have the walk, the procession, and the police didn't want us to do it for safety reasons because at the time there was an awful lot of road works going on around, and the police wasn't keen on us doing the procession you see, so that's why things sort of died last year.

There had, however, still been a Rose Queen in 2001 – but the committee had struggled to find a girl willing to take the part: 'You'd be like fighting for people; you'd like drag them off the streets,' said one woman. Another parishioner offered an explanation why this should have been:

> But we decided to drop that this year because the girls who were eligible for Rose Queen are Year Six, you see, and they think it's a bit naffy.

When asked if anyone had directly said that, she responded:

Well, not officially. [laughs] Unofficially. But, I suppose the answer to that is you drop the age group, don't you, for Rose Queen. ... that's one way of dealing with it. But, erm, I don't know. People just don't seem to want to make the effort. So I don't know what the answer is.

With regard to the decision this year to dispense with the prominent role previously given to the first communicants, the parish priest explained that the change had been forced by difficulties in obtaining insurance to cover the transport of children on the lorry, and by a growing awareness within the congregation of the need to ensure a safe environment for the children (particularly appropriate changing facilities). A rather different account of the reasons behind the change, carrying an implicit criticism of the first communicants and their families, will be noted in the analytical section below.

Stripped of these elements, the Field Day had effectively become a parish outdoor bazaar. Greater care had gone into the stalls, which were all now protected by small marquees, and several respondents were at pains to stress that the priest had not been required to lay out money in buying goods to be given as prizes as the congregation had given 'good quality stuff'. This had now become no more than a fund-raising event and family day out.

Analysis of the Event

The Meaning Given to the Event by its Participants

In his analysis of the Kingswood procession, Timothy Jenkins noted that participants in the walk who were not originally from the area (such as clergy) were more ready to offer an account of what was happening than the locals (Jenkins, 1999). This was also the case in the Field Day event. When asked in 1999 what it was about, several people were happy to describe what happened, but only one woman offered a rationale:

> The first communion children are the main people in our parish this year because it's their special year. The whole year is their special year – when they've received the sacraments – and then this is an added bonus to their day, you know.

On the other hand, the parish priest, who had only arrived in the parish in autumn 1997, and therefore for whom this was only the second experience of the event, offered a fuller explanation. He also regarded the first communicants as key, but rather than focusing upon their personal enjoyment, he framed his understanding of the procession in terms of the relationship between the Catholic and non-Catholic sections of the local community. He ascribed to his parishioners a 'ghetto mentality': 'There's them who are Catholics and there's the others who are outside the community. That's how it's always been here.' Within this perspective, he interpreted the event as an opportunity for Catholics to parade through their streets the guarantors of their future continuity, the first communicants:

They are the pride, they are the ones, they are the kings and queens of the day. Because the fact is, they are the centre of our community. They are the future of the community, so it's showing them off to the rest of the local community: this is our pride and joy. This is the Catholic community as we live our life. ... It's actually triumphalism. It's just showing everybody else that we're a very thriving community. And it's just showing off the Catholic element within this local area.

At first sight, such a statement appears to be the answer to the ethnographer's prayer! The priest's account introduces well-defined categories into the discussion, and invites a confident interpretation framed in terms of working-class sectarianism. The concept of a social unit such as the extended family using its first communicants to articulate a sense of its own identity has emerged from fieldwork I have conducted in the inner city of Liverpool (McGrail, 2003). My findings there suggest that the first communion event does indeed offer a stage from which a family can communicate to its neighbours a sense of its strength and self-confidence. The child, dressed in its elaborate and expensive costume, becomes the symbol of the family's social aspirations, while the first communion ritual and associated lavish gift-giving and partying permits the family to demonstrate its ability to fulfil social expectations, not least through the use of those consumer goods that are perceived within the local community as status markers. Thus, the event as a whole may be used to establish or maintain a place within the local social order. Theoretically, by inserting those same children into a corporate display, the broader unit of a parish might attempt a similar project. An analysis in terms of Bloch's (1992) concept of 'rebounding violence' is tempting: the community submits its younger members to a ritual of initiation so that it may then turn its aggression outwards: in this case, claiming the streets.

It is possible that the procession may at one period have fulfilled the function ascribed to it by the priest; there is nothing in the evidence I gathered to disprove that possibility. However, in terms of the event as staged in 1999, his explanation is problematic. In the first place, I found no supporting evidence for his sectarian interpretation; during the two years of my residence in the parish no member of the congregation ever raised the issue. Furthermore, although unaware of my Liverpool fieldwork findings, the priest's use of an 'anthropological' turn of phrase may have reflected his expectations of my interests. Then the relative ease with which the priest and his associates over the next three years accommodated an end first to the procession and then to the involvement of the first communicants raises two further questions. The first asks whether in fact there was a continuing need for an externally directed manifestation of the Catholic presence in the locale. The second focuses upon the internal preoccupations of the Catholic body, and asks how comfortably its leaders sat with the event itself.

These two questions relate to the most significant *dubium*. There were issues at play within the congregation in 1999 that suggest that the symbolic function of the first communicants was rather more ambiguous than was stated by the priest. The event that year conveyed a message not primarily to those outside the parish, but to the Catholic community itself – and, especially, to a particular group within it who were currently in dispute with the priest, his parish associates and the archdiocesan authorities. These two issues of the first communicants and internal conflict point to respectively long-term and short-term concerns within the parish. The short-term concerns were met simply by staging the event in 1999. The long-term issues have not been resolved, but an attempt has been made to reduce their visible impact by the radical changes in the nature of the event that took place over the three years that followed.

Short-term Issues: Conflict within the Parish

A core element in the parish priest's analysis of the event was his construction of non-Catholics as the 'other' before whom the procession was carried out. However, in this particular year there was a different group who are more likely to have been the intended audience. This was a body not outside the Catholic community, but within it – a number of parishioners who had recently withdrawn from active life in the parish. Until recently these people had enjoyed considerable influence within the parish, performing key roles in both its liturgical and social life. Significantly, it had traditionally been the task of a number of women within this group to organize the annual Field Day, which had been the most public manifestation of the group's presence and status in the parish. The women in the group gathered all the various elements in the parish into the event, and were able to grant or deny status, as it was they who chose the Rose Queen. Their men-folk occupied a prominent role within the procession, as it was they who carried the two large banners.

The operational base of this group had been the parish club, whose legal status as a members' club had offered to its committee considerable autonomy, effectively rendering them independent of both the archdiocese and the parish priest. This resulted in a situation that the archdiocesan authorities came to perceive as incompatible with the archdiocese's charitable status. Consequently, the authorities sought to regularize the situation by negotiating with the committee either a change in the legal status of the club or a rental contract consonant with the going market rate. Agreement was not forthcoming, and a deepening conflict was played out in the local newspapers and eventually in the civil courts. The parish became divided between those who supported the parish priest – the local agent of the archdiocese – versus the supporters of the club committee. As the conflict was played out, the members of that committee gradually withdrew from the various roles they had previously performed and eventually – reluctantly – handed over the club premises to the archdiocese. This was early in 1999. A new committee was then formed of close associates of the parish priest to operate the club under archdiocesan administration. This served to further focus and personalize divisions within the parish that were crystallized in the 1999 Field Day event, as its traditional organizers had withdrawn and a number of other women who had worked closely with the parish priest assumed their mantle. In 1999 it was essential that the priest and his collaborators staged the event: failure to do so would have been interpreted as a sign of the indispensability of the old guard and of weakness in the new order.

Long-term Issues: The Symbolic Role Played by the First Communicants

At the heart of the priest's account lay a concern that the parish community should be seen as enjoying present vibrancy and future viability. There was no evidence that this would have been of concern to those outside the parish; it was, however, a preoccupation of many within. The woman who stated that the first communicants were the 'main people in the parish' for that year hinted at this preoccupation. She identified as one of the outcomes of the Field Day the possibility of involving the families of the first communicants, whom she began to compare with her own, church-going family:

> And it does, we do find the children come, when they go on the lorry and that, we do find that they come to, erm, they come to the Field Day and maybe the parents participate in the Field Day as well. You know, I mean, this is where it is nice because you get people – I mean, I've always gone to Church, it's been no problem to me. And my children have always gone. I mean, my daughter was Rose Queen, you know.

The same concern emerged in the course of conversations carried out in 2002. One woman cited a perceived indifference of the first communicants and their families to any involvement beyond the first communion day as the motive for ending their highlighted role in the Field Day:

> There was forty odd children made their first communion. When we had the thanksgiving Mass and party there was only just on thirty turned up. So they don't – they seem to be interested in ... the actual day, and anything else concerned they don't seem to want to make the effort. So we decided to drop it this year.

The preoccupation expressed in both these instances is not for the parish's relationship with the outside world, but, rather, with issues internal to the Catholic community. To many within the parish the first communicants did not symbolize the self-confident continuity of their community – rather, they were an all-too-visible reminder that many within the church did not regularly participate in its life and worship. They were not guarantors of future continuity, but a potent reminder of the failure of the Mass-going element within the Catholic body to successfully reproduce its patterns of religious practice.

By contrast, however, there was a further body of children within the 1999 procession who presented a different vision for the future. This was the group known as the 'Little Church'. 'Little Church' (the commonest term) is part of a liturgical practice which has become increasingly prevalent in the English-speaking Catholic world. Its operation in the subject parish is typical. Each Sunday those twenty or so children of primary school age who attended Mass with their families were taken out of the church during the first part of the Mass by a number of female parish 'catechists'. The intention was to offer an experience of the scriptures that was appropriate to the children's stage of development. The movement from 'big' to 'little' church was ritualized according to a pattern common to many settings: at the start of Mass the priest called the children forward; he then gave a book of readings to one of the children, who led the rest in procession out of the church and into the sacristy area where their activities took place. The return was also ritualized: the children re-entered the church at the appropriate time as the homily ended and joined the procession that brought to the sanctuary the gifts of bread and wine and the collection. As they arrived at the sanctuary, they presented to the priest a drawing that they had made during their period away from the main assembly. This drawing was then displayed in front of the altar until the end of Mass.

The significance of this visible and celebrated group in the life of the parish was twofold. First, the children who took part were all by definition regular church attenders. As a body they could, therefore, represent to the practising section of the parish a more optimistic vision for its future than did the largely non-practising first communicants. Second, its entirely female body of catechists was made up of many who, as close collaborators with the priest, now formed part of the emerging power groupings in the parish. They included a number of those who had organized this Field Day, and the husbands of several were among the men who had been asked at short notice by the priest to carry the banners in the procession, replacing the men of the former leading group. The year 1999 was by no means the first time that the 'Little Church' and its catechists had walked in the procession; however, in that year many of the women enjoyed a new status within both the procession and the leadership structures in the parish as a whole.

There was an evident inequality in the visible impact of the two groups of children in the 1999 procession. The 'Little Church' walked with their parents and catechists in the main body behind their own small banner, rather than in the position of honour enjoyed by the first communicants. In the ensuing development of the first communion process within the parish, and the future course of the Field Day, the 'Little Church' was to emerge very quickly as the dominant model of children's participation in the Catholic community. This in turn carried implications for the promotion of a restricted sense of what constituted 'normal' Catholic identity and behaviour. When the first communion process for the next (2000) cohort of children began in the autumn of 1999 it had been radically restructured. Parents were informed that the educative process carried out in the Catholic school was to be complemented throughout the term leading up to the first communions by a series of special sessions that would take place each week during the principal Sunday Mass. In effect, the children who were preparing for first communion were to join the 'Little Church', of which they would now form a discrete group. This weekly participation was to be a pre-requisite for reception of the sacrament. The 'Little Church' model was enforced as normative.

Such an attempt to impose Sunday Mass attendance upon children and their parents as the sine qua non for access to the first communion ritual has emerged in other parishes in the archdiocese. In each location where the requirement has been introduced the aim is quite clear. It is to attempt, through the first communion process, to pattern the children, and through them the parents, into a habit of church attendance. A consistent picture has emerged across the various sites in which such attendance has been imposed. A very small number of parents refuse to engage with the process and effectively withdraw their child from the first communion programme. The majority bring their children week by week until the first communion day, and then cease to practise. It was evident from comments made at the 2002 Field Day, for example as noted above, that the effect within the parish had not been significantly different.

Conclusion: The Progressive Identification of the Catholic Community with the Sunday Congregation

The two events, and the contrasts between them, crystallize two different approaches to the identity of the Catholic community. The first sees the parish as a wide, inclusive body determined by baptism and family origins, that holds within it a range of differing patterns of affiliation to the liturgical assembly. The second is a narrower equation of parish with the Sunday-Mass-going population. The previously noted comments of one of the procession participants concerning distinctions in her childhood between 'practising' and (therefore) non-practising 'Catholics of the parish' should warn against any perception that this is a recent focus for contention. However, my own research into the celebration of first communion in the Liverpool inner city suggests that in the face of the changes outlined at the start of this chapter many within the Catholic community are retreating into a narrowing sense of Catholic identity.

This narrowing represents a particular Catholic reaction to the gradual process of the marginalization of mainstream Christianity in Britain. (For various interpretations of the impact of secularization in Britain, see Davie, 1994, 2002; Bruce, 1995, 2002; Brown, 2001.) While only a minority of Catholics regularly attended Mass during the century to 1950 (see Burke, 1910, and for a discussion of Catholic church attendance in London at the turn of the twentieth century, see McLeod, 1974), the parish nonetheless played a significant role in the lives of the majority as it formed the broad social setting within which they constructed their identity and formed their relationships. In the particular context of Liverpool, Catholicism was also strongly linked to Irish ethnic identity, not least in the face of considerable sectarian hostility (Gallagher, 1985; Belchem, 1992). While the hierarchy publicly lamented the general low church attendance rates, the sense that the Catholic community could not be limited to the Sunday congregation prevailed. Thus, Madeline Kerr's (1958) study of a Liverpool inner-city community noted that non-Mass-attending Liverpool Catholics expressed their Catholicism through participation in social and fund-raising activities and by joining parish processions.

However, as Catholics have moved progressively into the mainstream of English life during the second half of the twentieth century, the core parish institutions of the Sunday Eucharist, the school and the club have lost much of their significance as nodal points within a distinct Catholic subculture, and the network of relationships that in the past bound them together has become strained. In the subject parish this straining was manifested on two fronts: the conflict with the parish club and the removal of the first communicants from the Field Day. In both cases governmental legislation was cited as the catalyst for change, but broader underpinning discourses could be detected as an increasingly marginal Mass-going population moved away from the traditional broad construct of the Catholic community. As a consequence, the parish was becoming identified with the Sunday congregation.

When I revisited the Field Day in 2002, several participants argued that more of the Mass-going population were involved in the event than had been the case under the former regime. The parish priest said,

> One or two of the old guard have moaned because there's no procession. ... They thought it would end with them. Whereas it's been like a phoenix, it's raised – a whole new involvement of people – from the ashes. Like, now there's a whole group of people who've never been asked to be involved.

However, it is difficult to escape the impression that from being an event that still embraced the Catholic population in all its breadth, it had now become more internally focused upon the Mass-going congregation. What has 'risen from the ashes' is of a totally different order from that which went before.

References

Archdiocese of Liverpool (2000), *Towards Pastoral Regeneration in Liverpool City Centre: A Report to the Archbishop's Council and the Council's Response*.

Archer, A. (1986), *The Two Churches: A Study in Oppression*, London: SCM.

Belchem, J. (1992), 'The Peculiarities of Liverpool', in Belcham, J. (ed.), *Popular Politics, Riot and Labour: Essays in Liverpool History 1790–1914*, Liverpool: Liverpool University Press.

Bloch, M. (1992), *Prey into Hunter: The Politics of Religious Experience*, Cambridge: Cambridge University Press.

Brothers, J. (1964), *Church and School: A Study of the Impact of Education on Religion*, Liverpool: Liverpool University Press.

Bruce, S. (1995), *Religion in Modern Britain*, Oxford: Oxford University Press.

Bruce, S. (2002), *God is Dead: Secularization in the West*, Oxford: Blackwell.

Burke, T. (1910), *Catholic History of Liverpool*, Liverpool: C. Tingling and Co.

Davie, G. (1994), *Religion in Britain since 1945: Believing Without Belonging*, Oxford: Blackwell.

Davie, G. (2002), *Europe: The Exceptional Case. Parameters of Faith in the Modern World*, London: Darton, Longman and Todd.

Gallagher, T. (1985), 'A Tale of Two Cities: Communal Strife in Glasgow and Liverpool before 1914', in Swift, R. and Gilley, S. (eds), *The Irish in the Victorian City*, London: Croom Helm.

Hornsby-Smith, M. (1987), *Roman Catholics in England: Studies in Social Structure since the Second World War*, Cambridge: Cambridge University Press.

Hornsby-Smith, M. (1991), *Roman Catholic Beliefs in England: Customary Catholicism and Transformations of Religious Authority*, Cambridge: Cambridge University Press.

Hornsby-Smith, M. (ed.) (1999), *Catholics in England 1950–2000: Historical and Sociological Perspectives*, London: Cassell.

Jenkins, T. (1999), *Religion in Everyday Life: An Ethnographic Approach*, New York and Oxford: Berghahn Books.

Kerr, M. (1958), *The People of Ship Street*, London: Routledge and Kegan Paul.

McGrail, Peter (2003), 'The celebration of First Communion in Liverpool: a lens to view the structural decline of the Roman Catholic parish', unpublished PhD thesis, Birmingham University.

McLeod, H. (1974), *Class and Religion in the Late Victorian City*, London: Croom Helm.

Nolan Review (2001a), *Review on Child Protection in the Catholic Church in England and Wales: First Report*, London: Catholic Media Office.

Nolan Review (2001b), *A Programme for Action: Final Report of the Independent Review on Child Protection in the Catholic Church in England and Wales*, London: Catholic Media Office.

Ryan, D. (1986), *The Catholic Parish: Institutional Discipline, Tribal Identity and the Religious Development of the English Church*, London: Sheed and Ward.

Timms, N. (ed.) (2001), *Diocesan Dispositions and Parish Voices in the Roman Catholic Church*, Chelmsford: Matthew James.

Ward, C. K. (1961), *Priests and People: A Study in the Sociology of Religion*, Liverpool: Liverpool University Press.

Chapter 7

Congregations, Narratives and Identity: A Quaker Case Study

Peter Collins

Introduction

Ethnography – a method or set of methods typical of tightly focused, or 'intrinsic', congregational studies (see Woodhead, Guest and Tusting, this volume) – is not a matter of compiling statistics, testing hypotheses or establishing laws. Rather, ethnography is a facilitation of a more or less believable account of local or contextualized meanings. The central question ethnographers ask themselves is, 'What does this group do and how do they make sense of what they do?' (and doing here includes saying). It is about laying bare the processes involved in the production and expression of meaning. Moreover, doing ethnography is, as the eminent American anthropologist Clifford Geertz suggests, a matter of engaging in 'thick description' (Geertz, 1973, ch. 1), offering a detailed, nuanced account of a cultural phenomenon. In my own ethnographic research into a Quaker congregation in northern England (Collins, 1996), I found that, in attending carefully to the nuances of a Quaker Meeting, what became most striking was the economy of story-telling. The facilitation of 'thick description' became, in part, a recounting – a re-telling – of congregational stories, and my research an investigation into the role of these stories in the meaning-making process. This paper re-visits this research, reflecting on what became a narrative approach, and foregrounding the processes involved in the telling and receiving of stories as loci in the ongoing construction of congregational identity. I will first give an account of the theoretical underpinnings of narratology, before applying the insights of this approach in an analysis of a Quaker ministry taken from my own fieldwork. This will inform a final discussion of the value of a narrative approach in the broader study of congregations.

The Development of Narrative Theory

Narrative theory (or 'narratology') is primarily concerned with the ways in which stories are constructed and has been a significant component of literary criticism for a very long time, certainly since Aristotle's *Poetics*. During the last century, Vladimir Propp's proto-structuralist reading of folk-tales was extremely influential. Propp (1968/1928) examined many Russian folk-tales and found that each could be reduced to one of only a startlingly limited number of plots. After Propp, structuralist accounts multiplied, with various authors taking up narrative as a key concern (for example, Todorov, 1969, 1978; Lévi-Strauss 1970, 1973; Gennette, 1973, 1985; Culler, 1975; Barthes, 1977, 1982; Greimas, 1983, 1987). Apart from Lévi-Strauss, who wrote voluminously on myth, most of these authors have focused almost entirely on literary texts, as have those deconstructionalists who subsequently responded to the structuralist tradition (Culler, 1983; Derrida, 1986; Miller, 1992). More recently, academics have looked beyond the literary text in their attempt to extend narrative theory in history (White, 1973, 1981, 1987), ethnic studies (Bhabha, 1989, 1994), psychoanalysis (Schafer, 1981, 1992), economics (McCloskey, 1990), law (Jackson, 1990) and policy analysis (Roe, 1994). More recently, important strides have been taken by social scientists who have begun to identify and analyse narrative activity in social interaction. There is a growing understanding that narrative is centrally important not only to understanding fictional accounts but to social accounts more generally. When teachers, doctors, lawyers, cleaners, academics, migrants, housewives and others are asked to say what they do, they do so by means of telling stories. Plummer (1995), Bruner (1986, 1993), Spence (1982) and others have argued that stories are not only central to but are constitutive of social life. We not only tell stories to construe but also to construct our social worlds.

So what is narrative? The literature is now very extensive and there is a certain amount of disagreement over definitions (Riessman, 1993, p. 17). According to Gerald Prince (1987, p. 58) narrative is:

> The recounting (as product and process, object and act, structure and structuration) of one or more real or fictitious events communicated by one, two or several (more or less overt) narrators [tellers] to one, two, or several (more or less overt) narratees [listeners].

A more specific account is offered by Polkinghorne (1991, p. 136), who argues that 'Narrative is the cognitive process that gives meaning to temporal events by identifying them as parts of a plot.' He goes on to explain that narrative structure organizes events into various kinds of stories. Apart from 'public stories', which dwell on nations and national events, people simultaneously construct private and personal stories combining heterogeneous and sometimes chaotic life events into unified and understandable wholes. These are 'stories of the self' which provide the material from which we construct our personal identity and self-understanding. In the words of Barbara Hardy (1968, p. 5):

> We dream in narrative, daydream in narrative, remember, anticipate, hope, despair, believe, doubt, plan, revise, criticize, construct, gossip, learn, hate, and love by narrative. In order really to live, we make up stories about ourselves and others, about the personal as well as the social past and future.

Linde argues that 'Life stories express our sense of self: who we are and how we got that way' (Linde, 1993, p. 3). For Linde, perhaps the most critical outcome of the life story is 'coherence'. Coherence depends on two sets of relations: first, the proper relations between parts – at the word, phrase, sentence and perhaps higher levels – and between these parts and the whole; and second, the relations that determine when discourse is recognized and accepted as a well-formed example of its type. Linde (1993, p. 12) goes on to claim that coherence is less the property of a 'disembodied, unsituated text' and more the result of a sustained, cooperative effort by both speaker and listener. While the speaker endeavours to produce a coherent text, the listener (or more correctly, the 'addressee') attempts to understand it as a coherent text and to communicate that understanding.

Polkinghorne, Hardy and others usefully remind us that narrative is not confined to literary texts, that it operates on more than one level. Quaker written texts, including the best known – for example *Quaker Faith and Practice* and George Fox's *Journal* – are replete with stories. Moreover, these stories are commonly retold and embroidered by Quakers throughout the United Kingdom, and are in that sense canonic. I will go on to show how Friends themselves generate story-telling at a prodigious rate at Meetings and elsewhere. These are stories that are first introduced and sometimes later developed by individual Friends. But stories also lurk in the material culture of the Meeting House, in the furniture and fittings, in paintings and in the gardens that surround the building and so forth. These narratives are brought to life and circulated over decades and maybe longer periods, and partially constitute the memory of the Quaker Meeting. It is useful to separate out, at least for heuristic purposes, these levels or spheres of narrative. One particular advantage of paying proper attention to each of these narrative spheres is the gain in understanding the relationship, properly dialectical, between individual and society, crucially mediated by locale. It is not difficult to expose the ways in which these spheres of narrative are articulated, but it has rarely been attempted. A second advantage to this approach is the firm hold that is maintained on the centrality of human agency. I hope to show clearly that Friends bring their storied selves to Meeting and more or less consciously orient themselves to narratives which they find there – some primarily local, others more obviously canonic.

How might attending to this narrative process be useful to those involved in the study of congregations? Why pay so much attention to individuals and their stories? First, I would argue that all of social life comprises such stories, whatever else it might be said to consist of. Second, following Linde (1993), our very selves are constructs of such stories, indeed, consist of narratives, and any analysis of social agency is therefore enriched by adopting narrative as a perspectival tool. In this chapter, I take up this contention and attempt to 'thicken' it by further exploring the relationship between public and private stories in the ethnographic context of an English Quaker Meeting.

The Meeting as Narrative

There are around 500 Quaker Meetings in Britain. This chapter is based on ethnographic research carried out during the early 1990s in Dibdenshaw

Meeting (a pseudonym), a Quaker congregation in the north of England. Quakers have been meeting in the town since the 1660s and currently occupy a recently built Meeting House in the town centre. This is a typical Quaker Meeting in so far as it holds its weekly Meeting for worship on a Sunday morning from 11 until 12 o'clock. Numbers participating vary but the average is around fifty. A large proportion of participants work in the caring professions (education, social services, the health service) and, with one or two exceptions, are white. The Meeting House is in use most days, either by Quaker groups and committees or by a wide variety of outside groups – for example, Amnesty International, Buddhist groups, the local coroner – who rent rooms.

As I pursued my fieldwork as participant observer, I began to model the Meeting in a number of ways. I was continually brought back, however, to the kinds of talk that went on when Friends met, for example on arrival at the Meeting House:

> And how are you today?
> What wonderful weather...are you taking the boat out this afternoon?
> I don't think I've seen you here before...
> So, what did you think of the concert?
> What a shower – no chance of promotion now!
> I was very sorry to hear about your sister...

Almost always these opening remarks offer the invitation to construct a story. And so of all the various characterizations of meeting I considered, the one that makes most sense both emically (to insiders) and etically (to this outsider) is 'Meeting as narrative', or 'as story', if you prefer. After numerous readings of my field-notes I found that what came to stand out most luminously (and eventually in my memory of the events so represented) was the storied character of meeting. These tales, developed over months, often years, were primarily about participants themselves. Gluckman (1963) argued some time ago that gossip helps to bind people together, but narrative introduces a temporal and directional dimension and might be seen as the glue which holds people together over time.

Before going on to say something about the use to which I have put narrative analysis in my own work, an important distinction needs to be made. Clearly 'the recounting' can be done both by the ethnographer and by his or her subjects. As anthropologists have shown, it is possible to shine a great deal of analytical light on anthropological texts by re-presenting them as narratives, as stories anthropologists tell (Geertz, 1988; Van Maanen, 1988). Indeed, this is the gist of much of the 'new' anthropology. Some would doubt that there are any significant differences between the novel and anthropology, apart from the obvious difference of literary quality, which anthropology often significantly lacks. In any case, the ethnographer is, in a significant sense, a teller of tales.

I think it is more important, though, to point out that our subjects, members of the congregation, also tell stories and that if we pay proper attention to these, then we might also further illuminate the intricacy of social life. In relating the stories of individuals and groups we can identify the twists applied to structural rules which were once taken to be rigid, external and overarching. In fact, through their stories, we can see how ordinary people actually construct and reconstruct these structures only to unravel or embroider them in order to understand their world better. And we begin to see that the structures themselves are stories we tell ourselves.

Probably the most sustained attempt, apart from my own, to characterize the congregation in terms of narrative is that of James Hopewell (1987). Hopewell, priest and ethnographer, was until his untimely death part of a thriving American tradition of congregational studies. He argues convincingly that 'most parish idiom conveys and implies narrative' (1987, p. 46). In describing a number of parishes in which he worked, as teacher and/or minister, he adopts a broadly structural functionalist perspective in arguing that a congregation often does (and certainly should) develop a coherent 'story'. Although Hopewell develops a number of insights which I found useful in exploring possibilities in my Quaker ethnography, the result of his own analysis is a cross between Jungian 'archetypes' and Propp's 'morphology'. That is, he argues that there are a limited number of 'grand narratives' that the congregation might adopt and that some are more 'functional' than others. Given his pastoral motivation for undertaking the research, this conclusion is hardly surprising. However, the result is too simplistic, rigid and deterministic. Although Hopewell's account is undoubtedly inspiring in its groundbreaking approach, which foregrounds the fundamental place of story in the congregation, I do not feel that his account does justice either to the complexity of narrative or to the subtlety of congregations.

How, then, might narrative analysis be useful in helping us understand congregations in a way that builds on Hopewell but which also moves beyond the limitations of his approach? I have already mentioned that narrative analysis rings true in relation to my own ethnographic experience. I found that the trading of narratives in meeting was extraordinarily pervasive and quite transparent. A narrative also allows a central place for human agency; it is unlikely that the stories individuals communicate in meeting can ever amount to one coherent, seamless, narrative-cum-structure, as Hopewell suggests. Third, a narrative approach ensures that the voices of participants are properly heard. Fourth, the stuff of narrative derives not only from the words that individuals trade in conversation and in writing, but also from the many and varied acts carried out in everyday life. Narrative therefore makes meaningful the whole range of social interaction. Finally, if we accept a play of different spheres (or levels) of narrative, we allow for a dynamic congregation within which there is cooperation and contention, negotiation and confrontation, thus providing space for the consideration of power and difference within congregational life (see Ward, this volume).

Quaker narrative(s), I will argue, may be identified as operating at several 'levels': prototypical (or individual), vernacular (locally defined) and canonic (ascribed within Quaker tradition). During the early stages of my fieldwork, I was aware only of spoken discourse and considered this a central part of what Rapport (1993) calls 'talking relationships'. However, as time went by I became more sensitive to the shape of interactions between participants and realized that narratives were spun in many other, unspoken, ways. For now, though, I will relate just a single instantiation of narrative from the many which I noted during my fieldwork. What follows is a reconstruction of one spoken ministry. A Quaker Meeting for worship lasts an hour and consists, for the most part, of participants sitting still and in silence. Every now and again someone might stand and say something...

> We all have gifts and abilities...but we don't always use them well...remember the parable Jesus told about the talents...many people have used their abilities to glorify God and quite rightly so, just think of the great works of Bach and Handel...think of the Medieval artists and the extraordinary frescoes people like Giotto painted.... Yesterday we watched the Kitsons using their talent for acting.... I attended two performances of Talking Threads yesterday...I listened to every word...they were the most moving performances I have ever experienced...and each gave me spiritual inspiration that will last me the rest of my life...we should all be very grateful to them.

So what have we here? This is Michael, a member of the Quaker Meeting at Dibdenshaw, offering spoken ministry during Meeting for Worship one Sunday in 1992. We can understand such contributions better if we consider them in the light of the three 'orders' of narrative delineated above.

Canonic Narrative

This order provides the widest contextualization of this particular talk or discourse. Quakerism grew up at a time of great social upheaval, around about the time of the English Civil War during the early seventeenth century. George Fox, a Leicester shoe-maker, began travelling around the north of England, preaching as he went. He was, in the first place, extremely critical of the Church of England (and it is difficult for us now to imagine the power held by the Church at that time). He was not the only critic but he took more risks than most, interrupting sermons to tell congregations that tithes (a local tax and the clergy's main income) were wrong, that it was not necessary to have a degree from Oxbridge in order to preach, and that the Established Church owned too much land at a time when agricultural labourers were going hungry and being shouldered off common land because of enclosure. He went further, arguing that all were equal in the sight of God. He was frequently jailed for using the 'common' forms 'thee' and 'thou' when addressing the gentry and for failing to remove his hat in their company. He preached that outward symbolism and ritual was merely a diversion, that people should meet for worship in silence unless they felt moved by God to speak, and that women should worship along with men and should have equal rights to stand and speak, provoking tremendous loathing among Anglicans and others. This canonic narrative, or, if you like, set of narratives, illuminates and clearly legitimates Michael's talk. He, along with most if not all of those present, is aware of the canon; it consists of many stories which one is gently encouraged to learn. The very fact that

Michael spoke to people meeting for worship in a circle, sitting at the same level, none of whom was marked out in any way as a 'leader', that he rose in the silence and that those present listened in silence to what he had to say not only reflects but re-constructs or re-writes that canonic narrative. Furthermore, we observe here the extent to which narratives are embodied, generating norms of ritual practice as well as discursive style. It is worth noting that in the case of Quakerism the canonic is relatively clearly defined in a readily available text: *Quaker Faith and Practice*. In other congregational contexts, the Bible, Book of Mormon, Millennial Laws (among Shakers) and Qur'an might play a similar role. Of course, although *Quaker Faith and Practice* is a text, we would be mistaken to understand Quaker ideology as equivalent to it and somehow set in stone. Quakers bring the text to life through their interpretation of it.

Vernacular Narrative

This refers to the stories told of and by the local Meeting in Dibdenshaw, which perceives itself to be a community, a group of people with not only shared beliefs but also shared interests. Michael refers to the Kitsons, Quakers who are also professional actors. They wrote a play, a duologue in fact, celebrating the lifework of Fox and his wife, Margaret Fell. Persuading them to come to Dibdenshaw was no mean feat. The task was delegated to the 'Extension Committee', which had to ensure that at least forty people would attend in order to (a) provide a sufficient audience, and (b) finance the event. One Friend wrote to a number of local churches, mosques and Hindu temples, inviting their members to attend. On the day, many volunteers came into the Meeting House to prepare for the event, and a small display of Quaker literature, together with 'light refreshments', was organized. An ad hoc 'welcoming committee' was set up in order to take care of the Kitsons during their brief stay in Dibdenshaw. Michael's ministry alludes to this event, serving as a quietly oblique pat on the back for Dibdenshaw Meeting, a gentle celebration of its latest community-building achievement (cf. Cohen, 1985).

Prototypical or Individual Narrative

This is where careful ethnography takes centre stage, capturing as it does constructions of narrative particular to individual agents. When I heard Michael offer this spoken ministry I had come to know him very well. We had often spoken to each other about our pasts and particularly about our religious lives. He had, like me, grown up in Wales but unlike me had trained and practised as a minister in another denomination for more than thirty years. He had been expected to provide weekly or bi-weekly sermons and had, he told me, become quite adept at that part of the job. He was known as an eloquent speaker at Dibdenshaw. At the time of fieldwork, Michael was in his eighties, a bachelor and an avid attendee of all local and many national Quaker events. Here he is, among other things, flagging his commitment, his sense of belonging, his identity as a Dibdenshaw Quaker. It is important to note the multifariousness of these threads – clearly, any attempt at closure here would be pointless.

Michael's spoken ministry exemplifies and develops these three orders of narrative discourse. After the meeting for worship had ended, several Friends spoke to Michael about his ministry; some had attended the performance given by the Kitsons, others had not. Comparisons were made, comments passed, minor disagreements aired. In this way the prototypical narratives of individuals were braided, both one with another and with stories which belong primarily to the Meeting (vernacular or local narratives), and to the wider Society (canonic narratives).

What I would wish to emphasize, however, is the evident drive by all participants to create coherence in and across each of these spheres. This particular example, as well as those given below, strongly suggests a propensity to construct coherent accounts through sustained and cooperative effort, as described by Linde. However, whereas Linde is primarily concerned with the creation of coherence in the short term, I am more interested in the ways in which these multiple tellings cohere over a longer period of time, that is within the ongoing construction of congregational identity.

Both in and around the Meeting House (during meeting for worship, in meetings for church affairs, in the building itself and its furnishings) and away from the building (at social events and committee meetings held in Friends' homes) the presentation, exchange and reconstruction of narratives was omnipresent. For heuristic reasons, I have distinguished between three spheres of narrative: the prototypical, the vernacular and the canonic. Traditionally, sociological and anthropological theory has tended to privilege either the individual (as in methodological individualism) or the structural (as in structural functionalism). I have been developing my approach in an attempt to obviate such unhelpful dualism and also to give proper attention to the vernacular or local. It is inevitable that an action (whether it be a word during worship, the pinning up of a poster or the donation to Meeting of a rocking horse) may be contributing to a number of narratives which are at least partially connected, and which may be more or less consciously intended as a part of one or more narrative spheres. Furthermore, the prototypical narrative one has sought to communicate can be taken and appropriated by others who will adopt and adapt it in an effort to achieve coherence through their own narratives. Sometimes a participant will hear somebody being misrepresented and complain, thus engaging in a broader narrative; at other times they may let things pass. As Rapport (1993, p. 190) puts it, 'People can be said to be members of communities and living in individual worlds at the same time.' What seems clear to me is that participants perpetually contextualized (and thereby made meaningful) their contributions in Meeting with reference to what they saw as an appropriate narrative thread.

It is sometimes hard to distinguish between the spheres of narrative I have identified. It seems perfectly acceptable to claim that a single contribution might in time be granted status as prototypical, vernacular and canonic. And there are many complications, for example, what of the Friend who, by dint of local traditions surrounding eldership, stands during Meeting for Worship on the second Sunday of each month and reads from the 'Advices and Queries' (a chapter in *Quaker Faith and Practice*)? Would such a contribution not embrace all three spheres of narrative simultaneously? But this is probably not the place to narrow our focus to such an extent. Distinguishing between them may be important to the subject but may also be a methodological decision made by the analyst. This is a complex issue, requiring further research and analysis, but which I do not have the opportunity to pursue here.

A further issue relates to the manifestation and management of conflict within congregations. Though pacifist, we should not assume that the Quaker Meeting is free of conflict and contention. I presented a case study which did not involve conflict primarily because this is typical. However, there is no reason why situations and events in which individuals are in disagreement might preclude a narrative perspective. An individual might contribute to Meeting discourse in various ways and may justify that contribution with reference to his or her own past experience, the traditions of the local Meeting or to canonic texts. An individual or individuals who come to hold an opposing or alternative position might draw on the same pools of resources. As in the case of biblical texts, the Quaker canon is large enough and sufficiently ambiguous to allow those with different points of view to draw reasonably upon it. One minor contentious issue at Dibdenshaw surrounded the conversion of a lawned area behind the Meeting House into a 'wild garden'. As it was, the lawns were restful and attractive and had been cultivated by members of the Meeting (primarily vernacular narratives). Those who wished to create a wild garden proposed that Quaker testimonies supported the planting of 'wild' native species which would encourage further insect and bird life into the garden. Digging out a pond and creating raised earthen banks further encouraged debate between those who supported the venture and those who did not. The plan was initially discussed by a few interested members, who then asked for it to be included in a Preparative Meeting (PM) Agenda. PM is a business meeting open to all and anyone may speak on any item on the agenda. After the final contributor has sat down the clerk (chairperson) attempts to write a minute which captures the gist of all contributions. In this case the clerk felt that the Meeting should go ahead with creating a wild garden, even though one or two people had voiced concerns. Minutes of business meetings are generally very concise, but sometimes neatly encapsulate the competing narratives aired publicly by Friends.

An important tension (and source of narrative engagement) that exists in the Society of Friends nationally (and to some extent globally) is that which is claimed to exist between those of a universalistic inclination and those who might be thought of as Christocentric. This tension existed at Dibdenshaw but remained largely implicit, surfacing only on occasion. For instance, there were on the walls of one room in the Meeting House two pictures. The first was a Victorian representation of Christ suffering the little children to come unto Him, the second, a large, bright modernist depiction on cloth of the ten commandments by a Latin American artist. As if from nowhere a disagreement emerged over the relative merits of these works. The first was said to be racist, the second, unpleasantly 'loud'. Stories were presented in defence of each. The first had been a much-loved fixture in the 'old' Meeting House and was donated by a weighty Friend, respected by several generations of worshippers at Dibdenshaw. The second was bought after a number of fund-raising events from the local Oxfam shop. Here we have a fairly clear local instantiation of a canonical tension grounded in the tales told by individual participants. But there are at least two further twists to the story. The 'core' of those who presented narratives supporting the 'Jesus-with-children' picture tended to be from among the Meeting's 'old hands': local Friends and long-time participants at Dibdenshaw. Those whose stories tended to support the Latin American print were, by and large, incomers: younger Friends who had arrived relatively recently in the area and who were comparatively new to the Meeting. The second twist is that some Friends (both old hands and newcomers) contributed tales which sought to nullify or erase this tension, pointing out the inclusive nature of Quaker faith and doctrine (as presented canonically). In this way, different narratives are deployed in both the generation and attempted resolution of internal tensions, shaping both conflict and harmony within the congregation.

Conclusions

In this chapter I have examined the use of narrative analysis as a means of interpreting a specific congregation. Of course, congregations do not *have* to be represented as braided narratives and although I am inclined, on the basis of my fieldwork experience, to privilege a narrative perspective, it is clear that congregations are many other things too. My objective in proposing this particular analytical perspective is to stimulate further discussion through making suggestions, drawing comparisons and disclosing hunches. The problems most frequently levelled at an approach which takes narrative as the central analytical tool in understanding social interaction are twofold. First, narrative is often characterized as incorrigibly literary. This is hardly surprising since it has primarily been used to analyse prose and poetry, that is, written texts. But this imposes upon the approach an unnecessary and to my mind unwelcome narrowness. Stories are most certainly and most obviously spoken and written but we can also widen our understanding of texts to include our bodies, our built environment, our patterns of production and consumption, and so forth. We rely upon stories to make sense of all these aspects of social reality. Stories are ubiquitous; we find them in the ways in which we move, clothe ourselves, eat, decorate our homes, work, play, worship. Second, narrative analysis is often accused of being apolitical, astructural and, ironically, ahistorical, focusing largely on the individual and shedding little light on the group (or, in this case, the congregation) or on wider society. I hope that the case study I have presented redresses the balance in both instances. Narratives are both embodied and are negotiated in dialogue with local history and congregational structures. Moreover, I hope to have shown that not only are individual stories partly derivative of canonic and vernacular stories, but also that these are partially constructed by individuals. We are presented with a dialectical process in which human agency retains its central place.

At present we tend to draw on a literary narrative analysis in making sense of all these social phenomena, but that is unsurprising given the infant state of the approach. At some point in the future it is likely that we shall need to move on from treating the built environment or the body *as if* they were written texts, because the analogy will eventually become limiting and therefore sterile. Linde (1993), for example, in her work on coherence, has forged a strong bridge between the literary and social-scientific approaches to narrative. We will before long establish a narrative of space as well as time. Furthermore, if we give equal weight, interpretative weight, that is, to the prototypical (individual or micro), the vernacular (local or meso) and canonic (universal or macro), then narrative cannot be condemned for its narrow indifference to the supra-individual or structural.

Jerome Bruner argues in *Actual Minds, Possible Worlds* (1986, p. 11), that narrative is one of two fundamental modes of thought: 'A good story and a well-formed argument are different natural kinds. Both can be used as means for convincing another. Yet what they convince of is fundamentally different: arguments convince one of their truth, stories of their lifelikeness...' In this chapter, I have shown the extent to which the involvement of participants in the congregation consists in their willingness to engage in the weaving of stories. If we, as observers and interpreters of social life, are to provide a believable, a lifelike, representation of congregations, then it follows that narrative must be central to this.

References

Bal, M. (1985), *Narratology: Introduction to the Theory of Narrative*, trans. C. van Boheemen, London: University of Toronto Press.

Barthes, R. (1974), *Introduction to the Structural Analysis of the Narrative*, trans. R. Miller, New York: Hill and Wang.

Barthes, R. (1977), 'Introduction to the Structural Analysis of Narrative', in Heath, S. (ed.), *Image-Music-Text*, London: Fontana.

Barthes, R. (1982), *Mythologies*, ed. and trans. A. Lavers, London: Granada.

Bhabha, H. (ed.) (1989), *Narration and Narration*, London: Routledge.

Bhabha, H. (1994), *The Location of Culture*, London: Routledge.

Bruner, J. (1986), *Actual Minds, Possible Words*, Cambridge, MA: Harvard University Press.

Bruner, J. (1987), 'Life as narrative', *Social Research*, 54 (1), 11–32.

Bruner, J. (1993), *Acts of Meaning*, Cambridge, MA: Harvard University Press.

Burke, K. (1945), *A Grammar of Motives*, New York: Prentice-Hall.

Charon, R. (1993), 'Medical interpretation: implications of literary theory of narrative for clinical work', *Journal of Narrative and Life History*, 3 (1), 79–98.

Cohen, A. (1985), *The Symbolic Construction of Community*, London: Routledge.

Collins, P. (1996), 'Auto/biography, narrative and the Quaker Meeting', *Auto/biography*, 4, 27–38.

Cortazzi, M. (1991), *Narrative Analysis*, London: The Falmer Press.

Culler, J. (1975), *Structuralist Poetics: Structuralism, Linguistics and the Study of Literature*, London: Routledge.

Culler, J. (1983), *The Pursuit of Signs*, London: Routledge.

Dandelion, P. (1996), *A Sociological Analysis of the Theology of Quakers*, Lampeter: Edwin Mellen.

Derrida, J. (1986), *Of Grammatology*, trans. G. C. Spivak, Chicago: Chicago University Press.

van Dijk, T. A. (1988), *News Analysis*, Hillsdale, NJ: Lawrence Erlbaum.

Fox, G. (1952), *Journal*, ed. J. L. Nickalls, Cambridge: Cambridge University Press.

Franzosi, R. (1998), 'Narrative analysis – or why (and how) sociologists should be interested in narrative', *Annual Review of Sociology*, 24, 517–554.

Freud, S. (1953), 'Beyond the Pleasure Principle', in Strachey, J. (ed.), *The Standard Edition of the Complete Psychological Works, Vol. 18*, London: Hogarth Press, pp. 1–64.

Freud, S. (1977), *Case Histories I*, Harmondsworth: Penguin Books.

Freud, S. (1979), *Case Histories II*, Harmondsworth: Penguin Books.

Geertz, C. (1973), *The Interpretation of Cultures*, New York: Basic Books.

Geertz, C. (1988), *Works and Lives*, Stanford, CA: Stanford University Press.

Genette, G. (1973), *Narrative Discourse: An Essay in Method*, trans. J. E. Lewin, New York: Cornell University Press.

Genette, G. (1985), *Narrative Discourse Revisited*, trans. J. E. Lewin, New York: Cornell University Press.

Gluckman, M. (1963), 'Gossip and scandal', *Current Anthropology*, 4, 307–316.

Greimas, A. J. (1983), *Structural Semantics: An Attempt at a Method*, trans. D. McDowell, R. Schleifer and A. Velie, London: University of Nebraska Press.

Greimas, A. J. (1987), *On Meaning: Selected Writings on Semiotic Theory*, trans. P. J. Perron and F. H. Collins, Minneapolis: University of Minneapolis Press.

Greimas, A. J. (1990), *Narrative Semiotics and Cognitive Discourses*, trans. P. J. Perron and F. H. Collins, London: Pinter Publications.

Hardy, B. (1968), 'Towards a poetics of fiction', *Novel*, 2, 5–14.

Heath, S. (1976), 'Narrative space', *Screen*, 17 (3), 68–112.

Heath, S. (1981), *Questions of Cinema*, London: Macmillan.

Hopewell, J. (1987), *Congregation: Stories and Structures*, London: SCM Press.

Jackson, B. S. (1990), 'Narrative Theories and Legal Discourse', in Nash, C. (ed.), *Narrative in Culture: The Uses of Storytelling in the Sciences, Philosophy, and Literature*, London: Routledge, pp. 23–50.

Jakobson, R. (1990), *Jakobson on Language*, ed. L. R. Waugh *et al.*, London: Harvard University Press.

Kleinman, A. (1988), *The Illness Narratives: Suffering, Healing and the Human Condition*, New York: Basic Books.

Labov, W. (1972), 'The transformation of experience in narrative syntax', in Labov, W. (ed.), *Language in the Inner City*, Philadelphia, PA: University of Pennsylvania Press, pp. 352–396.

Lévi-Struass, C. (1970), *The Raw and the Cooked*, trans. J. Weightman and D. Weightman, London: Cape.

Lévi-Strauss, C. (1973), *From Honey to Ashes*, trans. J. Weightman and D. Weightman, London: Cape.

Linde, C. (1993), *Life Stories: The Creation of Coherence*, Oxford: Oxford University Press.

McCloskey, D. N. (1990), 'Storytelling in Economics', in Nash, C. (ed.), *Narrative in Culture: The Uses of Storytelling in the Sciences, Philosophy, and Literature*, London: Routledge, pp. 5–22.

Maines, D. R. (1993), 'Narrative's Moment and Sociology's Phenomena: Towards a Narrative Sociology', *Sociological Quarterly*, 34 (1), 17–38.

Miller, J. H. (1992), *Ariadne's Thread: Storylines*, New Haven, CT: Yale University Press.

Mishler, E. G. (1986), *Research Interviewing: Context and Narrative*, Cambridge, MA: Harvard University Press.

Norrick, N. R. (2000), *Conversational Narrative: Storytelling in Everyday Talk*, Amsterdam: John Benjamins Publishing Company.

Plummer, K. (1995), *Telling Sexual Stories: Power, Change and Social Worlds*, London: Routledge.

Polkinghorne, D. E. (1988), *Narrative Knowing and the Human Sciences*, Albany: State University of New York Press.

Polkinghorne, D. E. (1991), 'Narrative and Self-Concept', *Journal of Narrative and Life History*, 1 (2/3), 135–153.

Prince, G. (1973), *A Grammar of Stories*, The Hague: Mouton.

Prince, G. (1987), *Dictionary of Narratology*, Aldershot: Scolar Press.

Propp, V. (1968) [1928], *The Morphology of the Folk-Tale*, Austin, TX: University of Texas Press.

Quaker Faith and Practice. The Book of Discipline of the Yearly Meeting of the Religious Society of Friends (Quakers) in Britain (1995), London: Britain Yearly Meeting.

Rapport, N. J. (1993), *Diverse World-views in an English Village*, Edinburgh: Edinburgh University Press.

Riessman, C. K. (1993), *Narrative Analysis*, London: Sage.

Roe, E. (1994), *Narrative Policy Analysis: Theory and Practice*, London: Duke University Press.

Rosaldo, R. (1989), *Culture and Truth: The Remaking of Social Analysis*, Boston, MA: Beacon Press.

Rosenwold, G. C. and Ochberg, R. (eds) (1992), *Storied Lives: The Cultural Politics of Self-Understanding*, New Haven, CT: Yale University Press.

Roth, P. A. (1989), 'How narratives explain', *Social Research*, 56 (2), 449–478.

Sarbin, T. T. R. (ed.) (1986), *Narrative Psychology: The Stories Nature of Human Conduct*, New York: Praeger.

Schafer, R. (1981), *Narrative Actions in Psychoanalysis*, Worcester, MA: Clark University Press.

Schafer, R. (1992), *Retelling a Life: Narration and Dialogue in Psychoanalysis*, New York: Basic Books.

Shotter, J. (1998), 'The dialogical nature of our inner lives', *Philosophical Explorations*, 3, 185–200.

Spence, D. (1982), *Narrative Truth and Historical Truth: Meaning and Interpretation in Psychoanalysis*, New York: Norton.

Stringer, M. (1999), *On the Perception of Worship*, Birmingham: Birmingham University Press.

Todorov, T. (1969), 'Structural analysis of narrative', *Novel*, 3, 70–76.

Todorov, T. (1978), *The Poetics of Prose*, Oxford: Blackwell.

Van Maanen, J. (1988), *Tales of the Field: On Writing Ethnography*, Chicago: Chicago University Press.

White, H. (1973), *Metahistory*, Baltimore, MD: Johns Hopkins University Press.

White, H. (1981), 'The Value of Narrativity', in Mitchell, W. J. T. (ed.), *On Narrative*, London: University of Chicago Press, pp. 1–25.

White, H. (1987), *The Content of Form: Narrative Discourse and Historical Representation*, Baltimore, MD: Johns Hopkins University Press.

Young, K. (1989), 'Narrative Embodiments: Enclaves of the Self in the Realm of Medicine', in Shotter, J. and Gergen, K. J. (eds), *Texts of Identity*, London: Sage, pp. 152–165.

Chapter 8

Congregational Cultures and the Boundaries of Identity

Timothy Jenkins

I contend that congregational studies will most likely prove fruitful if the social anthropological method is included in the repertoire of methods adopted. I hope in this chapter to explain why this is so.

This chapter is necessarily condensed and somewhat abstract in its argument, for rather than presenting a case study it draws upon an already published ethnographic account of Kingswood in Bristol ('The Kingswood Whit Walk' in Jenkins, 1999, pp. 77–220), to which I must refer the interested reader to substantiate my claims. That study was based on intensive participant observation conducted over two-and-a-half years, focusing in particular upon the collection of more than sixty family histories. This material was supplemented by research in the local collections of the municipal libraries and the archives of local newspapers, and shaped by comparison with monographs from the community studies tradition and social history. The topics that emerged concern the importance of families in the occupation of a locality, the scansions of local history and how these are registered locally, and the forms taken by – and interactions between – local character and institutions. In a phrase, the account maps what I have termed 'local particularity': the ways of life that create a sense of identity that relates to a particular place. This is a thoroughly ethnographic concern.

The argument here touches upon a number of connected questions that are allowed by such an account: the role that congregations play as local organizations; the relation of these congregations to more widely held social values; the ways that congregations include and exclude various persons, groups and issues; and how congregations deal with conflict. These topics are organized around a central question: who goes to church?

I advocate a social anthropological, rather than a sociological, approach; the chapter therefore begins with questions of method, for these will determine the kind of materials that count as evidence. It then turns to a consideration of indigenous categories, essentially those relating to a conception of personality, or identity. This leads in turn to an exploration of the sophisticated capacity of these classifications simultaneously to generate and to make sense of the events of everyday life. Only then is it fruitful to discuss the factors determining church attendance (which are of such interest to sociologists of religion). Finally, it is possible from this focus upon congregations to suggest how the discussion might contribute to other topics in the sociology of religion.

An Anthropological Approach

What is implied in adopting an anthropological approach when considering congregational behaviour? I suggest four criteria for consideration. The approach implies, first, instead of taking the congregation as a predefined isolate, looking at the human context in which the congregation is set, and seeing how the group under consideration manifests more widely held forms of understanding and behaviour. Second, rather than reaching too quickly for externally generated criteria, such as class or gender, or imagining the uncritical adoption of such external criteria by the subjects of the study (variants upon the internal colonialism thesis), the approach demands we look at indigenous processes of classification, of making sense, whereby actors simultaneously define and evaluate both themselves and others. Third, because such acts of classification are claims made to the recognition of others, who grant or withhold that recognition, and who, by doing so, likewise make a claim to be able to do so legitimately, the social order is made up of a manifold of such negotiations, of claim and recognition, or mutual interpretation – interpretation which is not, however, a matter of mutual transparency, but of mutual definition, and even of mutual misunderstanding. A way of putting this is to say we are dealing in *persons* rather than *individuals*: that 'a man's real life is that accorded to him in the thoughts of other men by reason of respect or natural love' (Conrad, 1983). Finally, we should note that because the processes of classification implicate persons in collective processes, there are parallels between the processes defining persons and those defining institutions. In particular, persons will in large part define who they are by belonging to particular collectivities – such as congregations – or by failing to do so. Likewise, collective groups will show many of the same characteristics as the persons who make them up, evaluating, defining and excluding, so that boundaries become very important. In this perspective, we are dealing with the negotiation of boundaries rather than with bounded entities with definitional powers, and therefore with the evaluative function of human activities, not with concretized cultures or identities.

These four criteria all implicate specific targets. I consider the first two, taking the congregation as a predefined isolate, and the too-ready assumption of the positive reality of certain sociological categories, in a review of Bruce (1995) and Davie (1994) (see 'Two sociological approaches to religion' in Jenkins, 1999, pp. 25–39). I also have in mind the isolates created by often good ethnographic studies of social groups, including congregations. There is discussion of the third criterion, concerning mutual interpretation or misunderstanding, in a consideration of fieldwork as a way of gaining adequate knowledge of other forms of life (see Jenkins, 1994). I am aiming at models of social structure that take communication as the basis of social intelligibility, such as both functionalism and structuralism; in fact, transparency is not a common feature of the social. And behind the fourth criterion is a concern with theories that make actors' behaviour a function, reflection or product of their social situation, as if they lacked all intelligence, power of interpretation and initiative. I would point to the criticism of such theories in

Bourdieu (1977) and Herzfeld (1987), which are exemplary in this regard (see also Jenkins, 1994 and, for wider discussion of the implications of the fieldwork method, Dresch, James and Parkin, 2000).

To return to the argument, the simplest clue is to say that we are looking at indigenous categories, that these are fundamentally evaluative or moral, and that social facts are made up of the interactions of these embodied judgements. There is an additional twist, to say that the social scientist shows in all important respects the same characteristics – classifying, evaluating, demanding recognition of his or her claims, within a community of judgement – and that therefore one should ask what is being done when one approach or another is adopted. At this stage, let us note simply that most human actors in complex social situations take their own understanding to be the truth of the situation, rather than a way of negotiating a path through it. This incomprehension adds to the force of the description of the social fact as a meeting of mutual misunderstandings. But some social science approaches likewise impose a single perspective or frame to 'explain' an event or forms of behaviour. These accounts inevitably have an unsatisfactory air in that they seem to lie to one side of what is the case, they are incomplete and miss much of what is going on, while at the same time offering a version which bears some relation to the events on the ground. Bourdieu (1977, chapter 1) has drawn attention to the fact that, in their partiality and claims to completeness, these accounts resemble those that informants will give. The parallels between local practice and social scientific accounts are a constant of this kind of work.

Ethnography: Indigenous Organizing Categories

The district of East Bristol and Kingswood, where the study was carried out, is urban and industrial, and the population is predominantly working or lower middle class, with an elite consisting of skilled workers and self-employed men. In this milieu, the complex of values that defines both personality and many features of institutional life may be termed 'respectability'. A claim to a degree of privacy and respect is made up of various mutually supporting components. These comprise personal qualities, or virtues, such as thrift, continence, sobriety and self-discipline; certain material conditions, such as regular employment, a skilled trade and decent housing; the support of others, and in particular, a family life based upon such values and opportunities; and finally, the recognition of others, often in the form of membership of certain local organizations, such as a working men's club, a Friendly Society, or a congregation. In brief, respectability is made up in equal parts of inner restraint and outward reputation. It is the negotiation of a claim to merit a certain recognition, and the granting – or not – of that esteem, and this negotiation has a strongly collective aspect, binding together families and persons in a joint endeavour, defining the significance of belonging to a spectrum of local institutions.

To elaborate this conception: because they are a collective phenomenon, displayed in the fine detail of such matters as where you live and what your work is, how you spend your time and with whom, where you appear and how you behave, the values of respectability are continually being expressed and negotiated in everyday life, and this most acutely in issues of discriminations and boundaries. For the collective nature of the values simultaneously makes an egalitarian assumption that the people with whom one shares this kind of life are one's equals, and, on the other hand, therefore demands a strong sense of boundedness, excluding those persons who are judged not to hold or promote these embodied ideals. It is the potential of exclusion that gives tension to the business of claim (to personality) and recognition.

Claims in such a world are advanced very carefully, and are negotiated in a silent way that usually avoids outright refusal. Direct refusal is of course itself a breakdown of the values at stake, in particular the value of restraint. Hence there is a spectrum of forms of belonging, a series of ways of advancing claims of participation without rebuff. The churches and chapels are central – though not unique – institutions locally, organizing the 'field' in which these values operate, and families and persons take part to differing degrees. The spectrum of participation runs from attending jumble sales to asking for the occasional offices, to sending children to Sunday School, to belonging to satellite organizations, to attending occasional services, to being part of the congregation, to taking office or exercising leadership. The whole of local society is organized by the values of respectability, but there is a spectrum concerning to what extent people can expect to embody – and embody publicly – these values.

These values are of such significance that, in effect, everybody locally without exception would claim to be respectable, or to embody these values, for the claim is effectively to be a person: it is the local form of being human, and nobody claims not to be human. Nevertheless, a distinction needs to be made between the business of classification and the complexities of everyday life. On the one hand, as already suggested, the category contains a strongly motivated sense of judgement, both in the sense of a claim made to a certain status, or personality, and in the sense of the anticipated reception of that claim, an evaluation of personality. Contained within the category of respectability, there is its opposite, fecklessness. This may be an empty category, in the sense that nobody would claim to embody it, but it has a potential force in terms of judgement. It can be characterized by lack of restraint, or instant gratification, and so by drinking not sobriety, spending not saving, and disorderly, conflictual behaviour, such as fighting and adultery. It is therefore frequently associated in practice with such matters as family breakdown, irregular employment and poor housing. And in public terms, it is expressed in terms of a loss of reputation, and exclusion from local organizations, membership of which is a part of the proclamation of a certain character.

This question of fecklessness is, I emphasize, a categorical matter, the product of the negation of the values of respectability. However, on the other hand, for persons who find themselves in parts of the social field well away from the central focuses of value, the opportunity to express these values will be experienced differently. So, for example, if membership of a local institution – a chapel or a club – is an expression both of a person's restraint and their reputation, away from those institutions reputation may be established less by restraint than by competition, and a different kind of social persona erected upon such bases as being generous to family and friends, being able to settle an affront by fighting, without recourse to the law, and establishing one's honour by drinking, seduction, and even criminal activity. This kind of behaviour is of course open to being classified by others as unrespectable: it lends itself to judgement in the terms of respectability. But it is also generated by the values of respectability, such as collective solidarity, endeavour and self-sufficiency. It is another expression of the play of the principles of equality and exclusion, for only one's equals are one's friends and rivals.

This double optic, of the same values leading to quite opposed consequences depending upon where in the social field they are active, both lends more force to the anxiety that motivates the judgements, and produces strangely parallel figures, of both heroes or leaders, and of followers, or graded participation, in each sphere of possibility. The field of possibility in which each human life constructs itself and is constructed, in an unending apprenticeship of the potentialities collectively embodied, is both complex and fraught.

The Production of Everyday Life

This complex of values has a remarkable capacity, therefore, to generate very different styles of behaviour, which can then be classified in very different ways. I want now to remark upon the coherence of these articulated opposites. There is certainly a mutual incomprehension between actors in the various parts of local society. Each has their own, positive version of the local values that they embody, but each is blind to the motivations of the other: there is a structure of mutual misapprehension. The significant feature to which I wish to draw attention is that apparently opposed values contain within themselves the power to generate their contrary. I call this (in an ugly phrase) the 'co-inherence of opposites'. It might be claimed that even if, for a variety of demographic and economic reasons, the whole local population appeared at the 'feckless' or 'personal honour' end of the spectrum, without remainder and therefore without any sustainable institutions conferring and transmitting respectability, nevertheless that population would contain the possibility, as circumstances changed, of developing such institutions: of re-establishing three generations living locally, for example, and clubs to which only a certain kind of person could belong, and even chapels. This is not, then, an account that seeks to deny change, but one that recognizes that a local population will receive change upon the basis of certain resources, and that therefore change itself will have a certain structure. Even the 'unprecedented' is made sense of through historically constituted categories and, especially when the categories are as complex and flexible as the case we are considering, this has consequences for any sociological understanding of change.

It is desirable, then, to develop a more rounded account of the processes at work before discussing the question – upon which we clearly already have some material – of who goes to church. Certain refinements are needed in contemplating the place of an outside gaze, such as the one the sociologist brings to bear. First, the question of 'restraint' needs to be taken seriously. 'Respectability' and 'fecklessness' are not precisely local terms, although there are forms of speech, turns of phrase that allude to them. They could not be explicit categories. If restraint is a high value, laying out the principles upon which judgements are made is itself a questionable business. A decent discretion is crucial both to understanding the subject matter, and to embodying it. For this kind of work implicates myself and my practice, ourselves and our practice; this is because we are part of the picture. We are actors in the broader society that regularly brings a gaze to bear upon local society, in which encounter misunderstandings are exchanged, as I have already outlined.

Moreover, local society has always existed in such a relationship with a fitful metropolitan gaze. In the past, it has sometimes involved sending in the troops rather than the sociologists, and it is experienced in the present in the potential insensitivities of imposed forms of government, taxation, schooling, social services and so forth. And local society survives by presenting aspects of itself that match up to the categories being employed to judge it. This matching up is a quite unconscious process, an example of practical judgement exactly parallel to that by which different parts of the local order both judge and ignore one another.

Further, in the case of which I am speaking, the potential misreading includes an inversion of values. In summary, in local society, those who can embody best the notion of respectability, and who within their own world subscribe to collective, egalitarian and strongly bounded values, form the core, or the point of maximum definitional intensity of local identity. They, and the organizations to which they belong, to a great extent organize the social space, in the penumbra of which others live, to varying degrees. In these latter cases, as one moves towards the 'edges', the values are manifested under quite another aspect, one that can be characterized as individualist, competitive and promiscuous (or dissolving of collective boundaries). The inversion to which I refer is that, from the perspective of the metropolitan gaze, the former appear to be an anachronistic survival of a premodern, kin-and-status-based social order, while the latter appear to be modern, contractually oriented individuals. Then one can tell a different story, essentially a version of the transition to modernity, which places the weight – and the future – upon people who, in local terms, are at the edges of society, not the centre. The 'transition to modernity' is quite clearly an actor's account, one way of getting through the complex reality, rather than an adequate mapping of that reality.

There are numerous versions of this metropolitan re-reading of local categories: a well-known case is the Marxist account which labels the skilled artisan as a reactionary creature in thrall to bourgeois ideology (respectability as hypocrisy), while identifying the truth of the working class as residing in the unskilled proletarian worker. There are many features of local life that will support this (mis)reading. For example, the aversion to conflict and struggle contained in the virtue of restraint, and the local focus of collective values which ignores international class solidarities; likewise, the undifferentiated nature of the proletariat, with a certain aptitude for violence, which nevertheless has belied its promise to generations of intellectuals. In confronting these problems, we come to the heart of my dissatisfaction with much contemporary sociology: it is not that it is wrong, but that it is partial, and it unconsciously adopts a perspective that is at variance with local evaluations, so that, effectively, indigenous voices are effaced. This is, I repeat, the guise under which local society has long existed, so it is better to see the sociological account, with its too-hasty mappings, as one type of player on the ground, with characteristic affinities.

And the crucial strategy that we can invoke to counter the forms of blindness produced by the clarity of such broad apprehensions is to pay attention to the scale at which human beings make sense of life, and the associated temporalities of their interactions. One way of putting this is to say that we might look neither to global schemes and overarching categories, nor to individual actions and their sum, but to the intermediate scale of collective life: to the institutions of civil society. Sociology in practice arose as a concern for the well-being of the institutions of civil society, against the twin threats of the claims of the totalizing state and the fragmentation implied by the market, against overweening authority and isolating greed. In advocating an anthropological approach, I am doing no more than promoting a focus upon the basics of the sociological discipline, finding an appropriate way of apprehending the complex life of civil society and its component bodies.

Who Goes to Church?

Among these component bodies is the church, and so we may consider the life of the congregation – in this way finally reaching the point of the excursion. We might sum up the important aspect of the argument so far by suggesting that people who go to church in this area both embody a form of public good, and are able publicly to sustain the claim to represent that public good. Put like that, it might be the case that very few people will feel able to go to church on a regular basis, and the people who are prepared to take on this role will tend to be older and better established. In general, they are more central figures to the local order. And for this reason, too, there will be more women involved than men, because women are central to the ordering of local society, while men are peripheral. (This issue is explored, and the evidence for it considered, in Jenkins, 1999, pp. 109–140.)

As has been suggested, a far wider spectrum of people will make more limited claims to embody a public good through occasional participation in the church and its penumbra. Men often do this through their wives, families through their children. The penumbra in which claim and recognition are negotiated therefore includes family services, Sunday Schools, youth organiza-tions, the occasional offices, para-church organizations such as sewing groups, women's meetings and so forth, and sales and fêtes. Since people participate too through members of their families of birth, not simply of marriage, and kin can spread widely, it is likely that very few persons in the area are left entirely untouched by these forms of participation. On this basis, it is possible to hold a reasoned distrust both of statistics and of attitude surveys, for attendance is a poor measure of this kind of participation, and attitudes, too, even if well discerned, are a poor guide to these deeper solidarities of belonging.

Instead, we might think of this sort of participation in terms of a division of symbolic labour. On the one hand, persons who go to church are those who, to different degrees, claim to represent widely held values of a common good. On the other hand, a certain recognition is granted those claims by a far wider population, who thereby in a less public way subscribe to these values, and claim less ostentatiously to embody them themselves. We are concerned with the expression of a particular form of being human, with how people are 'persons', and the churches and chapels have a role in the economy of the life of that specific human being. That is why it can be claimed that organized religion is a way of paying attention to the possibility of and conditions for human flourishing.

Within such a scheme, nobody thinks of him (or her) self as non-human, or makes a claim to be such. Nevertheless, few people unambiguously embody these values of human flourishing (and they, under the protection offered by their unassailable position, may be guilty of enormities). Most people negotiate themselves a place, through claim to a persona and recognition of that persona, in the field of evaluation constructed through values and their inversions, boundaries and solidarities, as I have outlined. And persons placed towards the edges will not embody public good so much as private honour. 'Flourishing' takes on a reduced scale of implication; what I termed 'fecklessness' is perhaps best understood as a concentration upon the establishing of personal honour. Here one can glimpse the curiously aristocratic values of the unrespectable, concerning, for example, attitudes to display, women, cuckoldry, courage, violence, rank and privilege, legality, lying, literacy and even time (cf. Pitt-Rivers, 1977, p. 36; cited in Jenkins, 1999, p. 201). There is a good deal that could be said about the opposition of aristocratic mores to plebeian values in this society, not least to note the contrast between a concentration upon style and form on the one hand, and sincerity of heart and content on the other. It is worth remarking in a sentence that this linking of private honour with the concentration upon style makes this aspect of local culture more compatible with current intellectual or academic form, for which restraint, or things left unsaid, and the calculations of responsible behaviour are less a priority than the articulation of paradox in the pursuit of personal distinction. But to return to our current interest, such people in local society will not be much drawn to church-going, although they may bring children to baptism, or daughters for marriage, and the men may participate through the activities of their wives.

There are therefore two concomitant social forces to be taken into any account of church-going and its variations in such an area. The first is the division of labour, or representativeness, and the second, the opposition of public good and private honour. As has been made clear, a good many factors are concerned in deciding whether an individual is able to claim to personality by representing public good or private honour. These include regularity of employment, the learning of a skill or trade, housing, health and so forth. Economic, demographic and other wider movements are translated in these factors. Within this frame, all sorts of particular factors contribute: how a person deals with their fate or fortune (their habits, skills and flair), to what extent they are supported by spouse and family, and so on. It is worth remarking, too, that the outcome, in a person's life, is evaluated locally entirely in terms of character, of virtue in its various forms, or the lack of it.

Because persons condense a constellation of causes in this fashion, we might conclude two things in the optic of our concerns. First, even small congregations continue to represent a real option, or symbolic focus, in such communities, and second, that how many people participate will itself be a function of a great many independent factors. To consider for a moment the question of a diminishing church attendance: in this perspective, it implies a decline in the number of persons who feel able to uphold in public a claim to embody a form of public good. In these terms, secularization is an increase in the representation of private honour and a decline in that of public good. This is a serious matter; it has been a topic of concern in a broad way at least since the French Revolution, but it is worth observing both that these alternatives are co-inhering opposites, and that the stock market in moral currency changes all the time. And the challenge for churches is – as it always has been – to engage with and express new forms of public good as they emerge, rather than simply to perpetuate old engagements.

Topics in the Sociology of Religion

How then do the local churches and chapels respond, beyond passively registering changes in intensity and density of the population? I will make a number of observations that touch upon enduring debates in the sociology of religion. These topics include the distinction between church and sect, the nature of cults, new religious movements and the New Age, grasping the processes of secularization, and the concept of civil religion (for a convenient entry-point and review, see Hamilton, 2001).

First, as I have suggested, the representation of and participation in a public good concerns a sphere much wider than that of the Church. The factors at work will include such national aspects of public life and perception of social being as education, health, ecology and family life, as well as the forms of political and economic life. And because it contains a meditation upon human flourishing and the conditions thereof, the Church – or the churches, in their various forms and with their various agendas – will contribute to these developments of perception. The Church, nationally and locally, both exhibits the contradictions of the wider society and offers an interpretation of those contradictions. It offers an example of practical or embodied social thought, in this way demonstrating the sociological truth that human actors actively engage with social forces as well as passively registering them.

Second, within the orbit of the churches and chapels as local focuses or institutions of respectability, there are different possible emphases. For example, it is possible to concentrate more upon matters of style and form; an emphasis upon ritual and the priesthood, as in the Anglo-Catholic form of churchmanship, will make the liturgical and social organization of the Church more available to those persons in the 'private honour' part of the local social field. A Low Church approach, however, rejecting form in favour of content, and emphasizing the necessity of purity of heart and sincerity of intention, and the priesthood of all believers, will tend to concentrate participation among the core respectable.

On the other hand, it is the case that, particularly in the latter kind of church which, in my experience, is currently by far the more common, there are two possible phases of activity. The first we might call 'mutuality': a quiescent, congregational phase, marked by social activity, when boundaries are relaxed and the many shades of the penumbra are quietly negotiated through differential participation. The other is the active, mission phase of increased religious intensity, when boundaries are tightly drawn and conversion from one state to another becomes the key event, and where signs of belonging – for example, charismatic gifts or covering the head – are demonstrated. The type of groups formed, and their activities, and the discipline of time adopted, clearly are related in each phase, but they are not identical. The distinction pertains both to different churches and to moments in the history of each.

Each phase has a limiting condition, where different demands are brought into contradiction, and the phase tends to convert into its opposite. (We are of course redescribing the church/sect distinction in some respects.) In the case of the mutual phase, the tendency to extend into everyday life will at the limit dissolve the boundaries of effort and self-discipline by which the respectable define themselves: there will be a sense of promiscuous mixing which will provoke people to leave and go to other congregations, or to hanker after revival. Periods of intensity – which may relate to external factors causing social instability – lead to an inwardness and an increase in the sense of the private person, but also, in the warmth of the experience, to the possibility of a loss of restraint, or at least of that potential interpretation. Charismatic gifts, such as glossolalia or being slain in the spirit, have an intensity akin to sexual pleasure, and they are shared in private, with all the accompanying possibilities of abuses of power, deception and self-deception, and the separation of interests of members of a family. And, as is notorious, congregations frequently split in the process of intensification, and public conflict is a dramatic display of loss of restraint.

There are therefore rhythms, within individual congregations, of burgeoning and decline, over a generation or two, and to understand the state of a congregation one needs to take into account its previous history. Many declining churches are suffering from the hangover resulting from a period of revival. Congregations, one might conclude, are maintained in a steady state with difficulty, although one might look too at all the congregations of an area, and detect a certain collective homeostasis, growth or decline over a longer period, which will relate to wider factors (as already mentioned).

I have touched upon the sociological distinction between church and sect in the light of the dynamic of the category of respectability; I would make one further point, in a similar spirit. The logic of distinction contained within the category of respectability allows an understanding of a range of contemporary organizations and movements, not necessarily Christian, which sociologists term new religious movements or New Age. Concerning the latter, the formation of a group around the exploration and transmission of a secret, whatever the 'content' of that secret, is a long-standing practice: it is part of the claim to personality, made independently of or polemically against the supposedly hegemonic, orthodox institutions of society. Such groups are loose organizations, to be found in the more individualistic part of the social field: they are less constrained by the values of respectability, but exploit its logic in the pursuit of a certain distinction, explaining suffering and attempting to control man's destiny. They indeed contain popular theodicies. Their dynamics too can be appraised within the framework proposed (I offer an account in Jenkins, 1999, pp. 223–237).

Concluding Remarks

In brief, the development of congregational studies clearly has the potential to contribute to the wider study of contemporary religion in the UK, and at the same time to engage with the categories of the sociology of religion. In order to fulfil this potential, I believe, it will need to be especially attentive to the business of the negotiation of boundaries, and to the motivations that are expressed in them. And it is only by adopting an anthropological approach, with its recognition of the active intelligence of social actors, that these negotiations and motivations can be properly investigated and explored.

References

Bourdieu, P. (1977), *Outline of a Theory of Practice*, Cambridge: Cambridge University Press.

Bruce, S. (1995), *Religion in Modern Britain*, Oxford: Oxford University Press.

Conrad, J. (1983), *Under Western Eyes*, Oxford: Oxford University Press.

Davie, G. (1994), *Religion in Britain since 1945*, Oxford: Blackwell.

Dresch, P., James, W. and Parkin, D. (2000), *Anthropologists in a Wider World*, Oxford and New York: Berghahn.

Hamilton, M. (2001), *The Sociology of Religion*, London and New York: Routledge.

Herzfeld, M. (1987), *Anthropology Through the Looking Glass*, Cambridge: Cambridge University Press.

Jenkins, T. (1994), 'Fieldwork and the perception of everyday life', *Man*, 29, 433–455.

Jenkins, T. (1999), *Religion in English Everyday Life*, Oxford and New York: Berghahn.

Pitt-Rivers, J. (1977), *The Fate of Shechem*, Cambridge: Cambridge University Press.

PART THREE
THEORETICAL AND
METHODOLOGICAL
ISSUES

Chapter 9

The Messiness of Studying Congregations using Ethnographic Methods

Frances Ward

Introduction

I do not think it was very long into my research project that I found out that it was true, as Beverley Skeggs comments again and again: doing ethnography is a messy business (Skeggs, 1995). And the messiness does not go away. The processes of turning observed life into text are messy, full of difficult questions that have to be faced. And even after the fieldwork is done and the text produced, unresolved issues can remain, leaving the author with complex questions about the practice and ethics of becoming involved in a congregation as a researcher.

So how does it begin? You have a research project that suggests fieldwork, rather than documentary texts, or statistical data (although during your project you may well want recourse to these other types of data as well). Perhaps you want to research something that is not easily quantifiable – the attitudes of people to change, or nuanced value systems, or complex interactions between congregational members, or as Penny Becker does, conflicts over identity (Becker, 1999). Your research interest takes you towards the methods of data collection that only ethnographic methods can supply, with the project requiring your physical presence in a congregation over a length of time in order to gather data. It requires that you observe what goes on, and from your observations, from organizing interviews and transcribing the results, keeping a journal, noting different interactions between people, you accumulate various jottings and written material that will be more or less useful in supporting your hypothesis in a convincing manner. The writing begins on day one, and evolves continually as the reflective process deepens and extends. The end result is a text which has a thesis that is argued through and which relies upon the qualitative data to carry the day. So from the beginning the ethnographer is concerned with writing, writing down the lived experience in which they participate, attempting to capture something plausible that will take forward the reader's understanding of what is under investigation. The production of ethnographic research can be fraught and complex, and is often an emotionally charged process as well (Behar, 1996). A process that is personal, for it involves an ongoing chunk out of your life, much of which is rendered invisible in the neat and polished final text. A process that hides another sort of messiness, the constant questions of the relations of power and the positionality of everyone involved, including you as the researcher. Doing ethnography creates some sort of order out of the messiness of life, both the life of the congregation and, often, your own life as author. It is the production of a coherent text from the scraps and fragments of life.

I examine here the different stages of the production of the ethnographic text of fieldwork I did in an inner city congregation in a large city in northern England. The first stage was the initial entry into the field. The second stage can be categorized as the time of participation, when I interviewed congregational members, and made copious notes and charts of the interrelations I observed. The third stage, of writing up, was a time of withdrawal from the congregation, a time complicated by external factors and a lack of communication. The final stage, when the text was completed, still left awkward questions. To whom did this piece of work now belong? What now of the relations with the congregation that had developed over the months? What about publication, or would this involve betrayal of one sort or another?

As I explore each stage, I note the background reading that enabled me to reflect further on what I was doing, and address methodological questions as they emerged in response to the way in which the project itself changed and developed. I hope that the processes of observing, writing, reflecting and writing further here will mirror the unfolding story of a research project that had all the tensions and satisfactions of ethnographic research.

Stage One: Making a Start

My initial research proposal was to do an ethnographic study of three congregations of different Christian denominations, investigating 'corporate identity', a concept that so intrigued Hopewell, among others (Dudley, 1983; Dudley *et al.*, 1991; Hopewell, 1987; Browning, 1991), and which continues to hold the attention of researchers (Becker, 1999). I was interested to discover how each understood itself and formed such identity in dialogue with its own tradition and with the traditions of the others. I was particularly intrigued to find out how the informal structures of communication, particularly gossip, consolidated – and fragmented – corporate identity (Heilman, 1976; Spacks, 1986; Hopewell, 1987). I decided to start with the Anglican congregation, basically because the access was easiest: I knew both the then rector and the curate reasonably well. The congregation had been 'researched' before, and being an Anglican myself, I would be on home ground, as it were. So I talked informally with that rector, and with the curate, outlining my project.

Perhaps the most obvious and immediately noticeable feature about this church at the time was its rector. For twelve or thirteen years his strength of personality and flamboyance had left its mark upon the church's liturgical style and engagement in local political issues and community concerns in a social context that had undergone much change and upheaval. In many ways his type of leadership gave this church a particular ethos and corporate nature. Then, just as I was about to start the project, it was announced that he had been appointed to another post.

With this unforeseen movement, my initial plans of doing a comparative study of the different denominations within the area became more difficult. His imminent departure would create too many variables between the congregations. So instead I decided to focus solely upon this Anglican church, and to study its internal dynamics during the period of the interregnum. The vacuum left after the departure of a strong leader would make more interesting the notion of 'corporate identity'. I talked informally with the curate and when it was clear that he would be happy for the research to continue, I wrote to the Bishop to clear the proposal with him and also negotiated with my employer for the time to initiate and carry forward the project. I talked with the Parochial Church Council (the P.C.C.) and, before the rector left, introduced the research project to the congregation as an exploration of the notion of 'corporate identity'. I explained that I would be with them over the next few months, observing worship and P.C.C. meetings and social gatherings to investigate what held them together as a group. The rector was to be leaving within a fortnight or so, so essentially I was beginning my research as an interregnum began. It was to extend into the beginning of the incumbency of the next rector.

I attended most Sundays, sitting up in the balcony, making copious notes of where people sat, their interactions, and the roles that individuals played within the practices of worship. Coffee followed the main service, and again I mapped where people sat, whom they regularly talked with. A few then adjourned to the pub and I would accompany them, making mental observations that I would write up later on. I also collected other forms of data during that period – material from interviews (I interviewed two-thirds of the congregation), observations, and local primary documentary sources.

The notion of 'corporate identity' started to unravel. I was taken further towards a consideration of the power dynamics within the congregation than Hopewell seemed to contemplate, though Becker's use of 'new institutionalism' (1999, p. 11) in her study of *Congregations in Conflict* offers a fascinating approach to the subject. Unlike her, though, I turned more towards Foucault and his analysis of power as the negotiation with dominance. I found myself asking: Who constructs the 'corporate identity' of this particular congregation? Who is dominant here? Who subordinated? Whose interests are served by the status quo? What or who gave the congregation cohesion? How did members, especially black members, of whom there was a majority, and women, again of whom there was a majority, negotiate their places within the body of the congregation? In the face of such dominant white leadership as I suspected the rector gave, how did members register any discontent? What did members *really* feel about the liturgy at the church? Did all feel equally at home with what it offered? This plethora of questions raised concerns about power relations between different cultures and races, and the part played by gender.

The North American literature within the discipline of congregational studies at the time I was writing was largely produced within a white Protestant milieu, and although latterly there has been growing attention to questions of racism and gender (Wind and Lewis, 1998; Bennison *et al.*, 1999), it seemed to have very little to offer to enable an adequate analysis of the institutional forms that might emerge within a church congregation. The more I read within the field, the more it appeared benign and blind to such uncomfortable issues (Becker's book being the exception).

To provide the analysis I felt necessary, I turned to the work of Michel Foucault. Foucault, particularly in his *Discipline and Punish*, suggested that the construction of an institution makes material the interests of the status quo, which in turn serve the dominant subject. By 'dominant subject' here I had in mind Foucault's portrayal of modern man in his essay 'Man and his Doubles', where 'man' only makes his appearance 'in an unavoidable duality' with its others ([1966] 1994, p. 326). Such a subject sustains itself in power by cloaking its own presence and by projecting 'otherness' onto those who are different: black, women, gay and lesbian people, people of different class. If that 'subject', within the Church of England, is taken to be the dominant white Anglo-Saxon culture, then how might 'others' negotiate their presence?

There was a wide diversity of people who worshipped regularly in this congregation, from eleven different countries of origin, from many different denominational backgrounds and from Anglican churches with a different ethos. They continued to come to this church, often having sampled other Anglican or Catholic churches, because it was welcoming, and gave them enough spiritual sustenance. They felt at home, yes, but to varying degrees. I began to be interested in how 'at home' members felt in this congregation. As I interviewed members, the different ways in which they negotiated with the dominant practices and ethos started to emerge. There was plenty of evidence suggesting that there was not the same sense of ownership of the liturgy among black members that I heard from the Anglo-Saxon interviewees.

The congregation, under the leadership of rector and curate, took awareness of racism extremely seriously and worked hard to counter and challenge racist attitudes both within its own culture and in wider society. This was the time of the Stephen Lawrence Inquiry and the MacPherson report into 'institutional racism' within the police forces of the UK, and such language came easily to one of the leading white men, when I interviewed him. Talking of the black members of the congregation, he made the comment:

> And that's because we, the white race, have kicked them in the balls too many times. That's the institutionalized racism bit, if you like. And I accuse the Church of England of being institutionally racist.

In this first stage of the research I had already begun to refocus the central question. The initial notion of 'corporate identity' had now developed into an investigation into institutional racism and gender. When this happens in a project that does not involve fieldwork, it is a straightforward process of re-assessing documentary data thus far accumulated. When your research involves people, how beholden to them are you to keep them informed of changes of direction you are taking? I had moved from the initial 'contract' I had established with the congregation and the rector (who was long gone anyway). Should I go back and re-negotiate? With whom, though? And risk in the process disrupting the delicate business of gaining trust? With that rector gone, I did talk at length with the curate about where my thinking was going. At no time, however, during the period of my field research did it seem appropriate to talk with members of the congregation as a whole to bring them up to date. It would have been disruptive, and also it would have made a difference between those I had already interviewed and what they said, and the people I was yet to interview. And, anyway, who would I have selected? Was my thinking in a sufficiently coherent state to be discussed? For various reasons the ground shifted, and a widening gap emerged between where I was going with the research and the understanding that most members of the congregation had of what I was doing. But with hindsight, perhaps I should have talked more. Perhaps I should have set up from the beginning a group of congregational members with whom to consult about such matters, or used the P.C.C. more readily to air the progress of my research. As it was I continued, with a vague sense of disquiet.

Stage Two: The Time of Participation

The time of involvement in the congregation – when I was attending most Sundays and working hard to get to know people, asking them if they would be prepared to be interviewed, listening for any throw-away comments that would take me further on my investigation of institutional racism – was a time of constant negotiation. Who was I, anyway, to be asking such questions? How would I use what was said? How would talking to me affect the relationships that an individual might have with others? What happens if you find yourself potentially exposing people in ways they might not like? Should what you write be shown to them before publication? I broached this difficulty with one of my interviewees, during the field research, and he said that I should go ahead and write the way I saw it, regardless of how I thought it would be received. This was my account, he said to me. And ultimately that is what I did. But it was not comfortable, and still is not comfortable with people with whom I gained trust.

Uncomfortable stuff, and easily hidden within research texts. Any reading of the American literature based upon ethnographic research in congregations – from Carl S. Dudley's pioneering text *Building Effective Ministry* to Hopewell's *Congregation*, or Ammerman *et al.*'s *Studying Congregations*, or Don Browning's *Fundamental Practical Theology*, to various other Lilly Endowment Inc. and Alban Institute publications – does not make visible the difficulties. Brynolf Lyon (2000, pp. 257–271) outlines the plethora of research approaches to the congregation, from quantitative and qualitative methods, to be found in the range of studies such as those I have just listed. He draws attention to the appreciative attitude to be detected towards the congregation, and an increasing concern with capturing the 'thickness' of congregational life – its complexity, and the complexity of ways of interpreting it. Researchers often report a sense of discovery, a sense of encountering 'otherness' within the congregation: he writes 'Each [researcher] reports the sense of discovery, the disorientation from their own assumptive worlds which eventually led them to a more appreciative awareness of the strange and resistant complexity and power – the otherness, if you will – of congregational life' (2000, p. 263).

But so positive! Where is the conflict, the concern with power, the dissonance in such literature? Neither Hopewell nor Browning, to name but two who used ethnographic methods, sufficiently recognize, I believe, the difficulties they must have encountered. Becker notes how intractable conflicts can be, and how what she found entailed a change in the interpretative focus in her work (1999, p. 5), leading her to turn to methods of institutional analysis, and thereby contributing an important new element in congregational studies. I went in another direction. Investigating that 'otherness' within a congregation is fraught, I found, especially as I tried to explore the relationship between different 'others' within the congregation. I turned now to the field of feminist ethnography for a greater appreciation of the practical difficulties I was encountering.

Feminist ethnography makes no bones about the relationship between ethnography and autobiography (Behar, 1996; see also Atkinson, 1990). *Women Writing Culture* (Behar and Gordon, 1995) explores gendered reflexivity and observation, the relationship between ethnography and literature, the writing of otherness from the perspectives of colour and gender. The authors write in dialogue not only with the male tradition of ethnography, but with women of colour, with the women who have been traditionally *observed* by the white male, rather than conversed with (1995, p. 6). They write with awareness that cultural difference is to be found *here* as well as *there*, and indeed *here* is a relevant and accountable field for the exploration of identity and difference. The contributors to *Women Writing Culture* consequently write from a standpoint of greater political awareness and accountability than is found in mainline (male) ethnography, like Clifford and Marcus's *Writing Culture* (1986). They write with an understanding gained from '... feminist literary criticism ... that writing matters tremendously for women; that how we plot ourselves into our fictions has everything to do with how we plot ourselves into our lives' (Behar and Gordon, 1995, p. 15).

The feminist ethnographer who has engaged most profoundly with the challenge presented by the difficulties of doing ethnography is, I believe, Kamala Visweswaran (1994). Writing from the perspective of a second-generation woman from the Indian subcontinent living in America, she returned to India in 1986 to research the part played by Tamil women in the struggle for liberation from British rule in the 1940s. Her collection of essays, fables, diary entries and reflections provides a fertile source of material on identity, transculturalism, power and positionality, all rich seams for my own investigation of how members of a congregation negotiated their differences within one church.

Her autobiographical experience of cultural displacement and hybrid identity gives her profound insights into the practice and the discipline of ethnography and its relationship with literature. She refuses the general ethnographical trends of 'making sense', and reads against the grain of the usual construction of community, preferring to focus her analysis upon disrupted places and times. This focus provides a distinctive and radical approach that uses literary means to achieve a different practice of ethnographic research. 'My aim', she writes, 'in advancing a variety of narrative forms in these essays is to expose both processes of disaffection and rupture as well as the construction of community and identity' (1994, p. 15).

It is to the silences and interruptions that she is drawn as a feminist ethnographer. She is interested in those who did not want to speak with her. She struggles with her failures, for she believes that it is in the times of incoherence and in the gaps between meanings that the other is to be found. 'I want to claim', she says, 'shifting identities, temporality, and silence as tools for a feminist ethnography' (1994, p. 50).

Visweswaran acknowledges Clifford's work on allegory (Clifford and Marcus, 1986), and makes explicit her own allegorical trope, 'betrayal'. In her work with women who resisted British culture, she found that they were often brought into conflict with their own cultures. There were many different social and political positions, revealed between herself and the women and also between the women themselves, and these differences, she argues, can best be theorized by the allegory of betrayal. Her chapter entitled 'Betrayal: An Analysis in Three Acts' tells the story of three women and Visweswaran's attempts to extract from them the story of their child marriages. Her desire for information left her feeling inquisitorial and resulted in a betrayal of confidences. She asked herself 'What kind of knowledge was I policing, anyway? And what kind of confession did I hope to produce?' (1994, p. 47).

Such ethnography requires a different epistemology. Visweswaran follows Donna Haraway (1991) in seeing 'truth' and 'knowledge' as produced within situation and context. In doing so she comes down on one particular side within an ongoing debate within ethnography. Paul Rabinow (1986, p. 242) drew a distinction between two different directions in contemporary ethnography, spearheaded then by Clifford Geertz (1973, 1983, 1989) on the one hand, and James Clifford (Clifford and Marcus, 1986) on the other. Although it may, at first glance, seem that Geertz and Clifford are both about the same business, that of interpreting culture, they differ in crucial respects. Geertz may use literary concepts like text, discourse and author, but for him the task is a scientific one – the scientific description of culture, of otherness, of the field 'out there'. For James Clifford, the 'other' cannot be located scientifically 'out there' in the field, but is always the creation of the anthropologist, inscribed in the written text. Clifford writes ethnography aware of the many and various tools, such as allegory and irony, that are used to establish the authority and plausibility of the construction of otherness, an otherness that is inevitably symbiotic with the self who writes. 'Scientific' questions of objectivity and suchlike become meaningless as textualization opens up complexities and constructions of self and other, of positionality, of power, of silence and absence hitherto unseen by traditional ethnographers. Geertz (1989), on the other hand, acknowledges in his work the impact of textualization upon the discipline of ethnography, but remains firmly of the belief that the ethnographer's primary work is done in the field, followed by the secondary analysis of writing up 'here' what was noted down 'there'. He recognizes some of the difficulties this task presents, like the hitherto invisible position of the ethnographer as writer (1989, p. 10), and the 'gap', as he calls it, of 'getting "their" lives into "our" works [which] has become ... morally, politically, even epistemologically delicate' (1989, p. 130).

Nevertheless he grieves the passing of the secure realism of the past, the 'facts, descriptions, induction, and truth' (1989, p. 137) of former ethnography, now made unstable by the textualized attention to writing of such as James Clifford. Visweswaran's focus upon betrayal, omissions, silences and partial truths locates her firmly within the constructivist, textualized strand, allowing her to explore the relations between her own subject position and what and how she knows. Always incomplete, situational and relational, her ethnographic accounts make visible the ideological constitution of knowledge as produced from positions and standpoints of power between people.

Visweswaran tells the story of a woman who would not talk with her, who refused to be her subject. The woman refused to allow herself to be named – calling into question the very practice of naming. In doing so, the woman sustained herself as an enigma, thereby subverting Visweswaran's theorizing. That the woman refused to disclose anything about herself frustrated Visweswaran's attempts to move towards research closure, or even to establish her own authority as researcher. The woman forced Visweswaran to rethink the relationship between her own subject position and the subject position in which she put her interviewees. For her this becomes 'the ground of a feminist ethnography' (1994, p. 67). What might here be termed a failure is re-figured by Visweswaran and becomes another factor in the constitution of knowledge. Failure and silence are not just signs of epistemological crisis but also are configured within the epistemological construct of ethnography (1994, p. 99).

The women who refuse to speak, who refuse the subject position imposed upon them by ethnographic practice, subvert the epistemology that traditional ethnography relies upon. Visweswaran locates feminist ethnography at the site of betrayal and failure where knowledge is necessarily a negotiation between different power-laden subject positions. Her writing expresses not only voice and text, but also resistance and silence. Visweswaran brings the expression of power and agency through silence to the foreground. In shaping such a notion of power and agency, Visweswaran is listening not so much to what is *said*, and how, but to the *not-said*. She has an ear for the different sorts of silence, which can be the refusal to say, as well as that which goes without saying, and that which cannot be said (1994, p. 51). Silence means many things, both in interview and in text. The silences and omissions in the construction of her text mark her own examination of the power differentials inherent in her research. Visweswaran betrays us, her readers, by refusing to fill the silences. In adopting such a method, and in constructing such an epistemology, she subverts the traditional pillars of ethnography.

As I interviewed members of the congregation I encountered many ways in which silence could be used to register resistance. These came to light particularly when the new incumbent arrived. For example, 'silence' can be understood in terms of the amount of illness, which increased noticeably. On one occasion the curate commented to me that 'people are very fragile – Edith,

Audrey not well. Andrea has stopped coming'. And in my journal during the same period I wrote:

> After [the service] I went to the pub with Audrey and she opened up. She is feeling very nervy and doesn't like the atmosphere though she says [the new rector] is fine during the week. She said that no one turned up in time to deacon and she didn't because she didn't feel well enough and that she'd done it for all the past weeks. Gordon she says has been at the altar for the last five weeks. Edith is off with her nerves. Margaret's been told not to sing the antiphon and she's wondering whether she should bother coming.

During the interregnum and before, there was a dominant discourse in place that was very secure. When the new rector arrived, she entered the arena with different ideas, and a different set of theological and social values. She did not choose to share 'the Peace'. This upset many members, especially black members. For example, in interview Mary told me that many of her friends were wondering if it was because the rector did not want to shake hands with black people. And Gaynor told me:

> G   She don't come down, and she don't take your hand and she don't go up with the offering. You know, [the previous rector] always come down, and walk behind you, and come up at the communion. She don't do that. She don't come down and shake your hand like [he] did–
>
> F   –In the Peace?
>
> G   In the Peace, yes. So, I mean, probably that's her ways.

Jonathan, a leading black member, also wondered about the reasons why the new rector did not exchange the Peace.

> J   I think [she], well, it may be a bit superficial, but that may be the way she goes about things. In the first place she doesn't welcome people to the [church], and there's also the meeting after the service and tea and coffee and all the rest. I think, er, pleasantries are nice. And then I don't think she also goes around to do the handshake after the Peace, and some members are wondering why she doesn't do that.
>
> F   Have they been wondering to you?
>
> J   Yes, sometimes they do, wondering why she doesn't go around.
>
> F   And why do they think she doesn't?
>
> J   Well, they don't know. <laughter> I always think of asking [the curate] why she doesn't do that. I don't know whether he also knows. <laughter> Er. I think about twelve members of the church have observed that she doesn't welcome people and doesn't go around, I think.

Whatever the reason for the new rector's decision not to share the Peace, it was interpreted with an unease by black people that was not shared by white members, who did not invest the same significance in the lack of social intercourse. In other ways the new rector disrupted familiar ways, and provoked, as we see with Jonathan's comments above, gossip within the congregation.

My interest as a researcher led me to attempt to read from sub-groups within the congregation how they gauged the welcome they received, and how ready they were to absent themselves if they did not feel 'at home'. There was a real sense of withdrawal from the new rector among black members. Any dissent only emerged explicitly once, when Stella was asked to raise the matter in the P.C.C. meeting. Largely, though, people seemed to register their unhappiness by illness and staying away. Paul left permanently. As a gay white man, he was vocal in opposition to the changing ethos, threatened to leave while I was still attending, and did so a few months later, to worship at the local Roman Catholic church.

Writing up such encounters and reflecting upon what I was hearing left me acutely aware of the vulnerability of black people, and other 'others', to the vagaries of the dominant culture in which they might find themselves. The reasons to be silent, or to gossip because few other means of dissent were available, or simply to have a 'sickie', echoed what Visweswaran described as strategies of non-involvement. It was not so much with me that members, at this stage, refused to participate, but with a particular dominant discursive culture that they did not like. The last two stages did, though, call into question my engagement as a researcher, and the difficulties of writing up the life I had shared, and of leaving a congregation that had undergone such transitions.

Stage Three: Writing Up

I have already said how an ethnographer has to write from beginning to end. In a continual process of drafting and redrafting, the final text takes shape from bits and pieces, from snatched snippets of conversation, from seemingly arbitrary observations. The power of the author to cut and paste is the crude power to delete some voices, some perspectives, in favour of others. As you turn the lives of others into text, the burden of responsibility lies heavy. For whom are you writing? What style do you use? What do you select or omit (intentionally and unintentionally)? Throughout the research project a clear-cut distinction between research and 'writing up' proves impossible. And that power to select is not straightforward, either. It was difficult and extremely time-consuming to transcribe the interviews, especially those of people whose accent I did not hear well, or whose first language was not English. I found myself skipping chunks of tape-recording that I could not understand, of which I could not remember the details of the original conversation. Racism by default, perhaps. And then I would leave out of consideration some aspects of the data that I did not think would be ultimately relevant, and then return at a later date with surprise to the original notes, wondering how I might have missed that little gem of a comment. As I shaped the coherent final text, I was much more aware, often, of what I was omitting – of the losses and fragments that had no place, and of the mess that textual order left behind.

Stage Four: The Aftermath

Leaving the field of research can be a painful business. You have got involved: the concerns and business that have occupied you for a number of months now need to be left behind. My leaving was precipitated by the arrival of the new rector. There was no negotiation with her at all. Despite my offering at least twice, by letter before she arrived, and then face to face, to talk my research through with her, it quickly became apparent that my presence as researcher was not welcome at all. Her silence effectively meant I had to go. So between the period of her arrival in October and January the following year, I gradually withdrew from the fieldwork, completing some last interviews while continuing to observe the changes that occurred. Gordon, the same person who made the comment about 'institutional racism', was determined to work with her. He changed through this period in his attitude to me. As a former churchwarden he obviously took his loyalty to the rector seriously. This meant that he shifted ground noticeably after she arrived. In November I made the following note:

> Pub time was interesting. Gordon said 'so you'll be leaving us soon'. I said, 'well, that's the best'. He said 'it's been good' (talking in the past already). I said it needed to come to an end sometime.
> Later Audrey asked me quietly how I was – 'all right', I said. And I asked her. 'All right on the surface' she replied. 'But bruised underneath?' She nodded.

I found myself here caught in the middle of shifting alliances and loyalties – in the midst of changes that disrupted me as well as many of the members of the congregation. In many ways I think I found myself empathizing with the hurt and sense of betrayal that congregational members felt as well-established and familiar patterns of worship were changed.

It was at this time that I withdrew from the congregation as well, so I was left with impressions which of course were one-sided and probably did not do justice to the new rector's full ministry. She introduced changes that disrupted the settled patterns of the former dominant discourse, and after twelve or thirteen years of a particular way of doing things at the church, when members had become accustomed to the previous style of leadership, it was inevitable, you might say, that a new rector would have that effect. The observations at the tail end of my field research were very important to me, however, in that I was able to see how the congregation responded to potential conflict and disturbance.

Subsequently, I had other encounters with the original gatekeepers, neither of whom, for different reasons, were happy with my account of the story of this congregation over a difficult transitional time. The curate was made unhappy by some of the interpretations I made, especially about how illness was used as a form of resistance. The former rector criticized how I portrayed him and his 'highly autocratic leadership style', arguing that he spent many years trying to break a highly dependent tradition of 'Father knows best'. He was also not happy with my over-emphasis, as he saw it, upon worship, arguing that there were many black worshippers who actively chose Anglicanism over more

Pentecostal forms of worship. To be fair, it was not me, but many of the interviewees who described him as autocratic, and I was at pains to point out that during his years there, the congregation had sustained an unusual degree of diversity, and empowerment of many of the members, to his credit.

It was brought home to me just how difficult it can be to use ethnographic methods to interrogate such notions as 'institutional racism'. The former rector, indeed I myself, belong to a dominant Anglican ethos which uses its liturgical practices to sustain its culture, in which white people tend to feel more at home than black people. To research the ways in which such a culture perpetrates itself takes the ethnographer into territory where dominance may be challenged uncomfortably, and where the text itself will betray the means of its own dominant production.

Conclusion

I hope to have shown through this account that ethnographic methods, though most rewarding in many ways, are not without difficulty. This is a particular case study, but, I would argue, any ethnography worth its salt will run into questions of power which will permeate practical and ethical issues. Within a congregation the difficulties of making these visible may well outweigh the advantages, and perhaps this is why congregational studies can seem such a benign discipline. I am left with a real sense of unease as a result of doing the research. Yet I also feel that I honestly tried to understand some of the workings of institutional racism and the dominance of Anglo-Saxon culture within Anglicanism, using ethnographic methods to good effect.

With the benefit of hindsight, I would from the beginning be much more focused on where I ended up: institutional racism within the discursive practices of the Church of England, as analysed by an ethnographic study of a congregation. I would engage much more with members on this question, and negotiate throughout with participants and gatekeepers about the progress of my reflections and research. But hindsight is easy. And as only ethnographic methods will do for some subjects, the risks need to be taken. It is worth getting stuck into the mess, especially if those who study the congregation are prepared to engage with cutting-edge questions about church life in the world today.

References

Ammerman, N. T. *et al.* (eds) (1998), *Studying Congregations: A New Hanbdbook*, Nashville, TN: Abingdon Press.

Atkinson, P. (1990), *The Ethnographic Imagination: Textual Constructions of Reality*, London and New York: Routledge.

Becker, P. E. (1999), *Congregations in Conflict: Cultural Models of Local Religious Life*, Cambridge, UK, New York and Melbourne, Australia: Cambridge University Press.

Behar, R. and Gordon, D. (eds) (1995), *Women Writing Culture*, Berkeley: University of California Press.

Behar, R. (1996), *The Vulnerable Observer: Anthropology that Breaks your Heart*, Boston, MA: Beacon Press.

Bennison, C. *et al.* (1999), *In Praise of Congregations: Leadership in the Local Church Today*, Boston, MA: Cowley Publications.

Browning, D. (1991), *A Fundamental Practical Theology*, Minneapolis, MN: Fortress Press.

Clifford, J. and Marcus, G. E. (eds) (1986), *Writing Culture: The Poetics and Politics of Ethnography*, Berkeley: University of California Press.

Dudley, C. (ed.) (1983), *Building Effective Ministry: Theory and Practice in the Local Church*, San Francisco: Harper and Row.

Dudley, C. *et al.* (eds) (1991), *Carriers of Faith: Lessons from Congregational Studies*, a Festschrift in honor of Robert W. Lynn, Louisville, KY: Westminster/John Knox Press.

Foucault, M. ([1966] 1994), 'Man and his Doubles', in *The Order of Things: An Archaeology of the Human Sciences*, trans. A. Sheridan-Smith, New York and London: Routledge, pp. 303–343.

Foucault, M. ([1975] 1991), *Discipline and Punish: The Birth of the Prison*, trans. A. Sheridan-Smith, London: Penguin.

Geertz, C. ([1973] 1993), *The Interpretation of Cultures*, London: Fontana.

Geertz, C. ([1983] 1993), *Local Knowledge*, London: Fontana.

Geertz, C. (1989), *Works and Lives: The Anthropologist as Author*, California: Stanford University Press.

Haraway, D. (1991), *Simians, Cyborgs, and Women: The Reinvention of Nature*, London: Free Association Books.

Heilman, S. (1976), *Synagogue Life: A Study in Symbolic Interaction*, Chicago: University of Chicago Press.

Hopewell, J. ([1987] 1988), *Congregation: Stories and Structures*, ed. B. Wheeler, London: SCM.

Lyon, B. (2000), 'What is the Relevance of Congregational Studies for Pastoral Theology?' in Woodward, J. and Pattison, S. (eds) (2000), *The Blackwell Reader in Pastoral and Practical Theology*, Oxford: Blackwell, pp. 257–271.

MacPherson Report into The Stephen Lawrence Inquiry (1999), see www.official-documents.co.uk/document/cm42/4262, 24/02/99.

Rabinow, P. (1986), 'Representations are Social Facts: Modernity and Post-Modernity in Anthropology', in Clifford, J. and Marcus, G. E. (eds) (1986), *Writing Culture: The Poetics and Politics of Ethnography*, Berkeley: University of California Press, pp. 234–261.

Skeggs, B. (ed.) (1995), *Feminist Cultural Theory: Process and Production*, Manchester: Manchester University Press.

Spacks, P. (1986), *Gossip*, Chicago: University of Chicago Press.

Visweswaran, K. (1994), *Fictions of Feminist Ethnography*, Minneapolis: University of Minnesota Press.

Wind, J. P. and Lewis, J. W. (eds) (1998), *American Congregations*, 2 vols, Chicago: The University of Chicago Press.

Chapter 10

Are Congregations Associations? The Contribution of Organizational Studies to Congregational Studies

Helen Cameron

Introduction

The purpose of this chapter is to discuss how the academic field of organizational studies can contribute to the study of congregations in the UK. The case will be made by looking at whether the term 'association' is a useful definition of five case study congregations.

Before embarking on this task, it is important to acknowledge that there are significant barriers to making use of organizational studies in this way. First, there is the diversity of academic disciplines that deal with organizations and the very different levels of visibility they have within academic life. Second, there is the culturally embedded ideology of managerialism, which asserts that the well-managed organization can achieve its mission and so resolve social problems. Third, there is the widespread assumption that all organizations are bureaucratic in form and so lessons from one can easily be translated to another. Fourth, there are the rationalistic and utilitarian assumptions that pervade much organizational writing and that are at odds with the more interpretative mindset within which most religious professionals are formed. Such is the seriousness of these barriers that many of those who participate in congregational life feel instinctively that organizational language is inappropriate and even hostile to their endeavours.

Let me give my own reasons for persisting in trying to make use of organizational studies in the task of studying congregations. First, I want to take seriously the work, both paid and unpaid, that goes on in congregations. Much of this work has remained invisible to those who research congregations because they tend to interview paid professionals. Second, I want to take seriously the desire of congregations to reflect what they believe in the way that they act. Most congregants are seeking to act in a way that authentically resonates with their beliefs, but experience a gap between the aspirational language of the liturgy and the reality of maintaining a human institution while enacting its mission. Third, I want to take seriously the experience of the local church practitioners I teach. They tell me that the way their work is organized can affect whether it fulfils or frustrates their individual ministry as well as the corporate mission of the congregation.

The next section examines the barriers to the use of organizational studies in more detail. Following that I set out the method by which I hope to illustrate the contribution of organizational studies. The concept of association is defined, and then five case study congregations are introduced and compared to the concept. A discussion of the differences between concept and case study takes place before, finally, the conclusion assesses the diverse reality of congregations and reappraises the barriers and benefits outlined in this introduction.

The Barriers Examined

Having briefly outlined four barriers to making use of organizational studies, this section examines them in more detail. The first barrier is the confusing array of academics who study organizations and the fact that the ones who are most relevant to congregations are likely to be the least visible to the non-specialist. By far the largest and most visible group are the management academics who work in business schools. Their focus is mainly on the workings of large private sector businesses. Business executives provide a ready and lucrative audience for their research findings and teaching (Burnes, 1996). Within most business schools there is now a subset of academics who study the public sector, again usually the larger bureaucracies of the state (Ferlie, Ashburner *et al.*, 1996). A much smaller group, found in some business schools and social policy departments, studies the voluntary sector, focusing on its particular characteristics (Harris and Rochester, 2001). As well as academics, the discipline of management has spawned 'gurus' (Peters, 1987) and consultants (Hammer and Champy, 1993) who commodify techniques and sell them to practitioners (Micklethwait and Wooldridge, 1996).

A much smaller and less visible group of academics studies organizations from within particular social sciences, for example psychology (Argyris and Schon, 1978), sociology (Collins, 1998) and anthropology (Darrah, 1996). These academics bring the focus and methods of their own discipline to bear on organizational phenomena. A number of those taking a sociological approach are applying critical theory to dethrone the claims of managerialism (Parker, 2002).

Given the public prominence of writers on management and their focus on large bureaucratically structured organizations, it is hardly surprising that those interested in congregations feel safe in dismissing all writing on organizations. I want to argue that writers in the sociology of organizations (this chapter makes use of Weber) and writers on voluntary sector management (Harris, 1998a) can be of use (Abzug, 1999).

The second barrier to using organizational studies is the ideology of managerialism that confidently asserts that social and economic problems can be resolved through 'good management'. Pattison (1997) has illustrated the weaknesses of this approach when applied to public sector organizations such as the National Health Service. He argues that a managerialist approach minimizes the difficulties of effecting change, underestimates the true costs of change and assumes that all change is beneficial. It is a decontextualizing approach which accords superabundant agency to the manager and assumes ready compliance by subordinates and customers/clients. Such is the pervasiveness of this ideology that it is unsurprising that it has some advocates within the churches. Nor is it surprising that those in the churches who are aware of the fallenness of human institutions should be wary of its exponents and want to rule out the sources upon which they draw.

The third barrier derives in some ways from the previous two. Given the focus of management academics on large bureaucratically structured organizations and the popularization of their ideas, it is easy to see why there is an assumption that the bureaucracy is the sole way of organizing a group of people engaged in a common task. It was Weber (1947) who first defined the bureaucracy and predicted its dominance in the modern world. The bureaucracy coordinates work through a hierarchy of officers who have the right to assign work to their subordinates and hold them to account. Those who work in bureaucracy are paid and their work is their livelihood. These features do not ring true of the work done in congregations, and so again the insights of organizational studies are in doubt.

The final barrier is the epistemological assumptions of much writing on organizations. There is a tendency to seek the same status as the natural sciences and to develop law-like generalizations that will apply irrespective of the type of organization or its context. This type of knowledge is largely unattractive to religious professionals who are educated in the skills of interpretation and are more sceptical of claims for the predictive power of theories.

Having set out the barriers, the chapter now moves on to work through an extended example of an organizational concept being used in an empirical study of congregations.

Method

The purpose of the extended example is to show how organizational studies can be used in a way that avoids the barriers and helps participants increase their understanding of their practice. Weber, the earliest sociologist to study organizations, looked at both the bureaucracy and the association as means of coordinating work. The dominance but unpromising nature of bureaucracy has already been discussed, so the associational form will be explored here. Weber's method was to construct an ideal type definition of a social phenomenon and then look at how real examples differed from that definition. By constructing an ideal type definition of an association, I hope to make progress in understanding what associational features congregations possess. From this it may be possible to understand better the way in which their work is organized. The next section constructs a definition, as a precursor to introducing a set of case studies and making comparisons.

Defining Associations

Weber argued that where people wish to undertake a task that is beyond the energies of one person, a division of labour results and so some form of social coordination is required. He predicted that one form of coordination, the bureaucracy, would come to dominate modern society, but he also felt that other forms of coordination, including the association, would persist.

Unlike Weber's 'ideal type' definition of bureaucracy, which has been returned to by scholars as a starting point for their own work (Jaques, 1951; Crozier, 1964; Mouzelis, 1967), I can find no similarly well-accepted definition of an association. Many authors discuss associations without setting out the characteristics by which they are to be recognized. In my review of the literature I found ten criteria that were referred to by more than one writer which, put together, could form the basis of an 'ideal type' definition with which empirical examples could be compared.

Smith and Freedman (1972) define voluntary associations as structured, formally organized and relatively permanent groups that: have offices that are filled through an established procedure; have periodic scheduled meetings; have qualifying criteria for membership; and have some formalized division or specialization of labour. Perrow (1970) concentrates on members as the distinctive feature of associations and looks at the resources they provide which make the work of the association possible. As well as lending their name to the association, they can contribute time and money and engage with decision-making processes. Jaques (1976) in his *General Theory of Bureaucracy* helpfully contrasts bureaucracies and associations. The features he emphasizes in associations are their membership criteria, their democratic decision-making and the requirement upon members to obey the rules of the association. Billis (1993) identifies the dividing line between bureaucracies and associations as being significant in defining the voluntary sector and detects an ambiguous zone in which some organizations adopt both associational and bureaucratic characteristics. Membership criteria define the boundary of an association, officers are appointed and decisions are made by voting. The approaching boundary with bureaucracy can be detected when paid staff are employed to do the core work of the association rather than purely to facilitate the work of the members. Knoke's (1990) major study of associations focuses upon membership criteria, members contributing resources and democratic decision-making as key characteristics.

Synthesizing the work of these authors, the following ten criteria emerge. Associations are formally constituted organizations. Access to membership depends upon meeting a set of criteria. Officers govern the association but are appointed by the members and are accountable to them. Associations have scheduled meetings to conduct their business. There is a formal division of labour to enable the work to be undertaken. Members provide resources for the association by paying subscriptions and giving time to its work. Decisions are made by democratic procedures. Continuing membership depends upon not transgressing the rules of the association. Where paid staff are employed, they support the work of members rather than undertaking the core work of the association. Of these criteria, all five authors endorse two, namely membership is by fulfilling criteria and decisions are made democratically.

Having proposed an 'ideal type' definition of an association, the chapter now moves to consider the empirical data. The study undertaken is described and a quick sketch of each of five congregations is offered. A table summarizes the comparisons between the five congregations and the definition, and then each criterion is discussed in turn.

The Case Study Congregations

The study from which the data are drawn is of five congregations that were undertaking social action projects designed to meet needs in their local communities. The research question aimed to explore the relationship between congregation and project as this was felt to underpin the issues presented by the participants as problematic. In order to explore this relationship, data were gathered about the membership of the congregation, the decision-making structures and the resources available to them. The study involved spending one month with each congregation and undertaking a mix of participant observation, interviews and documentary analysis. The congregations were located in two contrasting neighbourhoods of the same English city and belonged to four different denominations. A brief description of the five congregations is given. Pseudonyms are used throughout and some details have been changed to protect the identity of the participants.

The first three churches are located in Underhill, an inner city area with multiple sources of deprivation. All Saints is an Anglican church with 160 worshippers on the electoral roll. The congregants are one-third Asian, one-third Afro-Caribbean and one-third white. The congregation is governed by the priest with two churchwardens and the Parochial Church Council, which has sixteen members. The Anglican Church is the national church in England and calls its local churches 'parishes', believing that it is their role to minister to all who live within the parish boundaries.

Barton New Testament Church of God started in the 1950s when a group of immigrants from the West Indies started meeting for worship in each others' homes. In 1963 a former Methodist church was purchased. All 250 members are Afro-Caribbean. There is a full-time pastor and members are heavily involved in running the activities of the church. Activities are grouped into departments, supported by a director and committee. Ultimately decisions are referred to the pastor, who is advised by a Church Council.

The Christian Centre was formed in 1974 from the merger of two chapels. New buildings were erected at the same time as the surrounding housing estate was being built. It belongs to the United Reformed Church denomination and has 75 members and 40 adherents, half white and half Afro-Caribbean. There is a full-time minister and a full-time community worker. The ultimate decision-making body is the Church Meeting, which is a monthly gathering of members chaired by the minister.

The final two churches are located in Parktown, a prosperous suburb on the edge of the city. Divinity Road United Reformed Church is located in the shopping centre in Parktown. It has 300 members and 190 adherents, all of whom are white. The main decision-making body is the Church Meeting at which all members can vote. There are 20 elected lay leaders who meet monthly and transact much of the business. The church runs many groups and activities that require substantial input from members. There is one full-time minister.

Eastgate Methodists has 350 members, all of whom are white. It has one full-time minister and one full-time lay worker. Members are involved in sustaining the activities of the church. The congregation is governed by a Church Council with 44 members that meets three times a year. Eight committees undertake much of the day-to-day decision-making.

Comparing the Congregations with the Definition

The table on page 145 summarizes the comparisons between the five congregations and the ten elements of the 'ideal type' definition.

All five case study congregations met four of the criteria. All were formal organizations; all held scheduled weekly meetings; all undertook more work than could be accomplished by one person and had a formal means of dividing the work between officers and sub-units; all had membership criteria that an applicant had to satisfy before becoming a member. All the congregations had the normal trappings of formal organizations. They had names by which they were known and in which they held bank accounts and property. They all had buildings which were a focal point for their work. They all undertook sufficient work to require some form of coordination and had established means of dividing the work among their members. In a church, scheduled meetings for worship are a core fulfilment of their purpose. In addition to this there were also scheduled meetings for many other activities and for transacting business.

All had membership criteria that they used to decide who was eligible to join. The two URC churches had two levels of membership, member and adherent, with a greater expectation that members would be involved in the work of the congregation. Adherents were unable to vote, although they could attend Church Meetings. All Saints Church of England parish used three overlapping definitions of membership. One of those definitions, that all residents within the parish boundaries are regarded as parishioners and therefore entitled to use the services of the church, was ascriptive, requiring no conscious act of 'joining'. Electors were those who worshipped regularly at the church and were able to vote in elections to deanery and diocesan synods. Communicants were those who had been baptised and confirmed and so were eligible to receive communion.

Another point about membership that must be emphasized is that the formal membership was only a loose guide as to who participated in each congregation's activities. All congregations had members who did not participate in any activities, usually because of old age or ill health. All congregations had those who participated regularly in activities but who had never taken the step of becoming members. Rarely was any distinction made

Table 10.1 Are congregations associations?

Criteria	All Saints	Barton NT Church of God	Christian Centre URC	Divinity Road URC	Eastgate Methodists
Formally organized	Yes	Yes	Yes	Yes	Yes
Offices filled by procedures	Election and appointment	Appointment only	Election and appointment	Election and appointment	Election and appointment
Scheduled meetings	Weekly	Weekly	Weekly	Weekly	Weekly
Membership criteria	Parishioner Elector Communicant	Member	Member Adherent	Member Adherent	Member
Division of labour	Yes	Yes	Yes	Yes	Yes
Subscriptions	Planned giving encouraged	Tithes Offerings Gifts	Planned giving encouraged	Planned giving encouraged	Planned giving encouraged
Giving time for church work	Not expected	Expected	Expected	Not expected but encouraged	Not expected
Democratic decision-making	Some via representative	No democratic procedures	Direct democracy of members	By members and by representative	Some via representative
Obedience to rules	None enforced	Lifestyle rules enforced	None enforced	None enforced	None enforced
Paid staff do not do core work	Clergy do core work	Clergy do core work	Clergy do core work	Clergy do core work	Clergy do core work

Note: Shaded entries indicate where the criteria are *not* met. Comments on the match between the case studies and the criteria are in the body of the chapter.

between members and non-members in terms of eligibility to participate in activities other than decision-making.

Two of the criteria were not met by any of the case studies. First, none of the churches had subscriptions as a condition of membership. There were varying expectations about voluntary giving by members but these were not enforced as a condition of membership in the way a subscription might be. Barton NT

Church of God had the strongest expectations, asking members to tithe their income to the church, to make free will offerings on special occasions and to make gifts of money when particular needs arose. The other four churches all had planned giving schemes whereby members could make a regular contribution to the congregation. The absence of subscriptions does not indicate that the churches were not dependent upon their income from their members. All Saints benefited from a denominational subsidy but the others were self-financing and in addition made a contribution to their denominations. Nevertheless, the term subscription is not appropriate as it is commonly held to imply an obligation to pay and the withdrawal of membership if payment is not forthcoming. Second, all of the congregations had a paid member of staff, that is, the clergy, who undertook core tasks of the congregation as opposed to just supporting the work of members. Not all denominations have clergy, although the majority do, and their status as specially trained full-time religious functionaries inevitably gives them a central role in the work of the congregation (Harris, 1998b). For Billis (1993, pp. 163f) this would disqualify congregations as associations, pushing them into the category of agencies, a hybrid of association and bureaucracy. Clergy had an ambiguous status because although the money to pay them was raised locally, all except the pastor at Barton NT Church of God were paid centrally by their denomination. They were all recognized as having particular expert knowledge in matters of religious belief, which represented the core purpose of the congregation. All clergy held a central place in the decision-making structures in their congregations. Clergy did also have a role in facilitating the work of members, but their primary purpose was to exercise religious leadership, especially in the conduct of worship, a core activity for all congregations.

There were three criteria on which Barton NT Church of God differed from the other four congregations. First, Barton was the only church not to fill some of its offices by democratic procedures. All its officers were appointed, usually on the decision of the pastor. Following from this, Barton was the only church not to have some form of democratic decision-making procedures, where members had a vote on key decisions. The church placed a strong emphasis on the responsibilities of members but accorded them only an advisory role in decision-making. Finally, Barton was the only church to enforce rules about lifestyle and belief and to withdraw membership if rules were broken. Several authors mentioned adherence to rules as a characteristic of associations. Assent to the rules is seen as part of the criteria for being accepted as a member. In all the congregations except Barton NT Church of God, it was unclear what, if any, rules a member was agreeing to when they joined the congregation. For the other four congregations, members had to make a simple statement of belief. It was unclear whether this committed the member to carrying out the ethical injunctions found in scripture. Membership usually signalled a willingness to take part in the life of the congregation, but although there were expectations of donating time and money and attending worship, they were not always fulfilled. Barton NT Church of God, by contrast, had a detailed statement of faith and specific rules about lifestyle including sexual morality, financial dealings and the use of drugs. Apart from Barton NT

Church of God, it was very difficult to detect any mechanisms for acting if members deviated from the rules. In fact it might be better expressed that the other four congregations had sets of expectations that members fulfilled or failed to fulfil according to their individual conscience.

The remaining criterion was whether giving time to the work of the church was an expectation of membership. At Barton NT Church of God and the Christian Centre it clearly was. At Divinity Road it was strongly encouraged, but at All Saints and Eastgate Methodists it was not an expectation.

Discussion

From the table and the description given, it can be seen that no clear pattern emerges if my 'ideal type' definition of association is applied to the case study congregations. While these congregations clearly do have some features in common, there is also a great deal of variation between them.

At this point it is worth returning to the definition and asking how much divergence from an 'ideal type' is possible before the definition becomes meaningless. In the literature review, two criteria were identified as having widest support, namely, membership by fulfilling criteria and democratic decision-making. However, even these two core criteria are not met by all the congregations. All Saints had one definition of membership that was ascriptive rather than about meeting criteria. Barton NT Church of God had no democratic decision-making procedures. Even this strategy of limiting the definition to two core criteria does not allow all the case studies to be classified as associations.

One possible explanation for the diversity in the case study congregations is to link it to the different denominational polities they belong to. All Saints, as an Anglican church, seemed to be a collection of historical accretions in its organizational structure. The dominant role of the clergy seemed to come from a traditional society where the clergy were a social elite. Added to that were the bureaucratic developments of the diocesan administration (Thompson, 1970) and the associational developments of synodic government. Barton NT Church of God seemed to be a membership organization that had adopted some bureaucratic features (Beckford, 1975) such as dividing its work into departments and having a hierarchy of officers who reported to the pastor. The Christian Centre and Divinity Road can be characterized as participative democracies where every member was expected to take part in decision-making. In the case of Divinity Road, representative elders also played an increasingly important role in decision-making. Eastgate Methodists was a representative democracy with decisions being taken by elected and appointed representatives. The variation in denominational polities has explanatory value and shows how different understandings of divine authority inform human organizing.

To summarize this discussion, there seem to be problems in classifying all congregations as associations. They seem to exhibit many of the characteristic behaviours of voluntary associations while not conforming neatly to an 'ideal type' definition. Until the base of research on congregations expands, the best description that can be offered of congregations is a category of membership-based organizations defined as formal organizations where members are admitted according to publicly known criteria and where members provide the bulk of the resources for the work of the organization. Beyond this there would be an expectation that congregations had diverse means of coordinating their work.

Conclusion

In conclusion, this chapter asks whether congregations are associations. It then revisits the real barriers and potential benefits to using organizational studies to look at congregations.

This chapter has constructed a definition of 'association' and used it to examine case study congregations. The discussion of the cases has shown that while all the congregations had associational characteristics, none met the definition exactly. Congregations are diverse, and not even those in the same denomination will share all characteristics in common. This leads me to conclude that the literature on associations cannot be applied directly to congregations and that a more nuanced approach to the organizational analysis of congregations is required. Examples of this could include looking at how congregations make decisions and understanding how they mobilize resources of time and money from their members. In a culture where much of organizational life has been homogenized by managerialism, congregations stand out as a testimony to the variety of ways in which work can be organized and the range of beliefs and values it is therefore possible to enact.

Of the four barriers to using organizational studies, two seem to have held firm and two have been lowered to some extent. The barrier of the diversity of the literature on organizations was experienced when seeking to construct a definition of association. A keen eye for the disciplinary base of the author and their assumptions about organizations and management are vital. The second barrier, the cultural embeddedness of managerialism, is unlikely to be dented by the publication of a chapter such as this, although I hope I have shown that it is possible to disengage from this over-optimistic and prescriptive perspective.

The third barrier of assuming all organizations to be bureaucratic in form has at least been challenged. It is clear that congregations do not coordinate their work through a hierarchy of officers who have authority to determine the work of their subordinates. This should put congregations in a better position to challenge the assumptions of the other organizations they deal with, such as schools and hospitals. It may even generate an appreciation of the variety of ways in which humans can coordinate their work and the theological principles embedded in their own denominational polities.

The fourth barrier, that of using concepts in a predictive manner, has also, I hope, been lowered. The skills of interpretation in which clergy are schooled can equally be turned from sacred texts to the contexts in which they operate and to the institutions in which they work. The aim here has been to expose the diversity of congregational life and the need to develop appropriate rather than standard ways of working.

As well as examining the barriers, this chapter has also tried to build the case for the benefits of using organizational studies. Congregations have been taken seriously as places of work and it has been shown that expectations about the time and money members will give to congregations will affect what they are able to do. They have been recognized as organizations engaged in a substantial variety of work requiring a range of interactions between participants. The desire of congregants to live out their religious principles in the way in which they organize has been manifest in the variety of denominational polities and the way in which they are enacted in different contexts. The difficulties of this particular approach in the face of managerialism and assumptions about the dominance of bureaucracy have been noted. The desire to design work that is fulfilling rather than frustrating has been supported by identifying specific features of congregations (for example, methods of decision-making) that can, it is hoped, become the subject of overt discussion and design (Lovell, 1994).

Organizational studies does have a contribution to make to congregational studies. However, this contribution stands in the shadow of the discipline's preoccupation with bureaucratically structured, private sector organizations with an over-optimistic understanding of human agency. On the margins of the discipline, among scholars of the voluntary sector and organizational sociology, there are useful concepts that can help elaborate what the organizational characteristics of congregations are and supply appropriate models and concepts. These models can help practitioners interrogate their own assumptions, drawn from their experience and the imprint of managerialism on our culture.

In the UK, congregations have been pushed increasingly into the private sphere. Despite the visibility of their buildings, what goes on in them has largely escaped the attention of policy-makers and academics in the 1980s and 1990s. There are some indicators that this may be changing (Sweeney, 2001; Bacon, 2003). Attempts to import the US debate about faith-based welfare have led both Labour and Conservative Parties to suggest that congregations might play a role in social policy (Cameron, 2001). New Labour's search for something that will work in urban regeneration has led to a revived interest in grassroots organizations that are seen as being able to reach the parts government programmes do not reach (Finneron, Green *et al.*, 2001; Farnell, Furbey *et al.*, 2003). Of those grassroots organizations, congregations are attractive because they have regional and national superstructures that can talk to the local and national state. However, as such dialogue continues, the formalizing and universalizing tendencies of state funding have the capacity to undermine the organizational models that make congregations what they are (Addy and Scott, 1988). A greater self-awareness among congregations, and an increased awareness among academics and policy-makers of the organizational characteristics of congregations, may well help avoid crushing that which is informal and particular.

Organizational studies needs to be encountered as both an academic and a cultural phenomenon. Its concepts should be seen as provoking and provisional and not normative – hermeneutic tools rather than predictive generalizations. There is further work to do to sort out appropriate means of dialogue with other disciplines and this could well start by exploring understandings of human agency. Organizational studies raises issues about the relationship between academic and practitioner that are likely to be relevant to any emerging field of congregational studies in the UK. It has an ability to raise issues which are of immediate salience to practitioners but also to connect those issues to wider academic debate. Organizational studies has value because it raises issues rooted in the daily particular reality of congregations which can in turn spark broader questions about social engagement, policy and theology.

References

Abzug, R. (1999), 'Nonprofits in organizational sociology's research traditions: an empirical study', *Nonprofit and Voluntary Sector Quarterly*, 28 (3), 330–338.

Addy, T. and Scott, D. (1988), *Fatal Impacts? The Manpower Services Commission and Voluntary Action*, Manchester: William Temple Foundation.

Argyris, C. and Schon, D. (1978), *Organizational Learning: A Theory of Action Perspective*, Reading, MA: Addison-Wesley.

Bacon, D. (2003), *Communities, Churches and Social Capital in Northern Ireland*, Coleraine: University of Ulster.

Beckford, J. A. (1975), 'Organization, ideology and recruitment: the structure of the Watch Tower movement', *Sociological Review*, 23 (4), 893–909.

Billis, D. (1993), *Organising Public and Voluntary Agencies*, London: Routledge.

Burnes, B. (1996), *Managing Change: A Strategic Approach to Organisational Dynamics*, London: Pitman.

Cameron, H. (2001), 'Review of "Faith in Politics"', *Political Theology*, 3 (1), 109–112.

Collins, D. (1998), *Organizational Change: Sociological Perspectives*, London: Routledge.

Crozier, M. (1964), *The Bureaucratic Phenomenon*, Chicago: University of Chicago Press.

Darrah, C. N. (1996), *Learning and Work: An Exploration in Industrial Ethnography*, New York: Garland Publishing.

Farnell, R., Furbey, R. *et al.* (2003), *'Faith' in Urban Regeneration? Engaging Faith Communities in Urban Regeneration*, Bristol: The Policy Press.

Ferlie, E., Ashburner, L., Fitzgerald, L. and Pettigrew, A. (1996), *The New Public Management in Action*, Oxford: Oxford University Press.

Finneron, D., Green, L., Harley, S. and Robertson, J. (2001), *Challenging Communities: Church Related Community Development and Neighbourhood Renewal*, Durham/London: Churches Community Work Alliance/Church Urban Fund.

Hammer, M. and Champy, J. (1993), *Reengineering the Corporation: A Manifesto for Business Revolution*, London: Brealey Publishing.

Harris, M. (1998a), *Organizing God's Work: Challenges for Churches and Synagogues*, Basingstoke: Macmillan.

Harris, M. (1998b), 'A special case of voluntary associations: towards a theory of congregational organization', *British Journal of Sociology*, 49 (4), 602–618.

Harris, M. and Rochester, C. (eds) (2001), *Voluntary Organisations and Social Policy in Britain: Perspectives on Change and Choice*, Basingstoke: Palgrave Macmillan.

Jaques, E. (1951), *The Changing Culture of a Factory*, London: Tavistock Institute.

Jaques, E. (1976), 'Bureaucracy and Associations Contrasted', in E. Jaques, *A General Theory of Bureaucracy*, London: Heinemann Educational, pp. 87–96.

Knoke, D. (1990), *Organising for Collective Action: The Political Economies of Associations*, New York: Aldine de Gruyter.

Lovell, G. (1994), *Analysis and Design: A Handbook for Practitioners and Consultants in Church and Community Work*, London: Burns and Oates.

Micklethwait, J. and Wooldridge, A. (1996), *The Witch Doctors: Making Sense of the Management Gurus*, London: Heinemann.

Mouzelis, N. (1967), *Organization and Bureaucracy: An Analysis of Modern Theories*, London: Routledge and Kegan Paul.

Parker, M. (2002), *Against Management: Organization in the Age of Managerialism*, Cambridge: Polity Press.

Pattison, S. (1997), *The Faith of the Managers: When Management Becomes Religion*, London: Cassell.

Perrow, C. (1970), 'Members as Resources in Voluntary Organizations', in Rosengren, W. R. and Lefton, M. (eds), *Organizations and Clients: Essays in the Sociology of Service*, Columbus, OH: Merrill, pp. 93–116.

Peters, T. (1987), *Thriving on Chaos: Handbook for a Management Revolution*, London: Macmillan.

Smith, C. and Freedman, A. (1972), *Voluntary Associations: Perspectives on the Literature*, Cambridge, MA: Harvard University Press.

Sweeney, J. (2001), *From Story to Policy: Social Exclusion, Empowerment and the Churches*, Cambridge: Von Hugel Institute.

Thompson, K. A. (1970), *Bureaucracy and Church Reform: The Organisational Response of the Church of England to Social Change 1800–1965*, Oxford: Clarendon Press.

Weber, M. (1947), *The Theory of Social and Economic Organization*, Oxford: Oxford University Press.

Chapter 11

Priests, Parish and People: Reconceiving a Relationship

Douglas Davies

As a contribution to congregational studies this chapter develops the idea of the 'occasional congregation' to describe events that embrace large numbers of people but which differ from the repetitive gathering of ordinary church groups. Behind this discussion lie two closely related concerns, one theoretical and one methodological. The first relates to the view of human beings as desiring a sense of unity achieved through collective action, while the second notes that both sociology and theology have their own methods of dealing with this desire and the means undertaken to achieve it. Here it is worth distinguishing between methodology – as the study of methods and their appropriateness for different tasks – and method – as one particular way of dealing with that task. In terms of this chapter, two methods, theological and sociological, stand out as ways of analysing the sense of collective unity. Several others, such as psychology, history, or even architecture, could also furnish ways of dealing with this subject. It is also worth noting that this very idea of a unified sense of things is, itself, an assumption, albeit related to observations of the human condition and human history, and is one that assumes a distinctive form both in sociology and theology. Doctrine, the systematized form of religious belief created within religious traditions, has often been the way churches have worked out their understanding of social experience. Doctrine can also, in its turn, influence the way people seek to organize both their individual and community life. In terms of this chapter, for example, we can see how ecclesiology – the doctrine of how and why a church works – can be viewed as a church's own form of 'sociology'. Of course a church can, if it wishes, develop an explicit scheme of sociology, its own theory of how society operates and how its own theology should influence that operation; indeed several traditions have done this, not least in a variety of Christian social theories.

This chapter, then, takes up questions about human gathering or congregating, aware of the significant differences that can be brought to the topic by both theology and sociology, and choosing, for most of the time, to adopt a sociological rather than a theological form of analysis. Accordingly, we present empirical evidence on the congregational relationship between priests, parish and people which Anglican clergy have traditionally described as 'occasional offices' and develop it in a sociological direction, aiming at a theoretical reconception of large-scale events in terms of an 'occasional congregation'. We begin with the prime relationship between the individual and society – one that itself possesses both theological and sociological forms – as the broad background for dealing with the more specific issue of the relationship between priest, parish and people.

One and Many

To begin, we indicate how sociology and theology, each in their own way, take up the question of how the individual relates to the group of which they are a part. This link between individual and society is notoriously complex and forms one of the foundational concerns of sociology in general and of the sociology of religion in particular. The very notions of 'individual' and of 'society' are known to differ from culture to culture as well as in the theoretical schemes that reflect upon them (for example, Carrithers *et al.*, 1985). Classically speaking, Durkheim emphasized 'society', reifying the notion in a way that might be expected from a Frenchman with political concerns of his own. Simmel, by contrast, explored the nature of the 'individual' in a much more personal way, expressing aspects of his own religiosity as well as the late nineteenth-century emphasis upon personality. Weber, more than either of his sociological companions, pursued the relationship between individual and society through his emphasis upon action and the socio-ideological sources of social life, and in many respects this yielded a more balanced picture of personal needs and their social resolution. Similar points could be made for all major sociologists as also for psychologists who ponder the dynamics of human self-awareness and social interaction. Today's theoretical fashions have maintained this interest, albeit by adding additional circuitry through notions of reflexivity and a more explicit self-consciousness of the part played by power, history, context and gender in anyone's interpretation of their life-world or theoretical world.

In Christian theology the relationship between individual and group has been just as important as in sociology and has been interpreted in terms of particular doctrines. The covenant community of Israel provides an early model for people bonded together through a shared belief in their response to God. Much later the sacramental community of the church and the more intimate brotherhood and sisterhood of sects furnished models of community. At a more abstract level, Christology – the complex debate concerning the nature of Jesus and the relationship of his human and divine natures – set the scene that prompted and fostered new doctrines explaining the church as a corporate body that somehow participates in Christ's nature and of priests who also symbolize Christ within that body of believers. In Anglican theology this was most forcefully expounded by the largely forgotten, but intellectually important, L. S. Thornton (1928, pp. 439–455; cf. 1956, pp. 66–77). Baptism, Eucharist and Ordination, for example, are rituals that deal theologically with what could be expressed, sociologically, as the relationship between 'individual and society', albeit the sacred society of the church. Catholic, Orthodox and Protestant traditions each have their own distinctive theologies of these relationships with their own, further internal turns of interpretation as expressed in ways that have been appreciated by sociologists in, for example, Ernst Troeltsch's magisterial *The Social Teaching of the Christian Churches* (1931).

Congregation and Parish

The Church of England in the mid-twentieth century went on to ponder the significance of the relationship between individual and society in several important ways and at different levels of social and political life, not least in terms of the relationship between priest and people both in the context of 'congregation' and of 'parish'. While, at its more abstract pole, it sought a theological understanding of the sociological nature of humanity and of the church within it – an issue addressed at William Temple's influential Malvern Conference of 1941 – such abstraction always returned to the local and parochial domain and the combined worship and service of the parish and its potentially missionary congregation. This was influentially pursued by A. G. Hebert in his *Liturgy and Society* (1935), with Gregory Dix's even more influential *The Shape of the Liturgy*, constructing what were, in effect, sociological ideal types such as 'Acquisitive Man, ... Mass Man, ... Eucharistic Man', and seeking to relate ritual changes in social values to ritual change within the church (1945, p. xviii). It is, perhaps, particularly worth noting that both Hebert, one of the Kelham Fathers, and Dix, an Anglican Benedictine of Nashdom, were members of monastic communities and from that life-perspective attempted to relate individual and society.

Roger Lloyd has helped focus attention on these and other church leaders in a period when 'sociology through liturgy' was of profound theological concern (1950, pp. 107–111). These contributions reflect the distinctive nature of the Church of England, by law established as the state church, and demand that the distinction of 'congregation' and 'parish' become explicit. Furthermore, the pastoral ministry of priests ensured that it could not be ignored, as is clear in Joost de Blank – then Bishop of Stepney – and his analysis of 'the parish and its congregation ... its people ... the individual ... and the world church' in which he details the role of the parson in relation both to the gathered congregation and to the largely non-attending people living within the geographical parish itself (1954, pp. 23–64). This presaged the church's later ethical–pastoral emphasis expressed through, for example, Bishop David Sheppard's work, especially *Bias to the Poor* (1983; cf. 1974).

Simmel, Congregations and Leaders

This background discussion shows how congregations and congregational leadership pose an interesting arena for exploring various aspects of the relationships between individual and society, whether the stress falls on group, individual participant or leader. This complex interplay also affords one relatively clear example of the way in which ideology, in this case theology, may influence forms of human association, and brings us to our chosen topic of 'occasional congregation'. Here we begin with a brief theoretical issue from Georg Simmel, a scholar of Jewish background but a member of a Protestant Church for most of his life, who pursued a sociology of religion that was almost theological in its acknowledgement of the experience of the individual in relation to God as an issue that could not be simply reduced to social forces. Nevertheless, he fully recognized the significance of those social dynamics in shaping the way people might believe and live. Here we restrict ourselves to but one cluster of his ideas, that which links the religious desire for unity with God and the concrete fact of priesthood as a medium of religious leadership within congregations.

Simmel describes 'priesthood', by analogy with 'society' or the 'state', as an abstract unity ranged above all individuals and yet representing their interrelationships (1997, p. 114). Just as he sees religion expressing the purest and most abstract form of the 'human instinct' for unity, so he takes the priesthood to be a more concrete symbol of that abstraction, most especially in the classic case of the celibate Catholic priesthood. In that priesthood the individual priest is freed from ordinary kinship obligations in order to relate equally to all within his sphere of responsibility: because of that freedom he is able to embody something of that 'suprasubjective order' of things in relation to which people seek a degree of union under the pressure of the 'instinct for unity'. Meanwhile, the priest, himself, comes to be 'directed by a guiding force that embraces his personality', a force that is nothing less than a suprasubjective order of existence (1997, p. 193). While Durkheim would have been content to classify that 'order' as 'society', some other sociologists felt the need to qualify its enclosing social reductionism, as when Peter Berger engaged in some awkward theoretical movements with 'signals of transcendence' (Berger, 1971, pp. 72–75). Simmel is content to engage in a more open form of discourse and not only takes the priesthood to be an expression of a division of labour but a mode of behaviour in which the leader acts for all, to help them realize their own desire for involvement in a higher order of things. The congregation becomes a site within which human nature pursues its religious aspect.

Having alluded to the cultural contexts that give both 'individual' and 'society' their distinctive local meaning, it is worth adding to them the notion of 'congregation' as such. This is largely because I want to differentiate between regular and occasional congregations and, to do so, I must draw attention to some of the implicit assumptions that the very notion of a 'congregation' brings to mind in the ordinary English Anglican context. The variation over even the English word is great, ranging from the independent groups of Christians reflected in the history of, for example, the Congregational Church, to monastic congregations, or to the nine distinctive administrative departments of the Vatican. More immediate than those contexts is the idea of congregation found in the Church of England that provides the framework for this chapter. To read priesthood manuals, the many volumes of advice on how to be a clergyman that have served the Church of England in the relative absence of any established body of pastoral theology, is to see individual experience and a degree of legal necessity raised to the power of theology as far as congregations within parochial life are concerned. Few in the twenty-first century, for example, would follow John Watson's 1896 lectures on practical theology in which he likens a congregation, referred to in the feminine, as being 'like a college or a regiment' and requiring a certain *esprit de corps* (1896, p. 148). As the technical study of congregations now develops, as reflected in the other chapters of this book, it remains important to consider how particular groups think of themselves and how their leaders see them. The difference, for example, between a congregation and a 'parish' in England is potentially great for, as we will see below, to be a parishioner, even one whose name stands upon the register-roll of a church, does not necessarily involve a great deal of congregational involvement. Similarly, clergy often employ an implicit, and sometimes an explicit classification of groups, as when they see regular attendees at the Eucharist or some form of special-group meeting as somehow more sincere or genuine in their religious commitment than less frequent members or than those who largely attend other forms of service.

'Regular' Congregations

Empirical Background

For a direct analysis of these issues we turn to empirical material, in particular to the Rural Church Project conducted by myself along with two other directors, Charles Watkins and Michael Winter, and other colleagues, Caroline Pack, Susanne Seymour and Christopher Short, and published in four volumes of extensive descriptive statistics (hereafter, Davies *et al.*, 1990). A more popular form was also published as *Church and Religion in Rural England* (Davies, Watkins and Winter, 1991). This material was funded by Leverhulme and by the Church of England and also fed into the *Faith in the Countryside* report of the Archbishop of Canterbury. Much of the primary material used in this chapter is drawn from the original, four-volume research report, but is presented in terms of models and issues not employed there. Over 480 individuals were interviewed in the five English dioceses of Truro, Gloucester,

Table 11.1   Frequency of church attendance among individuals registered on their church and civic electoral rolls.

Frequency of Church Attendance	Church Electoral Roll (n = 148)	Civic Electoral Roll (n = 338)
Once or more per week	26%	7%
From once a week to once a month	35%	9%
From once a month to three times a year	12%	7%
Less than three times a year	7%	11%
No attendance	20%	66%
Total	100%	100%

Southwell, Lincoln and Durham. Of this random sample of the public, approximately 30 per cent had their names on the electoral roll of an Anglican parish. Since it takes additional personal effort to ensure that one's name is included within the church electoral roll, as distinct from the civic electoral roll of all citizens, we distinguished between these groups and found that for general church attendance over the preceding year.

While this showed a marked difference between those on the church roll and the public at large, there were some 20 per cent on the church roll who said they had not attended church, while of those not on the roll some 7 per cent reckoned to attend weekly, and 9 per cent more that they attended at least once a month. In general terms women were more frequently present than men and there were also differences according to age and occupation.

Here, however, I draw attention to attendance at special services, those that would furnish members for what I am calling occasional congregations. Those interviewed were also asked whether they had attended such special services over the previous year and we return to their replies in a moment, once we have set the very notion of congregations into one possible conceptual framework, organized in terms of space and time.

Space and Time

Two key features of congregations concern place and time, each disclosing the distinctive feature of Christianity at different periods of its history and each related to different types of congregational leadership. Harold Turner's study of sacred space within Christendom served as an important contribution to this aspect of practical Christianity through his description of the interplay between the two ideas of temple and meeting house (Turner, 1979). Turner showed how earliest Christianity turned from the Jewish motif of the temple as a house of God (*domus dei*) to places in which the congregation of the faithful gathered together (*domus ecclesiae*). These places of meeting could be houses or other locations, for their essential significance was manifest only when the congregation was present. With time, Christians built special meeting places that generated their own significance as holy places and developed into temples as places of intrinsic sacred power. But, this inhering sacrality does not express what some Christians see as a true expression of the faith and they, accordingly, protest against it, seeking to rid their places of worship of these attributes. Such Christians protest against what they see as artificial in this 'temple' motif and press for a return to the simplicity of the 'meeting house', to a state of what could be described as congregational simplicity.

This dialectic between temple (*domus dei*) and meeting house (*domus ecclesiae*), drawn from Turner's history and phenomenology of religion, can be roughly equated with Ernst Troeltsch's much earlier sociological account of the essence of Christianity as something lying in the dialectic between the ideal types of 'sect' and 'church' (Troeltsch, 1931). This is to say that there is a sense in which the meeting house matches the sect and the temple the church type of religious organization. Protestantism afforded one example of this as it sought to turn the sacred spaces of Catholic worship into preaching houses which were not deemed to be sacred in any special way. John Calvin, for example, rehearses the prophetic tirade against those who boast of 'the temple of the Lord, the temple of the Lord, the temple of the Lord' (Jeremiah 7: 4), only to affirm that 'the Lord acknowledges no place as his temple', except those places where his word is heard and devoutly believed (Calvin, J. *Institutes* IV. II. III). In much more recent times the Charismatic and Restoration movements have witnessed a growth of congregational venues far removed from traditional churches with the adopted name of house-churches, reinforcing Harold Turner's distinction. Temple and meeting house are, then, two types of meeting place that express differing theologies and, accordingly, differing expectations of popular participation.

Leaders: Priests and Ministers

These two types of religious places of worship and of religious organizations inevitably raise the issue of types of religious leadership. At its starkest, and in terms of ideal types, it is easy to distinguish between the 'priest' and the 'minister', with the priest leading a 'church' meeting in a 'temple' while ministers serve a 'sect' gathered in their 'meeting house'. The priest is a professional, belonging to a corporation that admits or may reject members and holds very particular powers in relation to salvation, while the minister is, essentially, simply one of the congregation at large who is selected to serve the others. In theological terms the priest is described as possessing a distinctive priestly character imparted through ordination, while, by contrast, the minister simply serves as the medium of expression of the 'priesthood of all believers', itself the essentially Protestant doctrine that brings to the congregation both a sense of its fundamental identity and a means of grasping its relationship with God.

While the distinction between, for example, the Roman Catholic priesthood and the Protestant ministry is relatively easily ascertained, there are contexts of some difficulty, as in the Anglican Church, whose emergence through the English Reformation and subsequent centuries of theological reconsideration has produced a mixed sociological reality. This is evident in the phenomenon of 'churchmanship' or ecclesiastical parties (Daniel, 1968; Absalom, 1971; Davies, 1993). Where the Anglo-Catholic tradition speaks and thinks of priests, the Evangelical outlook sees ministers, indeed, the very words 'priest' and 'priesthood' have been problematic precisely for this reason. While the latter part of the twentieth century witnessed some significant changes and a degree of weakening of these divisions, there have also been significant points of hardening of attitudes, as over the ordination of women. As we will see below, these issues of churchmanship also relate to the form of relationship linking leader and congregation. For our original research purposes we distinguished between Conservative and Open Evangelicals, Central churchmanship, Modern Catholic and Traditional Catholic churchmanship. We also introduced the notion of 'spiritual style' as a further refinement within these five churchmanship categories: the styles were Charismatic, Liberal and Radical (Davies *et al.*, 1990, vol. 2, pp. 18–25).

The Occasional Congregation

Against these broad generalizations on space, time and leadership I now turn my attention to a particular study of Anglican practice to highlight one category of 'congregation' that deserves particular attention since it is, of all, the easiest to ignore: let us call it the 'occasional' congregation. The occasional congregation describes an event, usually held in a church building, when people come together, often on an annual basis, to mark some seasonal or historical event or to mark a more unique occasion. Given the fact that Christianity has, for most of the laity in most traditions, come to be viewed as a religion whose corporate public life is enacted through weekly activities, it is all the more important to note variations from that norm. The major occasional congregations dealt with here are the more regular events associated with weddings, baptisms and funerals, as rites of passage, with Christmas and Easter as major festivals, and with Harvest Festival and Remembrance Sunday. These last two are more difficult to describe since neither is a historical Christian festival in the strict sense of the term.

Harvest Thanksgiving

Harvest Thanksgiving, as it was originally called, only became a form of practical and popular festival in English Christianity when the Revd R. S. Hawker of Morwenstow in Cornwall held the first of such services in 1843. This had something of a precedent in Lammas Day of medieval England, but its revival or popular invention in the nineteenth century was dramatically successful and spread throughout the British Isles. The Church of England recognized this by preparing a special form of service by 1862. In the largely rural parishes furnishing the respondents for the Rural Church Project, a total of 43 per cent of respondents said they had attended Harvest Thanksgiving the preceding year, offering something of a picture of the late 1980s in English parishes. Of those on the civic roll who attended very infrequently, Harvest was likely to be one of their three or fewer congregational involvements.

Remembrance Day

If the Harvest Thanksgiving was a major invented tradition of the nineteenth century, its twentieth-century counterpart, especially in the Church of England, is that of the Remembrance Day Service. The scarring effect of the First World War, with its dramatic levels of loss of life and burial of the dead in overseas cemeteries, ensured that the new Remembrance Day Service would come to hold a significant place in British life. In our group of respondents nearly one-third (30 per cent) had attended this event in their locality in the preceding year. It was more likely that these were people who also attended some other special service than was the case for Harvest Thanksgiving. The attendance at Harvest Thanksgiving for those not on the church roll was similar to attendance at Easter.

Table 11.2   Church attendance at Easter and Christmas among individuals registered on their church and civic electoral rolls.

	Church Electoral Roll	Civic Electoral Roll
Church attendance at Easter	72%	24%
Church attendance at Christmas	80%	39%

Easter and Christmas

Both Easter and Christmas rank, theologically and liturgically, as major Christian festivals. However, they attracted rather different levels of involvement among our sample, as Table 11.2 shows.

So, while Easter attracted 72 per cent of those on church electoral rolls, Christmas attracted even more, 80 per cent. Similarly, Easter saw 24 per cent of those not on the church roll attend, with Christmas gathering some 39 per cent. Christmas comes out as a more significant event in terms of number and raises the important question of the relationship between occasional congregations and social life at large. Formal religious activity cannot be separated from the wider social arrangements that may tend either to foster or hinder them. Here holidays and commercial aspects of consumerism become important, and Christmas easily outstrips Easter in the English context when it comes to the congregations occasioned by these events.

But there is an entirely different aspect of the wider social world that also affects occasional congregations, and it is that of the basic rites of passage. Here the prime emphasis lies upon the bonds of kinship, friendship and association rather than upon any specific religious festival. While it is, of course, true to say that weddings, baptisms and funerals each possess a distinctive theological and liturgical significance, it is not likely that they predominate in the reasons for attendance at those events. This certainly applies to funerals, since so very few Britons opt for any form of secular rite. Weddings are slightly more problematic in that secular rites are more predominant, while baptisms may now, more than ever, indicate something of an inclination towards a religious affirmation.

Weddings, Baptisms and Funerals

Whatever the religious motivation, the major emphasis here is placed upon weddings, baptisms and funerals as providing opportunity for occasional congregations to occur. In our sample, attendance at these events in the preceding year showed that 86 per cent of those on the church roll and 70 per cent of those on the civic roll attended either a wedding, baptism or funeral. The occasional congregations for these specific events associated with rites of passage also showed some marked difference in terms of the gender of participants than did the others, as Table 11.3 shows.

Table 11.3   Percentage of men and women who had attended various kinds of 'occasional' church service during the previous year.

Event	% of men attending	% of women attending
Weddings, Baptisms and Funerals	71	79
Christmas	36	63
Harvest Thanksgiving	34	51
Easter	25	49

This shows that at weddings, baptisms and funerals 71 per cent of the men attended, as did 79 per cent of the women, as contrasted with Easter, when 25 per cent of men attended and 49 per cent of the women. This shift is, proportionately, quite significant in that the rites of passage reflect the general population gender balance far more than the Easter attendees, who comprise, practically speaking, twice as many women as men. Once more, proportionately speaking, Christmas and Remembrance Day showed a close resemblance over the balance of males and females even though the absolute number of attendees is smaller.

These attendance and gender balance figures suggest a distinction between church-focused meetings that express kinship and wider community activities on the one hand (in rites of passage and harvest) and the other group that includes Christmas, Remembrance and Harvest. This group, itself, shows its own differences, with Christmas being supported more highly than Easter and with Remembrance Day being least highly supported in numerical terms. This gradation from one to another reflects the degree to which the occasional congregational event is embedded within the family and society at large. Social context is particularly important in that, for example, the relatively significant position of Harvest Thanksgiving in the rural society in which this survey was conducted would not be expected to be mirrored in urban or inner-city parishes. Similarly, for example, the age of participants varied considerably, with, for example, the highest Christmas presence coming from those aged between 35 and 44 (60 per cent) who might well be bringing children to church, as opposed to the 18 to 34 year olds (40 per cent).

Finally, one might further exemplify the social embeddedness of these occasional congregations in relation to social class. Table 11.4 compares the percentage attendance of six categories of social class for all the major events discussed above.[1]

---

[1] The classification system used here is a modification of that outlined in Galdthorpe (1980). Briefly, class 1 refers to high-grade professionals; class 2 to lower-grade professionals and managers; class 3 to small proprietors, including farmers; class 4 to low-grade technicians and supervisors; class 5 to routine non-manual workers; and class 6 to routine manual skilled or unskilled workers. For a more detailed statement of this classification system, see Davies, Watkins and Winter (1991), pp. 52–54.

Table 11.4   Attendance at various 'occasional' services among individuals of different social class categories during the previous year.

	Social Class 1	Social Class 2	Social Class 3	Social Class 4	Social Class 5	Social Class 6
Rites of Passage	74%	74%	80%	73%	81%	72%
Harvest Thanksgiving	43%	51%	48%	33%	45%	38%
Christmas	67%	59%	49%	53%	63%	38%
Easter	51%	46%	41%	47%	45%	24%
Remembrance Day	40%	33%	31%	33%	35%	20%

What is entirely obvious is the way that social class markers were relatively insignificant for participation in weddings, baptisms and funerals and also, though less so, for Harvest Thanksgiving. The difference between demarcated group 1 and group 6 is noticeable throughout these events.

Priest and Occasional Congregation

Having already introduced the notion of churchmanship in Anglican practice, we now return to it in detail to see how it might affect how the clergy relate to this particular category of occasional congregation. Our research evidence allows us to address this topic since some 572 clergy – from both rural and urban contexts – were included in the diocesan questionnaire survey with 101 also being interviewed at length.

One means of accessing the relationship between churchmanship and leadership lay in the aspects of ministry that the clergy regarded as rewarding. The greatest difference over rewards was, in fact, related to churchmanship, with Evangelicals stressing individual spiritual growth of people, church growth, preaching, cooperation with laity and training. The Anglo-Catholic clergy referred more often to youth and family work and to the occasional offices and work with the community at large. As far as our present themes are concerned, it is worth noting that while 13 per cent of Modern Catholics and 10 per cent of Traditional Catholics referred to the occasional offices, which basically relates to the baptisms, marriages and funerals highlighted in this chapter, and while 11 per cent of the Central churchmanship clergy also did so, these services were mentioned by only 5 per cent of Conservative Evangelicals and 6 per cent of Open Evangelicals. In line with this slight trend, both the Catholics and Central clergy referred more to the work of the priest in the community than did the Evangelicals. What is interesting is to see the way clergy of both Central and Catholic churchmanships stressed 'people' at large as a reward of their work, while the Evangelicals pressed the notion of 'personal growth' as well as of church growth. This seemed to show something of a difference between a more sacramental priesthood viewing itself as working out from the church into the community at large and an Evangelical ministry seeking the interior religious development of individuals and a congregation of spiritually developing selves.

Using–Abusing the Church

One direct question posed to the 101 clergy interviewed for the Rural Church Project directly relates to occasional congregations and asked whether they ever felt that 'people take advantage of the church for their own convenience in marriage, baptism or funerals'. To this, 74 per cent answered in the affirmative, 13 per cent in the negative and 13 per cent were unsure. The nature of this large positive response became obvious in the elaborations that more than two-thirds of this 74 per cent made. Essentially, these clergy divided into a slightly larger group (60 per cent) whose major attitude was that the Church of England was a state church and existed for people to use for these crucial moments in their life-history, and a smaller group (40 per cent) whose emphasis fell upon the pastoral opportunity provided by occasional offices, offices or services that the church has long viewed as a duty of English clergy (for example Forder, 1947, pp. 297–313).

Congregational Type

The clergy were also asked, very directly, how they viewed those under their care, whether they placed their own pastoral emphasis more upon the church as a gathered community of the faithful or upon all those living within their parish, or upon both groups (Davies *et al.*, 1990, vol. III, pp. 163–164). The overall response was that approximately 43 per cent referred to all resident parishioners, 23 per cent to a gathered congregation and 27 per cent to both resident parishioners and to the gathered congregation. In terms of churchmanship, some of these results were slightly surprising in that Catholics emphasized the gathered congregation more than Evangelicals; even so the gathered congregation was, generally, less imperious in the clergy's sense of obligation than the community at large. This reinforces the overall sense of commitment to such things as the occasional congregation.

When asked about the time spent on various aspects of ministry, the clergy reckoned that of their average 57 hours per week work load approximately 3 per cent went on what we have described as occasional congregations and another 4 per cent on social or community events not immediately church-focused (Davies *et al.*, 1990 vol. II, pp. 33–35). To this, however, we may add some significant proportion of the 12 per cent of time devoted to visiting, since some of this relates to visiting in association with funerals, often with people not immediately part of the regular church congregation. Still, this is an interesting result given that so many clergy clearly acknowledge the significance of the community at large to their ministry. It may be that their perception of the significance of total-parish concern is not directly related to the time spent on particular activities.

Other Occasional Congregations

It is against that background of ordinary 'occasional offices' and congregations that we now highlight the more marked form of gathering expressing a more developed form of 'occasional congregation'. This occasional congregation relates less to the standard rites of passage or the annual events of nature and nation and more to unique events that befall social life. While taking us beyond the occasional offices they, nevertheless, reflect events in which the church has been much involved in past centuries and continues to be today. Clear contemporary examples of these have been associated with the death of Diana, Princess of Wales, with the terrorist attack on New York's Twin Towers in September 2001 and with the death of Elizabeth, the Queen Mother, in 2002. Other local events that have gained national attention through the media involve certain murders involving children. The first two of these events led to major gatherings of many thousands of people at international, national, regional and local levels in events that were memorialist in nature. The Queen Mother's lying in state, by both similarity and contrast, brought some two hundred thousand people to file past her coffin in Westminster Hall (Paflin, 2002, p. 1). Although it has not been customary to think of such events in congregational terms, largely because the very notion of congregation has tended to be interpreted as a regularly constituted and identifiable group of people that meets frequently, it is hard not to see such gatherings as distinctly congregational in form. If that is allowed, then these groups become some of the most significant congregations in the world of the later twentieth and early twenty-first century.

While, historically speaking, very large gatherings have occurred in the past, as the historian John Wolffe (2000) has admirably shown, the role of the media in contemporary life has extended their influence into innumerably widespread contexts. To a certain degree it is very likely that large crowds and actual congregations gathered for unique events are informed by the cultural practice of ordinary congregations and by a tacit knowledge of analogous situations, and that those who lead them and speak at them are influenced by similar personal experience. Certainly, the media, especially television, play a significant part in taking up such crowd-focused contexts and relating them to actual congregational services held at key sites, whether in New York or Westminster Abbey. The very nature of television editing is able to bring to viewers a sense of the united nature of those outside and inside meeting houses and can even integrate various days in the overall process of popular response to key events. In some respects this exemplifies Simmel's notion of the 'desire for unity' mentioned in our introductory section. Be that as it may, to allude to viewers is to raise, albeit without further comment, the question of whether individuals or groups of viewers should be regarded as joint members of the actual congregations they view on the television.

At a much less expansive scale are the numerous events that are unique – in the sense that they may be, for example, memorial services for particular individuals – and bring together family, work and leisure associates as well as friends, involving that penumbra that may be part of any established congregation (Jenkins, 1999, p. 178). Indeed, to a degree, every marriage and funeral is of this kind, and the more influential a person has been in their life the wider this collection of individuals and groups at their funerary rites is likely to be. Ministers officiating at such events occupy a distinctive role in being a stranger to the great majority of those present, and as such their representative capacity becomes all the more dominant. In many English contexts the local Anglican bishop sometimes emerges as a spokesman or the primary ritual functionary but, when it is the parish priest who fills the role, he or she is expected to satisfy a generalized model of the priesthood and not to assert any sense of idiosyncratic eccentricity. This may be, for example, in contradiction to an individual minister's ordinary persona within the congregation that knows him well.

Conclusion

This chapter has pursued the ideas of the relationship between the individual and the group, showing how these may be approached either sociologically or theologically. It has also shown how priests stand in relation both to individuals and groups and how they come to express something of the dynamics of social solidarity. Moving beyond the occasional offices of ordinary rites of passage, we have elaborated the more marked version of group association linked with disaster or with celebrities as portrayed through the media, and we have identified such levels of engagement as the occasional congregation. This notion has allowed us to exemplify Simmel's hypothesis concerning the religious 'desire for unity' and the part played by ritual in achieving it. We have seen something of the way in which an ordinary church-focused event can become the model for a much larger-scale event involving many members of society and not only those who are regular church members. Within this account priests have emerged as persons mediating the relationship between individual and group both in the context of regular core congregations, on the one hand, and with occasional congregations, on the other. Theoretically speaking, these cases have been shown to provide one exemplary form of the sociological concern with the relationship between individual and society.

References

Absalom, F. (1971), 'The Anglo-Catholic priest: aspects of role conflict', in Hill, M. (ed.), *Sociological Yearbook of Religion*, London: SCM Press, pp. 46–61.

Berger, P. L. (1971), *A Rumour of Angels*, London: Pelican.

Blank, J. de (1954), *The Parish in Action*, London: Mowbrays.

Carrithers, M. S., Collins, S. and Lukes, S. (1985), *The Category of the Person: Anthropology, Philosophy, History*, Cambridge: Cambridge University Press.

Daniel, M. (1968), 'Catholic, Evangelical and Liberal in the Anglican priesthood', in Martin, D. (ed.), *Sociological Yearbook of Religion*, London: SCM Press.

Davies, D. J. (1993), 'Spirituality, churchmanship and English Anglican priests', *Journal of Empirical Theology*, 6 (1), 5–18.

Davies, D. J. (2002), *Anthropology and Theology*, Oxford: Berg.

Davies, D. J., Pack, C., Seymour, S., Short, C., Watkins, C. and Winter, M. (1990), *Rural Church Project Report*, 4 vols, Cirencester: Royal Agricultural College and Nottingham Series in Theology.

Davies, D. J., Watkins, C. and Winter, M. (1991), *Church and Religion in Rural England*, Edinburgh: T. and T. Clark.

Dix, G. (1945), *The Shape of the Liturgy*, London: Dacre Press/Adam and Charles Black.

Forder, C. R. (1947), *The Parish Priest at Work*, London: SPCK.

Galdthorpe, J. U. (1980), *Social Mobility and Class Structure in Modern Britain*, Oxford: Clarendon Press.

Hebert, A. G. (1935), *Liturgy and Society: the Functions of the Church in the Modern World*, London: Faber and Faber.

Jenkins, T. (1999), *Religion in English Everyday Life*, Oxford: Berghahn Books.

Lloyd, R. (1950), *The Church of England in the Twentieth Century*, Vol. II, London: Longmans, Green and Co.

Paflin, G. (2002), 'The public pageant', *Church Times*, 12 April, p. 1.

Sheppard, D. (1974), *Built as a City*, London: Hodder and Stoughton.

Sheppard, D. (1983), *Bias to the Poor*, London: Hodder and Stoughton.

Simmel, G. (1997), *Essays on Religion*, New Haven: Yale University Press.

Thornton, L. S. (1928), *The Incarnate Lord*, London: Longmans, Green and Co.

Thornton, L. S. (1956), *Christ and the Church*, Westminster: Dacre Press.

Troeltsch, E. (1931), *The Social Teaching of the Christian Churches*, trans. O. Wyon, London: The Macmillan Company.

Turner, H. W. (1979), *From Temple to Meeting House: The Phenomenology and Theology of Places of Worship*, The Hague: Mouton Publishers.

Watson, J. (1896), *The Cure of Souls*, New York: Dodd and Mead.

Wolffe, J. (2000), *Great Deaths: Grieving, Religion, and Nationhood in Victorian and Edwardian Britain*, Oxford: Oxford University Press for the British Academy.

Chapter 12

Denominational Cultures: The Cinderella of Congregational Studies?

Philip Richter

The role played by denominational cultures has seldom been widely considered within the field of congregational studies. When cultural analysis has been applied, there has been a tendency to focus on the particular and sometimes idiosyncratic local culture of individual congregations. Penny Edgell Becker has termed this the study of congregational 'idiocultures' (Becker, 1999, p. 10).[1] In this chapter, I will first try to account for the relative neglect of denominational cultures and then suggest why a stronger focus on denominational cultures might be called for and how it might be developed within congregational studies. I will then outline and discuss the findings of a recent qualitative study of denominational cultures in relation to congregational identities. Finally, I will suggest some ways in which the insights gained from this project may be taken up in future research.

Why Have Denominational Cultures Been Neglected?

One reason why denominational cultures have been relatively ignored within congregational studies relates to the perception that denominational loyalties are of lessening importance to churchgoers.[2] If individuals are increasingly switching their loyalties from one denomination to another (Roberts, 1984, p. 158), this might suggest that denominational cultures have become attenuated and that individuals attach little importance to specific denominational cultures, consciously or tacitly perceived. In Britain's increasingly post-Christian society, denominational labels have become less significant to churchgoers than shared Christian (counter-cultural) identity. Individuals may be more aware of stylistic, rather than denominational, differences between congregations. If they move into a new area they may, for instance, be looking

---

[1] The term was coined by Gary Alan Fine (Fine, 1987, p. 125).

[2] It is true that denominational switching may be more prevalent within North America, given its religious 'free market': historically, Europe has not had such a culture of choice. However, anecdotal evidence from university chaplains in the UK suggests that denominational allegiances appear to be of declining importance, particularly to young people.

for a congregation that is 'charismatic' or 'Anglo-Catholic' or 'evangelical' in style, rather than one of a similar denomination to the one they have left behind (Richter and Francis, 1998, p. 68; Bennison, 1999, p. 56). One of the interviewees (#6) interviewed for this study told me that when he moved he looked for 'good teaching and a leader who knows and loves the Lord and shows it'; he looked for 'honesty and reality, rather than habit'. Equally, individuals may look for a new church that, for instance, meets the needs of their children or is socially compatible or geographically convenient. Denominational cultures are likely to be more significant for religious professionals, who, in theory at least, are expected to act as carriers of their denomination's culture. Clergy[3] appropriation of their denominational culture may, however, have been adversely affected by training in an ecumenical context, which may have tended simply to presuppose that students have pre-existing 'relatively distinct denominational identities' and that they need to have their religious horizons expanded. Ecumenical initial ministerial training has not always taken account of the base from which students increasingly begin: 'denominational switching and the eclectic personal fabrication of religious orientations' (Gilpin, 1993, pp. 199–200; Roberts, 1993, p. 92). Clergy also have to reckon with the fact that 'switchers' may import different and novel cultural elements, potentially at variance with the leaders' interpretations of their tradition, into local congregations (Becker, 1999, p. 187).

Another reason why denominational cultures have received little attention within congregational studies may be the inherent difficulty of pinning down cultures that are themselves in process of change. 'Boundaries separating the denominations, once meaningful to believers, have blurred, with a resulting loss of clarity about doctrinal identity and distinctiveness' (Carroll and Roof, 1993, p. 13). Mainstream denominations are 'open systems' influencing and influenced by other denominations, as well as by elements of the wider culture (Roberts, 1993, p. 75). Even Evangelicalism, although cross-cutting denominations, is undergoing seachanges in its culture (Hunter, 1987). This is not to ignore the fact that denominational cultures have changed historically: United Methodist Connectionalism, for instance, has evolved seven different styles, each with their 'own grammar and rules touching form, substance, procedure and structure' (Richey, 1997, pp. 7–8). The new factor is not so much the fact of change as the perceived *pace* of change. Their increasing state of flux has stimulated recent quests on the part of mainstream denominations to rediscover and reassert their identity: for instance, the Baptist Union Denominational Consultation's *Five Core Values for a Gospel People* or the Methodist Church's *Our Calling* document. Although a measure of cultural diversity is essential within any denomination, especially in an increasingly globalized milieu, there are limits to the variety that a denominational tradition can brook, 'whilst still maintaining a coherent religious and cultural identity'

---

[3] Within a discussion of denominational cultures it is important to acknowledge, however, that 'clergy' is a term that is alien to some denominations, including most Free Churches.

(Bennison, 1999, p. 86). Such denominations, revisiting their cultural identity, may face an uphill task, however, given that, in the dynamic reflexive macro-culture of late modernity, individuals, and increasingly congregations, are suspicious of ready-made cultural blueprints: 'no longer able to count on [denominational] all-encompassing cultural values and beliefs and associated taken-for-granted strategies of action, [local congregations] begin to feel very much "on their own"' (Marler and Hadaway, 1997, p. 294).

The relative neglect of denominational cultures has also been encouraged by the particular methodology used by many 'intrinsic' congregational studies practitioners: 'thick' ethnographic description of local congregational culture, taking a cue from anthropological and sociological studies of local culture (for example, Geertz, 1973; Fine, 1987). The focus is on rich, elegant description of the particular idioculture of the local congregation. The plausibility of the analysis tends to be judged by factors such as its internal consistency and its elegance (Becker, 1999, p. 9), rather than its transferability or comparability.[4] Even where studies of multiple congregations have been carried out there has been little tendency to analyse them within denominational frames (for example Ammerman, 1997; Becker, 1999).

The Case for Taking Account of Denominational Cultures

I have rehearsed some of the possible reasons why denominational cultures have not featured strongly within congregational studies. These are not necessarily compelling reasons, however, for continuing to neglect the role of denominational cultures. Although denominational switching and more eclectic approaches to personal religious identity-formation have tended to attenuate denominational cultures, it is unlikely that denominational cultures have been completely superseded. When individuals switch between denominations they do not necessarily choose *any* alternative: 'differences in polity, in theological emphases, in use of language, and in styles of worship are significant enough that ... any three or four denominations may seem like possibilities, but certain others are viewed as beyond the range of acceptability' (Roberts, 1993, pp. 95–96).

Even similar styles of church participation can take on a tangibly different cultural feel within different denominational settings. For example, Linda J. Clark has drawn attention to the range of meanings that the evangelical hymn 'Amazing Grace' can have in different denominational contexts. Individuals within the Episcopal Church, for instance, who appreciated this hymn tended to imagine God as more 'mysterious' and 'judgemental' than their United

---

[4] Similarly, Timothy Jenkins's elegant ethnographic account of the local culture of Kingswood, while describing the role played by churches and, especially, chapels as 'nodal points' for the location, reproduction and transmission of cultural values of 'reputation, restraint and respectability', does not tend to differentiate their role in terms of denominational cultures (Jenkins, 1999, pp. 172, 161, 176).

Methodist counterparts. Clark suggests that this reflects the more formal and ritualistic style of Episcopalian worship, as well as its more sacerdotal concept of ordination (Clark, 1993, pp. 110–111).

Whilst individuals and congregations may have become more pragmatic and voluntaristic in relation to denominational cultural identity, this does not preclude the possibility that denominational cultures can function as '*resources* for the construction of local congregational models', albeit in non-determinative fashion (Becker, 1999, p. 187). As Ammerman notes: 'what each congregation cooks up ... is always a mix of local creativity and larger tradition' (Ammerman, 1998, p. 79). Congregations will be constrained to some degree by their denominational heritage and will not, for instance, be totally free to define their style of decision-making; this will partly depend on their denominational style of polity and the roles allotted to the ordained leadership. The parts played by 'creative interpretation' and by informal networks of power should not, however, be underestimated even in ostensibly highly centralized and hierarchical denominations (Ammerman, 1997, pp. 51–53). Congregations will also be constrained by denominational expectations attached to appropriate forms of worship. In his ethnographic account of worship in four Manchester congregations, Martin Stringer has drawn attention to the importance of externally sanctioned official discourses existing in and around worship that 'begin to set limits on the form and nature of the kinds of meaning that can be generated' (Stringer, 1999, p. 76). In Penny Edgell Becker's analysis of four common models of local religious culture, whilst in principle any congregation, of whatever denominational allegiance, might operate according to any of the four models, in practice there was a tendency for denominations to privilege one type of model over another. For instance, the 'house of worship' model, identified by Becker, was more likely to be operationalized by Roman Catholic congregations than United Methodist congregations, 'because [the former] has always fostered the centrality of worship as a transformative rite for the individual, while the other has a long history of emphasising the link between personal piety and social activism' (Becker, 1999, p. 187). It is true that Becker also found that local congregations did not always adopt denominational culture 'in any straightforward way'. Congregations with a hierarchical, rather than a congregational, polity, such as in the United Methodist Church, might, for instance, 'delegate the taking of stands on social issues to religious professionals' or to 'the connection' (Becker, 1997, pp. 279, 265). Nevertheless, local religious cultures are seldom completely idiosyncratic; they are patterned by the larger institutional environment that limits their range of variation (Becker, 1999, p. 7).

At present, the methodology widely espoused within congregational studies tends to yield only passing references to denominational cultures, but it is not wholly incompatible with a wider approach. 'Thick' ethnographic description of congregations, at a 'microscopic' and 'homely' level, is itself intended to yield 'insight into the larger and more abstract realm of cultural world view and values' (Tisdale, 1997, p. 59), which may have significant denominational resonances. As Penny Edgell Becker recognizes, if congregational studies exclusively focus on the particular and idiosyncratic, they will tend to ignore 'what the local cultures of [congregations] within the same institutional field have in common' (Becker, 1999, p. 11).

Defining the Terms

Before suggesting some ways of approaching the study of denominational cultures, it is important to clarify terms. What, for instance, is the difference, if any, between culture, ethos and identity? I am using 'denomination' in a non-technical sense, to denote any grouping of Christian congregations within a common polity. Hence the term would encompass, for instance, the Roman Catholic and Orthodox Churches, as much as the Methodist Church, Society of Friends, or Vineyard Movement. Culture is a more difficult concept to identify. In the influential handbook, *Studying Congregations*, Nancy Ammerman defines culture as 'who we (presently) are and all the ways in which we reinforce and recreate who we are' by 'what we do, what we make, and how we talk about ourselves': each congregation 'is a unique gathering of people with a cultural identity all its own' (Ammerman, 1998, pp. 78, 84). Notice that she tends to elide local culture and identity and associates culture with deeply felt and embedded sets of meanings rooted in the regular intimacy and interaction of a relatively small group. As Penny Edgell Becker has pointed out, this way of defining culture tends to privilege small-scale, thickly descriptive ethnographic studies of congregations. If, instead, culture were to be defined more in terms of, first, 'semiotic code' or 'sets of "rules" governing behavior' and, second, 'institutional practices', this would shift the focus away from 'subjective, deeply felt beliefs' and towards culture as 'a constraining ground and context of action' (Becker, 1999, p. 202). The broader level of analysis associated with this alternative way of defining culture is, arguably, more conducive to understanding the role played by denominational cultures within congregations.

This approach also has the merit of helping to distinguish between 'culture' and 'identity'. Within her definition of culture, Becker points out that individuals do not necessarily have deeply to feel, or be able to articulate, cultural codes and institutional practices. The term 'identity', on the other hand, is perhaps best reserved for explicit recognition and intentional ownership of an otherwise implicit culture: 'people may share a culture and not recognise elements in it; but they will name portions and elements of a common identity' (Weeks, 1993, p. 309), that is, those things that make their cultural group distinctive vis-à-vis others. Denominational 'identity', therefore, implies an ability to identify and articulate distinctive denominational 'dialect' and 'markers' (Carroll and Roof, 1993, p. 348). The distinction between culture and 'ethos' is somewhat more fuzzy. Following Geertz, Jackson Carroll and Wade Clark Roof define ethos as a subset of culture (alongside 'worldview' and 'values'): 'a people's "tone, character, and quality of their life, its moral and aesthetic style and mood" ' (Carroll and Roof, 1993, p. 16, citing Geertz, 1973, p. 127). Congregational ethos refers to the overarching 'character' of a congregation, often best expressed in imagistic, metaphorical language or story, serving to 'integrate many of the disparate meanings gleaned through thick description of congregational symbols' (Tisdale, 1997, p. 89). Although a congregation's ethos is, by definition, characteristic of itself, this does not preclude the possibility that a congregation's ethos might be affected by a denomination's ethos.

Methods of Studying Denominational Cultures

There are a number of possible approaches to identifying the characteristic culture of particular denominations. These include looking for common themes and patterns by means of:

  (i)   literature surveys of core texts from the denomination, for example programmatic historical texts, denominational 'mission statements', official websites, official reports (see Craske and Marsh, 1999);
 (ii)   interviews with selected church leaders (see Weeks, 1993);
(iii)   participant observation of a random sample of congregations selected from within the denomination, including, for example, observation of worship, governance and regular activities;
 (iv)   semi-structured interviews with a random sample of members selected from within the denomination;
  (v)   semi-structured interviews with selected individuals who are likely to have acquired a cross-denominational perspective.

There are advantages and disadvantages associated with each approach. The first two approaches, while relatively straightforward to implement, would tend to privilege 'official' accounts of denominational culture, which may, or may not, be reflected at a more grassroots level. The third approach, while potentially in depth and well nuanced, would require extensive fieldwork[5] and subsequent synoptic analysis, and this would have to encompass congregations of other denominations, otherwise it would be impossible to identify the distinctive characteristics of the given denomination. The fourth approach, while reflecting 'grassroots' perceptions of denominational culture, would, like the third approach, not necessarily be capable of identifying distinctive denominational characteristics. For such reasons I adopted the fifth approach for my study. One of the disadvantages of my chosen approach was that it tended to yield data relating to denominational identity, that is, elements of denominational culture consciously perceived and owned by individuals. Hence it would benefit from being complemented by other approaches, for instance, (iii). However, approach (v) is cross-cultural and would probably be

---

[5] For instance, Gary Dorsey's semi-journalistic, semi-ethnographic account of a single United Church of Christ congregation (Dorsey, 1998) entailed an entire year's field study.

the most economical way of assembling an inventory of denominational characteristics.

The Study

The study comprised a set of semi-structured interviews with six individuals who, because of their work and/or life history, were likely to display critical distance from their own denomination and a capacity for comparative overview of several denominations. I was essentially looking for individuals who were denominationally bi- or multi-lingual. Interviewee #1 was a network television producer with several decades' experience of outside broadcasting from churches of all denominations, himself a lifelong member of one denomination. Interviewee #2 was a county ecumenical officer whose job had accustomed him to a wide range of denominational milieux; he had himself switched denominations several decades ago and currently belonged to an LEP (that is, a united church). Interviewee #3 had returned to her native denomination after having attended a different denomination while living in mainland Europe for nearly twenty years. Interviewee #4, similarly, had returned to his original denominational roots after having attended a different denomination for an extended period while working abroad. Interviewee #5 was a member of a United Church who had switched denominations as a young parent 'for the sake of her children'. Interviewee #6 was the evangelical warden of a Christian conference and holiday centre whose job had given him the opportunity to observe visitors from a wide range of denominational backgrounds. The interviews lasted, on average, approximately one-and-a-half hours each.

I had originally intended to structure the interviews to try to reflect the range of cultural components identified by Nancy Ammerman and others. Ammerman summarizes these as 'activities, artefacts, and accounts', that is, 'what we do, what we make, and how we talk about ourselves' (Ammerman, 1998, p. 84).[6] In practice, it proved difficult to cover such a wide range of topics with individual interviewees and it was often more satisfactory to elicit themes that were of greater salience for the interviewee. Moreover, interviewees were not equally alert to the different cultural dimensions. As a sociologist, with extensive ecumenical experience, and in-depth personal experience of Methodism, I was aware that my interviewees' descriptions of denominational characteristics were often fairly limited, whether because they found it difficult to articulate them or because they had failed to notice them.

Sometimes it is important to notice what is *not* present, as well as what is present in a denomination's culture. This is easier for those with lived experience of several denominations, but will be limited by the types of

---

[6] For the sake of this study, because it has been widely adopted within congregational studies, I have simply operationalized the approach to studying culture devised by Ammerman *et al.*, without entering into wider discussions about cultural theory.

denominations experienced. For instance, when interviewee #5 was asked to list some of the indicators that might reveal to a casual visitor which denominations her (United) Church comprised, she mentioned: the 'non-conformist roof' (by this she meant a pitched roof, with internal struts and steel ties across the ceiling), the minister dressed in a suit 'like everyone else', the way the congregation typically dressed (women: Viyella, Alexon or Easton; men: suits), the warmth of the church – physical, aesthetic and spiritual – the lack of either an altar or a pulpit, the practice of receiving communion in individual glasses in one's seat, and the prominence given to the Bible, which would be ceremoniously carried into the church and placed on the communion table at the start of a communion service. Interviewee #5 had grown up within the Brethren, had later joined a Methodist Church and now belonged to a united Methodist and United Reformed Church. She recognized the minister's style of dress as more distinctively URC: the Methodist ministers she had known had typically been 'fully gowned up', usually with clerical collar and even stoles. The lack of a proper pulpit was also perceived by her as more distinctively URC: at her previous Methodist church 'you were well aware of the pulpit', which assumed particular prominence architecturally in the church. The warmth of the church, on the other hand, she perceived as distinctively Free Church, in comparison with Anglican churches which, in her experience, tended to be 'mostly medieval, stone walls, pews and cold'. Similarly, the style of congregational attire in the United Church was seen as reflecting Free Church identity, in comparison with two Anglican congregations with which she was familiar: one in the home counties where 'they all work in the City and dress down to go to church, but in designer labels' and another, more locally, where their dress tends to be one of 'genteel scruffiness'. Because of her denominational backgrounds, interviewee #5 missed some of the cultural clues that might have distinguished the United Church from an Anglican church: for example, the lack of hassocks, bells, 'bishop's chair', altar frontals, side altars, and so forth. Clearly, it is desirable to build up a picture of denominational cultures from a wide range of interviewees, with multichromatic experience of different denominations, allowing for geographical and class biases – some parts of Britain may, for instance, be more likely to retain more traditional Methodist church architecture, privileging the pulpit.

On the whole, it was easier within the study to get individuals to identify cultural items that surprised them in some way, rather than to articulate more 'taken-for-granted' dimensions of denominational culture. Either they had been surprised to find something within another denomination that had been different to their own or they had recognized that they were not seeing what they had expected to see.[7] Most of the interviewees claimed to have not previously given much thought to the details of denominational culture and identity. Sometimes one could detect a process of growing self-awareness of

---

[7] Roy Wagner (1981, p. 9) has drawn attention to the key role played by such 'culture shock' in making culture visible.

denominational characteristics within the interviews. For instance, interviewee #2 frequently peppered his conversation with phrases such as 'I've only just realized that!'

The process of uncovering perceptions of denominational cultural distinctiveness was a delicate one. Generally, interviewees were not able spontaneously to provide a list of denominational characteristics, when asked a question such as: 'What would you recognize as making your denomination different, in your experience?' It was important not to prompt them with leading questions, based either on the interviewer's own knowledge of denominational cultures or the interview schedule which derived from Ammerman's approach within *Studying Congregations*. In practice, whilst the interview schedule informed the interview, the most fruitful lines of approach tended to revolve around simple open-ended questions such as the following:

(i) 'Have you ever had the experience of being told: "You would say that, wouldn't you, you're a [here the person's own denomination would be inserted]"?';

(ii) 'Have you ever "put your foot in your mouth" when mixing in a different denominational context?';

(iii) 'Has anything ever surprised you about your experience of another denomination?';

(iv) 'Has anyone, from a different denomination, ever said to you: "That's not the way we do things around here!"?';

(v) 'In your interaction with another denomination, have you ever reached a personal "sticking point", when you have said to yourself: "So far, but no further"?';

(vi) 'What are the most valuable characteristics of your denomination, in your experience?';

(vii) 'Have you noticed any significant changes within your denomination?'

One additional, and, in practice, seminal question, which grew out of the experience of the study was: 'Can you think of a particular experience or event that helped you understand an aspect of a different denomination in especial depth?'

'Can you think of a particular experience or event that helped you understand an aspect of a different denomination in especial depth?'

To begin with the final question cited above, most interviewees were able to recall often deeply personally moving encounters with aspects of another denomination's culture in which both the strangeness and the authenticity of that culture had come home to them. For instance, interviewee #2 spoke of the 'deeply moving experience' of finding himself in a group of mostly lay Roman Catholics, discussing the Eucharist. An elderly woman, sitting opposite him, had looked at him and said, 'N is not a complete Christian, because he doesn't believe that the communion wafer and wine is fully turned into the body and blood of Christ.' At this point, one of the two priests in the group retorted, 'But I don't believe it like that!', whereupon the other priest, a traditionalist, had interrupted and said, 'We are talking about things so holy that I am going to stop you from carrying on this conversation.' For the interviewee, this had been a pivotal learning experience about how the communion elements tend to be treated within Roman Catholicism. Interviewee #4, similarly, appreciated that he was 'dealing with something he had not come across in this way before' when, as someone with Free Church denominational roots, he saw an Anglican lay reader 'with tears in his eyes as the bread was broken'. Interviewee #1 cited his experience of having attended a 'Funeral of Jesus' service in the White Russian Church in the Garden of Gethsemane one Easter: 'at one level everything was quite bizarre – the catafalque, nuns, priests, icons, kissing icons, and people chatting in the background – but I found it profoundly moving and began to have a sense of its meaning to the participants'.

'Have you ever had the experience of being told: "You would say that, wouldn't you"?'

In terms of this question, interviewee #1 said that others would attribute (Methodist) denominational special pleading to him when he questioned their 'lousy' hymn choices or when he stressed the importance of the congregation's role and their interactivity within worship.

'Have you ever "put your foot in your mouth" when mixing in a different denominational context?'

In terms of this question, interviewee #2 admitted to having 'mildly offended' a Quaker by giving them a title, not having understood their non-hierarchical ethos. He also confessed that he had misread denominational dress code, not realizing that he would be expected to dress much more smartly and formally at an Anglican Synod than at a Methodist or URC one, where ministers, in particular, often seemed to deliberately 'dress down'. Interviewee #5 spoke of how when she joined a Methodist Church, after having belonged to the Brethren, and started to run a Bible class, the minister had phoned her to tell her that 'someone was teaching the young people something non-orthodox about baptism'. 'Oh,' she replied, quite innocently, 'They're not teaching infant baptism, are they?' She said that it had never previously occurred to her that Methodists did not solely baptize believers. Interviewee #1 related how he had once misread the cultural cues at a broadcast of cathedral choral evensong and had asked the choir to give the hymn 'Rejoice the Lord is King' 'more wellie'. It was 'turned into a congregational whoop, with organ fanfare on top', which would have been perfectly fitting within Methodism, for example, but not at choral evensong.

'Has anything ever surprised you about your experience of another denomination?'

In terms of this question, interviewee #6 was surprised by the tendency of Pentecostal and House Church groups to be, in his experience, much more 'disorganized, untidy, noisy, late' and chaos-inducing than those of other denominations. He also noted that they were often 'dead keen to go to a [praise] meeting, to praise the Lord, to have their hands in the air, and really get immersed in what was happening, yet would not worry about their child who might be crying in the bedroom [in the Conference Centre]'. For interviewee #6, who identified himself as 'low church Anglican', this behaviour appeared neglectful and reflected 'wrong priorities' on their part. Further research may, or may not, bear out these apparent denominational differences of behavioural expectation. Interviewee #2, on the other hand, was surprised to find that the directions of Church of England and Roman Catholic bishops were 'creatively interpreted' by their clergy and laity, having assumed that a bishop's authority would be more akin to that of a university vice chancellor. Interviewee #3 was not only surprised, but rather horrified, to be asked, as a new member of the Anglican Altar Guild, to consume wine left over at the end of the Eucharist. The chalice was 'huge', there was 'so much alcohol to drink' and she felt quite drunk. Her Free Church background predisposed her to want to reverently dispose of the communion wine, but not to drink it 'as if some kind of magic had taken place'. She had also been responsible for washing and ironing the altar linen and had been astonished to be given four foolscap pages of instructions, with the motto 'Only the best is good enough for God' at the top. She was expected to 'wash the linen by hand, wrap it in a bath towel for two-and-a-half days, iron it on a bed so that the linen didn't touch the ground, and then roll it with tissue paper between'. She acknowledged that this was quite different to what she was used to and had begun to sense how 'incredibly powerful' these symbols must be in Anglican denominational culture.

'Has anyone, from a different denomination, ever said to you: "That's not the way we do things around here!"?'

In terms of this question, interviewee #5 related how she had found a particular Methodist Committee 'oppressive' in the way it functioned in that it was over-structured and 'it didn't seem to allow for any creativity or variation'. When she expressed her concern at this the District Chairperson had told her, half-jokingly, half-seriously, 'But this is the Methodist Church, what do you expect?'

'In your interaction with another denomination, have you ever reached a personal "sticking point"?'

In terms of this question, interviewee #5 spoke of her reluctance to call Orthodox priests 'Father' while at an international ecumenical gathering. She appreciated that this was causing offence and resolved the situation by jokingly agreeing with them: 'I'll call you "Father" if you call me "Mother"', which they did. This was a learning experience for her about Orthodoxy, but equally a point at which she felt the need to erect a cultural marker. Similarly, interviewee #4 had wanted, as a liberal Methodist, to 'mark that there were other ways of understanding the resurrection' when he belonged to an Anglican congregation with evangelical leanings. He had done this by often referring to David Jenkins, the Bishop of Durham famous for his radical thinking, in his lay preaching.

'What are the most valuable characteristics of your denomination, in your experience?'

In terms of this question, Methodist interviewees tended to cite exuberant hymn singing which lifted one's spirit (while acknowledging that Methodism was 'born in song', but not necessarily into trained, musically adept hymn singing); preaching that is challenging, thought-provoking and 'feeds' the listener; a sense of 'connectedness' within the denomination; balanced theology 'rooted in love for God and love of neighbour'; and pragmatic applied belief. Interviewee #1 pointed out that, in fact, in today's much smaller congregations, hymn singing can be 'hard work, a real effort' and 'a pale echo of [past experiences of] six hundred Methodists in a large chapel having a whale of a time at a Circuit Rally'. He went on: 'trying to recreate this with twenty-nine people in a chapel seating three hundred becomes hard work, instead of being a joyous moment'. But he claimed that many Methodists were still able to 'plug into [this experience] even if it's not there any more, through their memory of those larger events'. There are interesting parallels here with Martin Stringer's ethnography of worship, in which he suggests that worship 'works' largely through the memory of past experience, 'drawing together disparate memories within the scope of that experience, so giving a special significance to all other memories' (Stringer, 1999, p. 194). Arguably, hymn singing might constitute the source of that experience within Methodism. Although interviewee #6 claimed to have been an Anglican for thirty years 'almost by chance', he confessed that, within the Baptist church he currently attended, he 'missed enormously the richness of the words' of Morning Prayer and of Church of England Communion liturgy. He also missed a sense of drama in Eucharistic worship: 'there was a real build up to the Lord's table in the Anglican Church'.

'Have you noticed any significant changes within your denomination?'

In terms of this question, interviewee #4 had noticed that the 'hymn sandwich' structure of worship within the Methodist Church had tended to alter, in that the penultimate item was now the intercessory prayers, rather than the sermon. He suggested that this was giving less prominence to the preached Word. It would be worth exploring whether this change in liturgical sequence was related to a move towards a more interactional approach to worship within the denomination and a lessening of clergy status and authority, as Keith Roberts' ritual ethnography might suggest (Roberts, 1993, p. 82). Interviewee #1 cited another Methodist who had complained to him recently that 'We're getting shorter and shorter sermons'. In the context of a denomination where forty-minute sermons were once the norm, this statement implied that something important was being attenuated. Interestingly, in an Anglican context, it might have had quite opposite connotations! Exegetes of denominational cultures need to be aware of such nuances.

Inevitably, interviewees varied according to the degree of insight they had into the cultural features that were uncovered. Interviewee #1, for instance, not only noted that there was a different feel to hymn singing in a Methodist congregation than in an Anglican one, but also delineated a number of important differences. To some extent it is simply a truism to say that Methodist hymn singing is recognizably louder and more enthusiastic than Anglican. Interviewee #1 pointed out, however, that, at least in an Anglo-Catholic context, hymns tend to have a different purpose: 'hymns are not the main thing: they are usually there as buffers and as something to go alongside action that is bound to happen, such as a procession, the offering, or preparation of the altar. It's not that they don't care what the hymns say, but they are there almost as an adjunct to what the liturgy is doing alongside them.'

It might appear that a high proportion of the interviews focused on the detailing of fairly mundane cultural minutiae, although it is important not to overlook the degree to which a culture's symbolic structures are embedded in such everyday practices (Bourdieu, 1990). The interviews did, however, also encompass broader discussion of denominational identity and ethos. It is important, as in the study of individual congregations, not to presuppose a coherent or homogeneous cultural orientation on the part of any given denomination. For instance, there does not appear to be any significant correlation between denominational allegiance and the five different congregational self-images itemized by Carl Dudley and Sally Johnson (Dudley and Johnson, 1993).[8] It would also be important to correct for individual bias.

Generally, however, interviewees were often able to characterize denominations in ways that did not appear purely idiosyncratic. Interviewee #4, for instance, characterized the Methodist Church as an extended 'family'. He spoke of the 'warmth in connectedness', although times were changing, and whereas Methodism had once spoke of itself as a 'connexion of societies', it now tended to describe itself in terms of being a 'church'. The 'family sense' in Methodism, though attenuated, was still relatively strong compared to other denominations. He pointed out that, as an individual Methodist, you were 'a member of a class, which was part of a society, which was part of a circuit, with its visiting preachers [lay and ordained] who were a means of communicating with what went on elsewhere'. When a new minister came to a Methodist circuit one would tend to ask 'Does anyone know him/her?': not primarily to find out about her/him, 'but to place him within the family'. He appreciated the non-hierarchical nature of the family ethos of Methodism in which, for example, the District Chairperson would be referred to on first-name terms.

---

[8] Private correspondence with Carl Dudley, February 2001.

This interviewee's sense of Methodism's distinctive ethos is paralleled in other studies that have highlighted the importance of 'fellowship' (Marsh, 1999) and connectionalism (Richey, Campbell and Lawrence, 1997) for Methodist identity.

Interviewee #3 referred to Methodism's concern for social issues and suggested that this reflected a different ethos to Anglicanism. When, as an expatriate, she had belonged to an Anglican congregation, she felt that 'social issues were not high on the agenda'. She had demonstrated against the stationing of Cruise Missiles in Europe, but 'there was no church involvement: it wasn't even discussed'. She had also noticed that individuals of Methodist background were disproportionately involved in helping to run church activities. Here was a socially activist and 'hands-on' ethos, which might potentially be at variance with the possibly more inward-looking ethos described by the previous interviewee. Again, however, this interviewee's account of Methodism's distinctive ethos is consistent with that of other analyses (see Becker, 1999, p. 187).

Interviewee #1 suggested that some aspects of Methodist identity had been superseded recently: 'Methodists used to say that they were called "to spread scriptural holiness throughout the land"; nobody thinks like that any more!' He drew a distinction between 'historical differences' and 'those one would go to the stake over'. When asked about the Anglican ethos, he associated it strongly with the idea of being a national church, 'present in every parish, with a vicar in every parish to look after its people and serving the whole community, and not just those who happen to turn up on a Sunday morning – even if [Anglicans] are aware that it has broken down a bit'. This was, he suggested, 'their central perception of what the church is about'. This interviewee's sense of Anglicanism's distinctive ethos is also paralleled by other commentators (for example, Biles, 1999, pp. 127–128); the parish has been described on the Church's official website as 'the heart of the Church of England'.[9]

As well as illustrating one way of conducting research into denominational cultures, the findings of this study have also added weight to the case for taking denominational cultures seriously within the sub-discipline of congregational studies. Inevitably, since this was a relatively small-scale study, its findings are tentative and would need further corroboration and exploration.

Future Research Agenda

The insights gained from the study described above possibly provoke more questions than they offer answers. It is useful, in this respect, to highlight some important issues that might be taken up in light of these insights, and pursued within a future research agenda. Most notably, further research into the denominational factor might test the following hypotheses: that the longer an

---

[9] http://www.cofe.anglican.org/about/frame_means.html (accessed 16 August 2002).

individual is involved in a denomination, the greater will tend to be his/her absorption of the 'official denominational culture' (Weeks, 1993, p. 323); that there is less variation culturally within denominations than between them; that the greater an individual's involvement in the activities and governance of the denomination, the more likely is s/he to internalize a denominational culture. In order to test out these hypotheses, it would be necessary to conduct a wider range of interviews encompassing both longstanding and newer participants, with different levels of involvement in the denominations' activities and governance. In this chapter, I hope to have initiated an exploration of these issues, bringing to attention both methodological and empirical complexities, and offering some suggestions about how they might be tackled within the field of congregational studies.

References

Ammerman, N. T. (1997), *Congregation and Community*, New Brunswick, NJ: Rutgers University Press.

Ammerman, N. T. (1998), 'Culture and Identity in the Congregation', in Ammerman, N. T., Carroll, J. W., Dudley, C. S. and McKinney, W. (eds), *Studying Congregations: A New Handbook*, Nashville, TN: Abingdon Press, pp. 78–104.

Becker, P. E. (1997), 'Understanding Local Mission: Congregational Models and Public Religion in United Methodist Churches', in Richey, R. E., Campbell, D. M. and Lawrence, W. B. (eds), *Connectionalism: Ecclesiology, Mission and Identity*, Nashville, TN: Abingdon Press, pp. 265–285.

Becker, P. E. (1999), *Congregations in Conflict: Cultural Models of Local Religious Life*, Cambridge: Cambridge University Press.

Bennison, C. E. (1999), *In Praise of Congregations: Leadership in the Local Church Today*, Boston, MA: Cowley.

Biles, T. (1999), *Church Wardens I Have Buried: The Journal of a Country Vicar*, privately published, 36 Hound Street, Sherborne, Dorset, DT9 3AA.

Bourdieu, P. (1990), *The Logic of Practice*, Stanford: Stanford University Press.

Carroll, J. and Roof, W. C. (eds) (1993), *Beyond Establishment: Protestant Identity in a Post-Protestant Age*, Louisville, KY: Westminster/John Knox Press.

Clark, L. J. (1993), ' "Songs My Mother Taught Me": Hymns as Transmitters of Faith', in Carroll, J. and Roof, W. C. (eds), *Beyond Establishment: Protestant Identity in a Post-Protestant Age*, Louisville, KY: Westminster/John Knox Press, pp. 99–115.

Craske, J. and Marsh, C. (1999), *Methodism and the Future: Facing the Challenge*, London: Cassell.

Dorsey, G. (1998), *Congregation: The Journey Back to Church*, Cleveland, OH: Pilgrim.

Dudley, C. S. and Johnson, S. A. (1993), *Energizing the Congregation: Images that Shape your Church's Ministry*, Louisville, KY: Westminster/John Knox Press.

Fine, G. A. (1987), *With the Boys*, Chicago: University of Chicago Press.

Geertz, C. (1973), *The Interpretation of Cultures*, New York: Basic Books.

Gilpin, W. C. (1993), 'The Theological Schools: Transmission, Transformation, and Transcendence of Denominational Culture', in Carroll, J. and Roof, W. C. (eds), *Beyond Establishment: Protestant Identity in a Post-Protestant Age*, Louisville, KY: Westminster/John Knox Press, pp. 188–204.

Grierson, D. (1984), *Transforming a People of God*, Melbourne: Joint Board of Christian Education of Australia and New Zealand.

Hunter, J. D. (1987), *Evangelicalism: The Coming Generation*, Chicago: University of Chicago Press.

Jenkins, T. (1999), *Religion in English Everyday Life: An Ethnographic Approach*, Oxford: Berghahn Books.

Marler, P. L. and Hadaway, C. K. (1997), 'Methodists on the Margins: "Self-Authoring" Religious Identity', in Richey, R. E., Campbell, D. M. and Lawrence, W. B. (eds), *Connectionalism: Ecclesiology, Mission and Identity*, Nashville, TN: Abingdon Press, pp. 289–316.

Marsh, C. (1999), 'A Training-Ground for Forgiveness: Methodism and "Fellowship"', in Craske, J. and Marsh, C. (1999), *Methodism and the Future: Facing the Challenge*, London: Cassell, pp. 100–114.

Richey, R. E. (1997), 'Introduction', in Richey, R. E., Campbell, D. M. and Lawrence, W. B. (eds), *Connectionalism: Ecclesiology, Mission and Identity*, Nashville, TN: Abingdon Press, pp. 1–22.

Richey, R. E., Campbell, D. M. and Lawrence, W. B. (1997), *Connectionalism: Ecclesiology, Mission and Identity*, Nashville, TN: Abingdon Press.

Richter, P. (2002), 'That Elusive Methodist Identity: a Sociological Perspective', *Epworth Review*, 29 (1), January, 39–48.

Richter, P. and Francis, L. J. (1998), *Gone but not Forgotten: Church Leaving and Returning*, London: Darton, Longman and Todd.

Roberts, K. A. (1984), *Religion in Sociological Perspective*, Chicago: Dorsey Press.

Roberts, K. A. (1993), 'Ritual and the Transmission of a Cultural Tradition: An Ethnographic Perspective', in Carroll, J. and Roof, W. C. (eds) *Beyond Establishment: Protestant Identity in a Post-Protestant Age*, Louisville, KY: Westminster/John Knox Press, pp. 74–98.

Stringer, M. D. (1999), *On the Perception of Worship: The Ethnography of Worship in Four Christian Congregations in Manchester*, Birmingham: University of Birmingham Press.

Tisdale, L. T. (1997), *Preaching as Local Theology and Folk Art*, Minneapolis, MN: Fortress Press.

Wagner, R. (1981), *The Invention of Culture: Revised and Expanded Edition*, Chicago: University of Chicago Press [originally published 1975].

Weeks, L. B. (1993), 'Presbyterian Culture: Views from "the Edge"', in Carroll, J. and Roof, W. C. (eds), *Beyond Establishment: Protestant Identity in a Post-Protestant Age*, Louisville, KY: Westminster/John Knox Press, pp. 309–326.

Chapter 13

The Significance of Gender for Congregational Studies

Kristin Aune

Why study gender? In the 1970s and 1980s, those establishing Women's Studies courses in universities and colleges were giving this question much thought. Influenced by feminist politics, they saw that inequalities facing women in society were also visible in academia. As feminists had attempted to do in society, they aimed to reveal and eliminate inequality as regards women's comparative exclusion from academic knowledge – as subjects, objects, students and teachers. They argued that although scholarship claimed to be objective it was in fact 'androcentric' or 'phallocentric', with 'men's experiences and priorities being seen as central and representative of all' (Robinson, 1997, p. 2).

Over twenty years later the 'Why study gender?' question is still not taken seriously in the sociology of religion, nor in congregational studies – particularly in the UK (Walter and Davie, 1998, pp. 640–641). Yet, as this chapter will argue, gender should be of vital concern to those studying contemporary religion. This is so for three reasons. The first is that gender has become a significant field of academic enquiry. The second is that gender is a significant means by which social identities are established and, arising from this, a site of social conflict. The third is that gender is important for sociologists of congregations because a relationship frequently exists between congregational membership and gender.

This chapter has two major sections. The first half of the chapter offers a brief summary of the current state of research into gender in congregations – with a central focus on work in the UK – and provides illustrations and examples. This will be done with reference to the three reasons just outlined. In the second half of the chapter, in order to ground the chapter's argument in my own empirical work, I present material from a recent ethnographic study of gender in an evangelical congregation, considering whether and how gender is a means by which social identities are established and occupy a site of social conflict, and how the significant gender imbalance in the membership of the congregation influences its dynamics.

Gender as a Significant Field of Academic Enquiry

Gender within General Congregational Studies

While sociologists of congregations have not been quick to notice the significance of gender – classic texts such as Hopewell's *Congregation* (1987) fail even to mention it – the late 1980s saw interest increase. Authors of general studies of congregations finally began to attend to gender. For some of them, gender appears as a minor variable meriting only a paragraph or two. Others note the significant position gender issues occupy for the congregations they study. Most of this work is American. Ammerman's (1987) ethnographic study of a fundamentalist church reveals how 'Southside Gospel Church' employs a conservative understanding of the husband/wife relationship as a way of enforcing boundaries between the church and 'the world'. Stout and Brekus's (1994) historical study of a New Haven Congregational church is a paradigmatic study that foregrounds gender in order to explain one of the congregation's most significant features, its enduring gender imbalance.

In Britain, Briers (1993) and Charman (1995) focus on the evangelical charismatic 'House Church' or Restorationist movement (now called New Churches). Briers's ethnographic study of a congregation from the Covenant Ministries network reveals an ambiguous relationship between the movement and modernity. Covenant Ministries 'has offered itself as an antidote to the modern world, while simultaneously offering a spiritual affirmation of its underlying values' (Briers, 1993, p. 208). Briers shows how the congregation employs strict idealization of the nuclear family with distinctly separate gender roles to differentiate it from perceived feminist and gay emphases within society. Yet in doing this Covenant Ministries is simply sanctifying a family set-up that is more a modern Western construct than a biblical norm. Charman discusses New Church life in terms of empowerment and enfeeblement. Covert ethnographic observation in three congregations revealed that women's congregational roles were limited by a theology of male authority in marriage, church and society. Because of this limitation, 'empowerment is possible in men to a greater extent than in women who appear to meet a "threshold" earlier because they are undervalued by an expectation that they will comply with traditional female roles' (Charman, 1995, p. 382; see also pp. 281–289).

Jenkins (1999) gives substantial discussion of the social context of the Kingswood Whit Walk, a march that happens yearly on the morning of the Whit Bank Holiday, led by the churches through an area of East Bristol. Despite men's leading status on the day, the walk is planned and directed in advance primarily by women. The walk makes visible the central position of the family in Kingswood, and it is this family-centredness that explains women's dominance in the business of the walk.

Congregational Studies of Gender and Women

A further group of congregational studies concentrate exclusively on women or gender. American studies include Lawless's (1988) research into women in a

Pentecostal congregation in Southern Indiana and Davidman's (1991) ethnographic research into the increasing numbers of American women converting to Orthodox Judaism. In her investigation of women's extensive participation in evangelical congregations in Columbia, Brusco finds that women's conversions and congregational adherence can be understood as a means of raising their status (Brusco, 1995 and 1997). Gillespie's work on four Episcopalian congregations aims to remedy the fact that 'to date the least studied, least known element in the process of religious change is that involving the female segment of mainline church members in the United States' (Gillespie, 1995, p. 2). Prelinger's edited collection *Episcopal Women* (1992) brings together short historical and sociological studies of women in Episcopalianism. And Brasher's (1998) ethnographic work amongst American Christian fundamentalists demonstrates the paradox that fundamentalist women can gain power even though they inhabit congregations led solely by men. Through establishing parallel female-only spheres of activity women gain skills and opportunities which enable them to take control of their lives.

Turning to Britain, Sharp's (1998) PhD thesis addresses the 'discordant discourses' of male priests and their female congregants in the contemporary British Roman Catholic Church. Franks (2001) asks why women join British Islamic and Christian revivalist movements. Her Christian section involved limited participant observation of the evangelical charismatic Jesus Fellowship community and of a student meeting of a congregation from the New Church network Covenant Ministries. Franks focuses on four themes: marriage and female submission, rights and responsibilities, modesty and dress codes, and empowerment. She concludes that revivalist women adhere to a range of models of gender relations, not simply the conservative pattern. Women interpret their religious choices – which Franks views through the lens of rational choice theory – as empowering. Those in movements with conservative gender roles do not regard limitations on women's roles as restrictive, but as providing divinely ordained structures for women's flourishing. While a few feminist revivalist women are willing to challenge religious authorities, their challenge is reformist rather than radical.

Although not congregational studies as such, several other studies merit mention because of their qualitative research methodology. These concentrate on denominations or strands of Protestantism. The most unusual is Fulkerson's *Changing the Subject* (1994), which seeks dialogue between feminist theology and the sociology of religion. Griffith's *God's Daughters* (1997) is an ethnographic investigation of the evangelical charismatic Women's Aglow movement, a large American (now worldwide) women's prayer fellowship. In Britain, Baillie's work on women in evangelical churches in Belfast (2002) uses quantitative (questionnaires) and qualitative (interviews) methodological tools to ask whether women are 'imprisoned or empowered'. She concludes that while women in the homemaker role may be empowered by conservative evangelical idealization of domesticity, other women – those seeking public roles in society and the church – are imprisoned by it, as are women whose ambitions have been limited by evangelical constraints on their expected roles. Porter's (2002) similarly cross-denominational interview-based study of seventy women in different Northern Irish congregations demonstrates the significant, often unrecognized, contribution women are making to Northern Irish community, church and political life. Church structures often exclude women from leadership, and Porter shows how evangelical women negotiate their roles in such contexts.

The empowerment/disempowerment lens through which many of these studies examine congregational gender roles derives from second wave feminists' attention to ideas around patriarchy and women's empowerment. Yet this can be, as Woodhead (2002) has cautioned, a limited, contextually specific emphasis. It assumes that women's religious practices should be judged by specific criteria of what constitutes women's 'oppression' and 'liberation'. Modern feminists have often regarded religion as oppressive to women because it denies them autonomy (as Hampson, 1996 does), while neglecting the significance of religious practices to women worldwide for whom faith is not an optional extra (Woodhead, 2002, p. 332).

Postmodern Congregational Studies of Gender and Women

The turn to the postmodern manifests itself as a move away from second wave feminism as a distinctive movement, and from analysis that claims to address a monolithic 'women's experience'. Feminism has given way to contextually specific *feminisms*, and studies foregrounding women are being replaced by work on specific groups of women. Of these studies, only Aune (1998 and 2002), Foster (1992) and Toulis (1997) are British. Toulis (1997) and Gilkes (2001) attend to women's experiences in black churches. Toulis considers the negotiation of gender and Jamaican ethnic identity among Pentecostalists in a Birmingham New Testament Church of God congregation, showing how different models of identity converge:

> there are three categories of the person in the church: 'men,' 'women' and 'saints.' The construction of gendered persons ('men' and 'women') and the construction of persons as undifferentiated saints employs two different models: one model rests upon both the 'model for' the family provided by patriarchal 'Christian marriage' and the 'model of' the practical range in African–Caribbean kinship and domestic organization, while the other model is based on the 'model for' 'Christian identity'.
>
> (Toulis, 1997, p. 272)

Each factor – Afro-Caribbean and patriarchal Christian concepts of gender and a belief that Christian identity is genderless – moderates the others to produce gender identities unique to Afro-Caribbean Pentecostalism.

My own work addresses the status of single women in evangelical churches through an ethnographic study of an evangelical charismatic New Church congregation (Aune, 1998) and a larger questionnaire and interview survey of women from a variety of evangelical denominations (Aune, 2002). Both reveal how single women are marginalized within evangelical congregations, first in relation to married women, and second, along with married women, in relation to men. Foster (1992) combines both emphases in a study of women in black British churches. She shows that such churches can be pictured as two pyramids:

> The first pyramid is inverted and represents the 'female' Church. In this pyramid lies the spirituality, the life-giving and life-sustaining nature of the Church. The second is the upright pyramid. It represents the Church in all its patriarchal and hierarchical glory, and contains all leadership, juridical and priestly roles.
>
> (Foster, 1992, p. 47)

She also observes that substantial numbers of women (who make up between 65 and 95 per cent of black congregations) are single. The church's desire to stand out from perceived societal permissiveness has led it to privilege the married state, and single women are exhorted to pray that they will find a Christian man to marry. This response is, Foster believes, inadequate. Many single women refuse to accept involuntary celibacy and leave the church in search of partners.

Several American studies take as their female subjects Christian feminists. Stocks (1997a and 1997b) addresses evangelical feminists struggling to bring change to their congregations. Neitz's (1995) ethnographic work is on a loosely Roman Catholic women's spirituality group which has parallels with the Goddess, feminist neo-pagan and women's spirituality movements described in her earlier work (Neitz, 1993); one such group is the focus of Jacobs's (1993) ethnographic study. Trebbi (1993) provides a short account of the Women-Church movement of (largely Catholic) Christian feminists in America. As yet, no comparable British research has been conducted.

Congregational Studies of Men

As Women's Studies makes way for the more inclusive Gender Studies, there is a growing emphasis on men's social role, an emphasis linked to debates in the 1990s about the 'crisis in masculinity' (Horrocks, 1994; Clare, 2000), made visible in popular culture through the 1980s 'New Man' and 1990s 'New Lad' stereotypes. Congregational studies, accordingly, have paid some attention to masculinity. However, studies of this type are, as far as I am aware, exclusively American, mirroring the greater attention paid to the study of masculinity in the United States. Mamiya's (1994) mainly historical study reveals an African Methodist Episcopal congregation that has swum against the black churches' tide of low male membership by developing lay organizations for men. A clutch of studies have addressed the American evangelical men's Promise Keepers movement, which was born in the early 1990s and grew at an incredible rate, attracting a total of one million men at rallies at sports stadiums in 1995 (Balmer, 2000). Lundskow (2000), Cole (2000) and Bartkowski's (2000) ethnographic work shows how Promise Keepers mixes traditional and egalitarian under-standings of masculinity.

Gender, Identity and Social Conflict

Before exploring these wider issues in relation to my own fieldwork, it will be instructive to revisit some of the theoretical debate that has shaped the discussion of gender as a site of social conflict within religious groups. In this way we may begin to speak of relationships between the construction of religious values and the construction of gender identities.

Since at least 1800, and probably before, Western churches have attracted more women than men (Davie, 1994; Walter and Davie, 1998; Brown, 2001). Women do not only attend church more frequently: they score higher on surveys of religious and spiritual beliefs, and engage more in private prayer and Bible reading (Walter and Davie, 1998). Although America has a far higher church attendance level than Britain, the gender imbalance in religion is remarkably similar (Woolever and Bruce, 2000). In Britain, figures suggest that the gender disparity has increased in the last twenty years. In 1979, 55 per cent of church members were women. In 1989, this had risen to 58 per cent (Brierley, 1991, p. 24), and in 2001 to between 61 per cent (Wraight, 2001, p. 21) and 65 per cent (Churches Information for Mission, 2001, p. 9).

Historical and sociological research shows some relationship between gender traditionalism and Christian adherence; this is particularly true in certain denominations and traditions.[1] Distinctive attitudes to gender are a key feature of what Woodhead and Heelas call 'religions of difference'. Religions of difference enforce boundaries between the congregation and the 'world' outside, and the maintenance of 'prescriptive' difference-based gender identities contributes to this. Contemporary Christian congregations classifiable as religions of difference include evangelical Christianity and Roman Catholicism (Woodhead and Heelas, 2000, pp. 27–69). In conservative evangelical Protestantism, heterosexual marriage is seen as the ideal relational status. Within marriage the man is viewed as head of the household with ultimate responsibility for decision-making and financial provision. Women, meanwhile, have a submissive role and are expected to shoulder most of the childcare responsibilities. Preaching and congregational leadership are male domains, while women teach children and do administrative, domestic and other supportive tasks. In Roman Catholicism, marriage is highly valued for the laity, but the exclusively male clergy are required to take vows of celibacy. Motherhood is exalted, and women are seen as primarily responsible for their families.

---

[1] However, it is important not to overplay this relationship, as, for example, Callum Brown (2001) does in arguing that British Christianity has 'died' because of changing gender roles. While congregations have generally held conservative attitudes to gender, exceptions exist – the influence of evangelical Christian women in the formation of first wave feminism in the nineteenth century is a notable case in point (Banks, 1981; Rendall, 1985).

Conversely, the keener a congregation is to engage with those outside religion, the more flexible its gender roles. Woodhead and Heelas' category 'religions of humanity' describes this attitude. Religions of humanity value human experience, expecting it to play an important role in interpreting scripture and tradition. They look to bring divinity and humanity closer together, do not erect boundaries between humans, and appreciate difference only if it is non-prescriptive – if it is up to the individual to assert or avoid. Within contemporary Christianity, liberal Christianity conforms to this designation (Woodhead and Heelas, 2000, pp. 70–109). Marital gender roles are more fluid, divorce and remarriage more accepted and alternative sexual partnerships such as cohabitation or lesbian and gay relationships may be permissible. It is from within liberal Christianity that feminist theology has arisen.

One observation gained from in-depth study of congregations is the existence of 'congregations in conflict' (Becker, 1999). As Roof (1978), Wuthnow (1988), Ammerman (1990) and Hunter (1991) have shown in the American context, denominations (and to a lesser extent congregations) can be sites of theological, social and organizational conflict – even polarization. Often viewed as a conservative-liberal conflict, it roughly translates as Woodhead and Heelas' 'religions of difference' and 'religions of humanity'. What is particularly salient is that, as Becker (1999) has shown with reference to the congregations she studied, gender and sexual issues are the third most common causes of congregational conflict (see also Wuthnow, 1988, pp. 224–235 and Ruether, 2001, pp. 149–155 for evidence that gender is a key area of polarization in American congregations). Ammerman (1990) shows how the woman's role was a key issue of contention for the American Southern Baptists.

However, ethnographic studies tend to moderate, even contradict, 'culture wars' theses. Ammerman has cautioned against assuming a conservative-liberal polarization (1997, pp. 356–358), and, indeed, her work on the Southern Baptists (1990) revealed a conservative-liberal spectrum rather than a polarization. Similarly, Becker rejects the view that conflict over gender roles reveals a wide split between 'conservatives' and 'liberals', arguing that the 'liberal' stance on gender equality espoused by those in one congregation she observed derived not from societal norms but from evangelical feminist hermeneutics (Becker, 1999, pp. 127–130, 177–178). Moreover, as most research on gender in congregations shows, conservative congregations are not uniformly so, and often contain elements which militate against gender conservatism, either diluting it or producing transformations which would be seen as favourable for women.

Yet notwithstanding these hesitations, it remains true that, in Britain, gender is a site of social conflict for Christians. This conflict can occur within a denomination: the fight for women's ordination in the Church of England exemplified this. Although insufficient qualitative research has been conducted into gender in British congregations, studies by Briers (1993), Charman (1995), Aune (1998) and Sharp (1998) suggest the widespread presence of congregational conflict centred around gender issues.

Gender in a New Church Congregation

In the light of the foregoing remarks, I turn now to a more detailed exploration of some of my own research findings. 'Westside'[2] is a small charismatic, evangelical congregation belonging to the New Church network New Frontiers International (NFI). NFI is a part of what began to emerge in the late 1960s and early 1970s as the 'House Church' or 'Restoration' movement. Small, independent groups of Christians were surfacing, whose leaders began meeting together, inspired by their perception of a divine calling to 'restore the church'. Along with individual churches, networks grew up around key leaders, who became known as 'apostles'. Terry Virgo, NFI's founder, was one of these leaders. While they share many common features with earlier Classical Pentecostalism, Restorationists can be distinguished theologically by three features. First, they have an anti-denominational kingdom theology. They believe denominations are not in God's plan; rather, Jesus is establishing his kingdom on earth, and they are aiding its progression. Second, their ecclesiology is distinctive. They believe that churches should be led by divinely appointed apostles (overseers of groups of churches), prophets and elders (local church leaders). From their ecclesiology a third feature arises: the doctrine of discipleship. Restorationists believe that individuals' spiritual growth comes from submission to those in authority over them. Children submit to parents, wives to husbands and all to elders, who submit to apostles (Walker, 1998). NFI is still led by Terry Virgo, whose oversight extends to over two hundred churches or 'church plants' in the UK and several dozen overseas.

Westside, where I spent fifteen months in 2000 and 2001 as a participant observer, is situated in a British city. As fieldwork began, Westside had twelve adult members, and as it ended, twenty-four; the majority of members were female.[3] Most Westsiders are in their twenties, with the exception of two couples (the leader Chris and his wife Sarah, and supporting leader Mark and his wife Jane) who are in their thirties, one single woman in her late fifties (Jenny) and a married couple (Harry and Ann) in their early sixties. All but three of the twenty-four were white and most would be considered middle class. Because it is small, Westside is referred to as a 'church plant'. It was 'planted' a year or so before fieldwork began, when Chris and Sarah moved to the city in response to the encouragement of leaders in their previous NFI church. As well as attending congregation gatherings, I conducted interviews with twenty members, asking questions about attitudes to gender.

For the first six months, congregational activities centred around a weekly Wednesday evening 'house group' meeting at the home of Chris and Sarah or Mark and Jane. As it grew, a further house group was started on another evening. Group meetings were informal; the time was spent chatting, studying the Bible, listening to a talk given by a group member, singing (referred to as

---

[2] 'Westside' and names of all members are pseudonyms.
[3] By 'members' I am referring to regular attendees. Westside had not yet developed a formal membership policy.

'worship') and giving each other prophecies. Just after I left, Westside began a monthly Sunday service.

Gender as a Means by which Social Identities are Established

Gender is crucial to NFI's identity as a movement. Differentiated[4] gender roles were upheld from its inception. NFI's annual summer camp, Stoneleigh Bible Week, has always included seminars on gender roles, family life, marriage and women's issues. Teaching given there (by male leaders, or, in the women's seminars, by Virgo's wife, Wendy) puts forward a clearly delineated pattern of masculinity and femininity. According to NFI leaders, 'the family' is to be celebrated and supported. 'The family' is a nuclear family within which the husband takes the leading breadwinner role and his wife submits to him. She may work outside the home, but her main responsibility is to her children and husband. This pattern translates into local congregations, where overall leadership ('eldership') is restricted to men, and women's roles tend to be supportive (for examples of this teaching, see W. Virgo, 1998; D. Holden, 2000; L. Holden, 2000; Pettit, 2000; Betts, 2001; T. Virgo, 2001, pp. 301–303; Piper and Grudem, 1991, is the American text used most frequently within NFI). Such gender differentiation is believed to be 'biblical', and NFI leaders use a fairly literalistic method of biblical interpretation.

NFI's closed gender ideology arose from a number of social factors. Most significantly, although they mirrored the 1960s counter-culture stylistically, promoting free expression in worship, tongues-speaking, prophesying and praying for healing, Restorationist leaders perceived the counter-culture as a threat to the family and society. Not only did they reject pre-, extra-marital or homosexual sexual activity; they also conflated the 1960s 'sexual revolution' with second wave feminism, which led them to oppose feminist goals. Second, many House Church leaders had grown up in the Brethren, a movement known for believing that women should remain silent at church meetings. Third, leaders took inspiration from Argentinian Juan Carlos Ortiz, 'father of discipling and shepherding doctrines in their modern Protestant form' (Walker, 1998, p. 83) and from Orvil Swindoll and the American charismatic leaders known as the 'Fort Lauderdale Five' who established the discipleship doctrine in North America (Walker, 1998, p. 83). Integral to the doctrine was women's submission to their husbands and church leaders. Fourth, the debate over the ordination of women was the key issue for the Church of England in the 1970s (Hastings, 2001, pp. 610–611); it is likely that the House Churches wanted to avoid controversies by formulating a position early on. Fifth, Restorationist

---

[4] I have chosen, as far as possible, to avoid using the term 'conservative' for NFI's 'conservative' gender ideology. This is because some NFI members understand this as an offensive and inaccurate term. They eschew traditionalism or conservativism for its own sake, and instead see themselves as a radical movement who are returning to true biblical Christianity. Because of this, I have opted for the adjectives 'differentiated' or 'closed' (in the sense of 'non-negotiable').

gender ideology was fuelled by the rise of New Right Thatcherism, with its emphasis on the nuclear family.

While NFI's views on gender derive largely from this 1970s and 1980s social context, indications suggest that from the late 1990s this gender-differentiated ideology was reasserted; this can be understood as a backlash against Christian (notably evangelical) feminism. British Christian feminists were active from the 1970s, primarily in the campaign for women's ordination as priests in the Church of England (Davis, 1996). From 1985 to the early 1990s the British evangelical feminist organization Men, Women and God had a high profile amongst evangelicals (see Keay, 1987). In the late 1980s the American Council on Biblical Manhood and Womanhood (CBMW) was formed in opposition to evangelical feminism. In 1998 it established a British branch, of which Terry Virgo became a patron. At Stoneleigh that year, Wendy Virgo led a seminar suggesting that some NFI women needed to ask forgiveness for their 'Jezebellic Spirit' which they were using to manipulate and control men (W. Virgo, 1998). In 2000 Stoneleigh held more sessions than usual on gender, devoting six seminars to 'man in the new millennium' and four to 'women in the new millennium'. In 2002 Wayne Grudem, Vice President of CBMW, was invited to NFI's leaders' conference to conduct a plenary session ('Gender Confusion – The Way Forward') and seminar ('The Biblical case for why some roles should be restricted to men'). Thus NFI's backlash against feminism can be understood as two distinct waves: in the 1970s to 1980s in opposition to second wave feminism, and from the late 1990s in opposition to Christian feminism (which, in turn, can be understood as a Christian version of second wave feminism).

In 2001 Terry Virgo published his autobiography. In one chapter he details five areas in which NFI differs from some evangelical churches. The first is NFI's belief that women should not hold 'governmental' leadership roles or engage in authoritative preaching to men (T. Virgo, 2001, pp. 301–313). Virgo refers to the fact that observers jokingly referred to NFI as 'No Females Included', a charge he rejects, detailing women's extensive involvement in NFI congregations. I was already familiar with the 'No Females Included' label, and have lost count of the number of times I have explained that I am studying NFI to evangelical Christians who have responded: 'Aren't they the ones who don't have women leaders?'

Gender as a Site of Social Conflict

Because the particular focus of my research was a local NFI congregation, I had little opportunity to discern the presence or absence of gender-related conflict among the movement's leaders. But what I did find was congregational gender conflict. Notwithstanding Ammerman (1997) and Becker's (1999) contention that the conservative–liberal divide in congregations is weak, if it exists at all, my research *has* shown up such a divide, albeit one better resembling a continuum or spectrum. My interviews show that Westsiders' views on gender roles fall along a spectrum ranging from closed (or conservative) to open (or liberal). Three examples, from the closed end, middle and open end of the spectrum, illustrate this.

The opinions of Ann, who is in her early sixties, are the most gender differentiated. Ann believes men and women are 'equal but different'. Their difference should translate into different social roles: in particular, women's childbearing capacity means that their attention should be given to rearing children. Until her children were grown up, Ann generally stayed at home caring for them, despite her husband Harry's low wages. She believes it is important that children have their mother at home. Ann sees marriage as a more advantageous status than being single; this is presumably because she locates Christian gender identity for women in their childbearing capacity. Furthermore, she believes that pre-, extra-marital and homosexual sexual activity is illegitimate behaviour for Christians. Regarding congregational roles, Ann grew up among the Plymouth Brethren, who do not permit women to speak at congregational gatherings. She has since modified her views, but admits: 'I still think that in the church, that the women have to, you know, be sort of in submission to, um, to the male headship because I believe that's the way that God has said, you know – that Christ is the head of the church and the male's the head of the female.'

John is in his late twenties. His opinions would place him around the middle of the closed–open gender spectrum. John supports gender equality in society, and in particular in employment. Within the family, however, he thinks there should be differences. He believes he holds a particular responsibility towards his wife, which is part of what it means to be a man. Distinctive masculinity is important, John contends, and boys need fathers who are strong male role models. This does not, however, mean that he believes wives should submit to their husbands. John favours neither marriage nor singleness as ideal marital states. Like Ann, he believes sexual activity is not permissible for Christians outside marriage, but he is aware that biblical injunctions about sexual behaviour can be interpreted as culturally specific. Regarding congregational gender roles, John admits being torn between what he thinks he sees in the Bible ('men being chosen as primary leaders') and 'what I know experientially from life ... There are women in the church who are every bit as capable of doing, you know, doing everything that fellas do in church.' He adds: 'I think in a way I can always square what we do in Westside (with, like, having myself, Mark and Chris as the three, you know, main guys in the leadership team) with the fact that, you know, ... we always consult our wives in everything.'

Jenny, the only older single (divorced) woman, is a similar age to Ann. Her views, however, were the most open of all Westside members. She is opposed to differentiated gender roles in society, family or church, and believes that in the congregation 'roles should be according to individual preference and appropriateness'. She favours neither marriage nor singleness and is the only Westside member to accept gay and lesbian relationships and non-married heterosexual sexual relationships as valid lifestyles for Christians. She believes that lifelong monogamy is important, but that it is commitment, rather than the 'manmade' 'bit of paper', that is significant.

Because Westside is a new congregation, it lacks an official position on gender issues. During the fifteen months of fieldwork at the weekly house groups, there had been no outright restriction on women's roles. In an average meeting, men were a little more likely than women (1.3 times more likely) to hold a leadership role – worship leading, chairing (known as anchoring) the meeting or giving the talk or Bible study. However, when viewed in proportion to their number and attendance, this imbalance increases dramatically. In proportion to their number and attendance, men had over three times as many leadership opportunities as women. However, women (more often married women) were sometimes asked to take on these roles, and did so very competently. Surprisingly, men's greater participation was present in almost every area of congregational involvement: in proportion to their attendance, men were also more than three times more likely than women to make the tea and coffee for those arriving at the house groups. During the fifteen months, a leadership team of three men, Chris, Mark and John, was formed, with women explicitly excluded because of NFI's stance on male eldership. Some Westside members, particularly those unfamiliar with NFI, were unhappy with this.

Although as a movement NFI opposes female congregational leadership, my fieldwork shows that members of congregations are less likely to support gender differentiation. Six of the twenty Westside interviewees disagreed with male-only congregational leadership. Another six had not made up their minds, leaving only eight (just over a third) who agreed with NFI's opposition to female elders.

Lack of consensus among Westsiders makes it unlikely that in the long term their leaders can continue favouring men in leadership positions without facing opposition. As Westside was preparing to begin Sunday services, the role of women at those services became an important issue. Chris asked Mark, who is regarded as having good biblical knowledge, to prepare a draft paper on the role of women. Mark's paper begins: 'Perhaps the most contentious issue in contemporary evangelical Christianity is that of the role of women in the church.' It goes on: 'We are keen that Westside should not fall into the trap of sweeping this issue under the carpet ... we would prefer that whatever position we reach, we reach by honest prayer and rational study rather than by default.' The paper judges the issue important for three reasons:

1   church leaders are answerable to God for the way they develop those they lead (including women);
2   people visiting Westside could be put off if they perceive male domination;
3   if women have Bible-teaching abilities which they are forbidden to use, both the individual women and the whole congregation are unable to benefit from them. Mark weighs up what he sees as the central conflict:

> Living in Western Europe in the 21st century, it is absolutely contrary to our intuition that there may be some roles from which women are excluded simply on the basis of their gender. Yet there are passages in the New Testament which seem on the surface to say just that.

He finds that although the three reasons above are good arguments for removing restrictions in women's roles, the deciding factor must be 'the teaching of the Bible'.

Mark's paper reveals conflict between a closed and open stance on gender. Acknowledging the presence of a closed–open gender spectrum reveals that gender is but one factor in a much larger continuum. Westside, with the rest of contemporary British evangelicalism, vacillates between closed ('religion of difference') and open ('religion of humanity') positions. Closed evangelicalism, with its insistence on order, differentiation, rationality and literal interpretation of an inerrant Bible struggles against open evangelicalism, with its reflexivity, its openness to the supernatural movement of the Holy Spirit and its desire to heal divisions. Whether evangelicals can sustain this closed–open tension, or whether it will pull their congregations apart, is as yet unknown.

The Gender Imbalance in Westside

Westside's gender imbalance was greater than in the average congregation, with women constituting between two-thirds and three-quarters of members. Furthermore, by the end of my fieldwork, the majority of members (14 out of 24) were single women, a proportion more than double that of the average evangelical church (Aune, 2002, pp. 16–17). (Of the remainder, there were four married couples and two single men.) The gender imbalance in Westside has had three main consequences: it has raised the status of men, lowered the status of single women and, though it appears paradoxical, increased the opportunities available to women in general.

Because NFI, and some Westside leaders, believe that leadership is a characteristic men need to develop, nearly all the male Westsiders were given leadership responsibilities. By the end of my fieldwork, all but one of the men had led, or were about to lead, a house group. In contrast, less than a third of women held, or were to begin holding, an equivalent role. Westside's three overall leaders are also all male. At Westside, then, men have a high status. Men are also rated highly by single women looking for a partner, and this is connected to the second consequence of the gender imbalance: the reduction of single women's status.

In movements like NFI that locate ideal gender identity in marriage – only in marriage can women fulfil a submissive, childbearing role, and men a leadership, breadwinner role – single people's status is lower than married people's, and can only be raised by marrying. Furthermore, because NFI believe that Christians should marry fellow Christians, ideally preferring endogamy (marriage within NFI), church is the primary arena for singles to find partners. In a congregation like Westside, the lack of single men renders women's chances of finding a suitable partner almost non-existent. This creates feelings of desperation, powerlessness and rejection in single women, feelings exacerbated by the regular comments, jokes and matchmaking attempts of married Westsiders. One Sunday, at a nearby NFI congregation frequented by Westside, the preacher joked while announcing the 'offering' (collection):

> While the offering's still going round, let me say there's also a special two-for-one offer for any couples. Everyone has to put £5 in, and if you're a couple you only need

to put in £2.50 each. And if you're single and are going to ask someone out this afternoon – do you hear that, you singles at the back? – we'll give you £10. O.K.? (Congregation laughs.)

Imaginary financial privileges are announced for couples, ranking 'coupledom' twice as important as singleness. The need for single people to couple up is treated as so urgent that not only would they be required to give less to the church, but they would actually be given money to do so – more than double what a normal single person would be required to put into the offering basket!

Compared with married women, single women have reduced access to congregational leadership roles. This is generally not a conscious marginalization on the leaders' part. Jenny is 'Prayer Director' and coordinates Westside's prayer meetings, and a single woman in her early thirties, Marion, was, towards the end of my fieldwork, given responsibility for training house group leaders. However, on one occasion Chris said that he wanted more married couples to join Westside in order that they could lead evening house groups, demonstrating his preference for married group leaders. During a conversation, Jenny told me she was convinced that her single, middle-aged, status was the reason she had not been invited to lead a house group:

> Jenny: Middle-aged women are just used in supportive roles, although there's so many of them.
> KA: Like babysitting?
> Jenny: Babysitting and cooking.
> KA: But in this group you're prayer director. That's a role.
> Jenny: But it's patronizing. It was done to patronize me. I told Chris that. It's because they don't want me to lead a group.
> KA: Because you're single?
> Jenny: Because they only want couples and I'm a single middle-aged woman.

It is also true, however, that the prevalence of women at Westside has made them more visible and granted them more opportunities than they might have otherwise had. Observing a Westside gathering it would be impossible to designate it 'No Females Included'. Women are rendered highly visible by the lack of men in attendance. Moreover, because there are so few men, women have to take on many non-prohibited roles, including worship leading, playing musical instruments, giving talks in house groups, leading Bible studies and prayers, running the crèche and organizing social events. As I left Westside, Jenny was finally, due to her missionary endeavours that had produced a sudden influx of new local single women into Westside, given permission to initiate a new house group. After I left, I kept in touch with her and heard how, as this all-female group developed, women who in other house groups had previously been passive attendees became active participants, taking responsibility for the spiritual growth of their believing sisters.

As I write this, over a year after my fieldwork officially ended, the 'women issue' in Westside has yet to be resolved; this, perhaps, indicates its conflict-producing capacity. Westside continues in a 'default position' of male-only preaching, and few women lead Sunday services. Some single women have left the congregation: the gender imbalance and their desire for husbands has led them to a large evangelical Anglican church where they perceive a greater chance of finding partners. Men continue to lead and preach. Women continue to care for the children, sustain the congregation's social life and provide informal pastoral support for each other. Gender differentiation is holding out. But below the surface, a spirit of openness threatens change.

In Westside, like all congregations, gender is a lens through which social identities are constructed – and sometimes disputed. The advent of feminist scholarship in the last two to three decades has established the importance not only of studying gender, but also of letting gender transform our epistemology and ways of studying. Exploring gender in congregational studies will uncover the processes by which identities are formed and theology and the social interact. Moreover, in a post-Christian context, to look at a congregation's gender practices can also allow the observer to see beyond them. As Ursula King has written, 'Gender and religion are closely interrelated as our perceptions of ourselves are shaped by and deeply rooted in our culturally shared religious and philosophical heritage, even when this is rejected' (King, 1995, p. 2). And in the congregation, cultural gender ideologies and patterns may be challenged, morphed and rejected, even as they are affirmed and illuminated.

References

Ammerman, N. T. (1987), *Bible Believers: Fundamentalists in the Modern World*, New Brunswick, NJ: Rutgers University Press.

Ammerman, N. T. (1990), *Baptist Battles: Social Change and Religious Conflict in the Southern Baptist Convention*, New Brunswick, NJ and London: Rutgers University Press.

Ammerman, N. T. (1997), *Congregation and Community*, New Brunswick, NJ: Rutgers University Press.

Aune, K. (1998), 'Headless women? The role of single women in the contemporary evangelical church', MA dissertation, Centre for Women's Studies, University of York.

Aune, K. (2002), *Single Women: Challenge to the Church?* Carlisle: Paternoster Press.

Baillie, S. M. (2002), *Evangelical Women in Belfast: Imprisoned or Empowered?* Basingstoke: Palgrave Macmillan.

Balmer, R. (2000), 'Introduction', in Claussen, D. S. (ed.), *The Promise Keepers: Essays on Masculinity and Christianity*, Jefferson, NC: McFarland and Company.

Banks, O. (1981), *Faces of Feminism: A Study of Feminism as a Social Movement*, Oxford: Martin Robertson.

Bartkowski, J. P. (2000), 'Breaking walls, raising fences: masculinity, intimacy, and accountability among the Promise Keepers', *Sociology of Religion*, 61 (1), 33–53.

Becker, P. E. (1999), *Congregations in Conflict: Cultural Models of Local Religious Life*, Cambridge, UK and New York: Cambridge University Press.

Betts, M. (2001), 'Role of Women', audiotape, no publisher listed.

Brasher, B. (1998), *Godly Women: Fundamentalism and Female Power*, New Brunswick, NJ: Rutgers University Press.

Brierley, P. (ed.) (1991), *Prospects for the Nineties: Trends and Tables from the 1989 English Church Census*, London: MARC Europe.

Briers, S. J. (1993), 'Negotiating with Babylon: Responses to Modernity within a Restorationist Community', unpublished PhD thesis, University of Cambridge.

Brown, C. G. (2001), *The Death of Christian Britain: Understanding Secularisation 1800– 2000*, London: Routledge.

Brusco, E. E. (1995), *The Reformation of Machismo: Evangelical Conversion and Gender in Columbia*, Austin: University of Texas Press.

Brusco, E. E. (1997), 'The Peace that Passes all Understanding: Violence, the Family, and Fundamentalist Knowledge in Columbia', in Brink, J. and Mencher, J. (eds), *Mixed Blessings: Gender and Religious Fundamentalism Cross Culturally*, New York and London: Routledge.

Charman, P. J. (1995), 'The rival kingdom of the New Churches: empowerment and enfeeblement', unpublished PhD thesis, Department of Religious Studies, University of Lancaster.

Churches Information for Mission (2001), *Faith in Life: A snapshot of church life in England at the beginning of the 21st century*, London: Churches Information for Mission.

Clare, A. (2000), *On Men: Masculinity in Crisis*, London: Chatto and Windus.

Cole, R. A. (2000), 'Promising to Be a Man: Promise Keepers and the Organizational Constitution of Masculinity', in Claussen, D. S. (ed.), *The Promise Keepers: Essays on Masculinity and Christianity*, Jefferson, NC: McFarland and Company.

Davidman, L. (1991), *Tradition in a Rootless World: Women turn to Orthodox Judaism*, Berkeley, CA: University of California Press.

Davie, G. (1994), *Religion in Britain since 1945: Believing without Belonging*, Oxford: Blackwell.

Davis, C. (1996), 'Movement for the Ordination of Women', in Isherwood, L. and McEwan, D. (eds), *An A to Z of Feminist Theology*, Sheffield: Sheffield Academic Press.

Foster, E. (1992), 'Women and the Inverted Pyramid of the Black Churches in Britain', in Sahgal, G. and Yuval-Davis, N. (eds), *Refusing Holy Orders: Women and Fundamentalism in Britain*, London: Virago.

Franks, M. (2001), *Women and Revivalism in the West: Choosing 'Fundamentalism' in a Liberal Democracy*, Basingstoke: Palgrave Macmillan.

Fulkerson, M. M. (1994), *Changing the Subject: Women's Discourses and Feminist Theology*, Minneapolis, MN: Fortress Press.

Gilkes, C. T. (2001), *"If It Wasn't For The Women . . .": Black Women's Experience and Womanist Culture in Church and Community*, Maryknoll, NY: Orbis Books.

Gillespie, J. B. (1995), *Women Speak: Of God, Congregations, and Change*, Valley Forge, PA: Trinity Press International.

Griffith, R. M. (1997), *God's Daughters: Evangelical Women and the Power of Submission*, Berkeley, CA: University of California Press.

Hampson, D. (1996), 'On Autonomy and Heteronomy', in Hampson, D. (ed.), *Swallowing a Fishbone? Feminist Theologians Debate Christianity*, London: SPCK.

Hastings, A. (2001), *A History of English Christianity 1920–2000*, London: SCM Press.

Holden, D. (2000), 'Man in the New Millennium: In the Home', Stoneleigh Bible Week audiotape, Hove: New Frontiers International.

Holden, L. (2000), 'Women in the New Millennium: Nothing to Prove, Plenty to Enjoy', Stoneleigh Bible Week audiotape, Hove: New Frontiers International.

Hopewell, J. F. (1987), *Congregation*, Minneapolis, MN: Fortress Press.

Horrocks, R. (1994), *Masculinity in Crisis: Myths, Fantasies and Realities*, Basingstoke: Macmillan.

Hunter, J. D. (1991), *Culture Wars: The Struggle to Define America*, New York: Basic Books.

Jacobs, J. L. (1993), 'Women-Centred Healing Rites: A Study of Alienation and Reintegration', in Robbins, T. and Anthony, D. (eds), *In Gods We Trust: New Patterns of Religious Pluralism in America*, second edition, New Brunswick, NJ: Transaction Publishers.

Jenkins, T. (1999), *Religion in Everyday English Life: An Ethnographic Approach*, Oxford: Berghahn Books.

Keay, K. (ed.) (1987), *Men, Women and God*, Basingstoke: Marshall Pickering.

King, U. (1995), 'Introduction: Gender and the Study of Religion', in King, U. (ed.), *Religion and Gender*, Oxford: Blackwell.

Lawless, E. J. (1988), *God's Peculiar People: Women's Voices and Folk Tradition in a Pentecostal Church*, Louisville, KY: The University Press of Kentucky.

Lundskow, G. N. (2000), 'Are Promises Enough? Promise Keepers' Attitudes and Character in Intensive Interviews', in Claussen, D. S. (ed.), *The Promise Keepers: Essays on Masculinity and Christianity*, Jefferson, NC: McFarland and Company.

Mamiya, L. H. (1994), 'A Social History of the Bethel African Methodist Episcopal Church in Baltimore: The House of God and the Struggle for Freedom', in Wind, J. P. and Lewis, J. W. (eds) (1994), *American Congregations Volume 1: Portraits of Twelve Religious Communities*, Chicago and London: University of Chicago Press.

Neitz, M. J. (1993), 'In Goddess We Trust', in Robbins, T. and Anthony, D. (eds), *In Gods We Trust: New Patterns of Religious Pluralism in America*, second edition, New Brunswick, NJ: Transaction Publishers.

Neitz, M. J. (1995), 'Constructing Women's Rituals: Roman Catholic Women and "Limina"', in Ammerman, N. T. and Roof, W. C. (eds), *Work, Family and Religion in Contemporary Society*, New York: Routledge.

Prelinger, C. M. (ed.) (1992), *Episcopal Women: Gender, Spirituality, and Commitment in an American Mainline Denomination*, New York: Oxford University Press, Inc.

Pettit, L. (2000), 'Women in the New Millennium: Submission or Suffocation?', Stoneleigh Bible Week audiotape, Hove: New Frontiers International.

Piper, J. and Grudem, W. (eds) (1991), *Recovering Biblical Manhood and Womanhood: A Response to Evangelical Feminism*, Wheaton, IL: Crossway Books.

Porter, F. (2002), *Changing Women, Changing Worlds: Evangelical Women in Church, Community and Politics*, Belfast: Blackstaff Press.

Rendall, J. (1985), *The Origins of Modern Feminism: Women in Britain, France and the United States 1780–1860*, Basingstoke: Macmillan.

Robinson, V. (1997), 'Introducing Women's Studies', in Robinson, V. and Richardson, D. (eds), *Introducing Women's Studies: Feminist Theory and Practice*, second edition, Basingstoke: Macmillan.

Ruether, R. R. (2001), *Christianity and the Making of the Modern Family*, London: SCM Press.

Sharp, G. (1998), 'Patriarchy and discordant discourses in the contemporary Roman Catholic Church: the voices of priests and women in parish settings', unpublished PhD thesis, University of Plymouth.

Stocks, J. (1997a), 'To Stay or to Leave? Organizational Legitimacy in the Struggle for Change among Evangelical Feminists', in Becker, P. E. and Eiesland, N. L. (eds), *Contemporary American Religion: An Ethnographic Reader*, Walnut Creek, CA: AltaMira Press.

Stocks, J. (1997b), 'Voices from the Margins: Evangelical Feminist Negotiation in the Public Debate of a Small Denomination in the United States', in Brink, J. and Mencher, J. (eds), *Mixed Blessings: Gender and Religious Fundamentalism Cross Culturally*, New York and London: Routledge.

Stout, H. S. and Brekus, C. (1994), 'A New England Congregation: Center Church, New Haven, 1638–1989', in Wind, J. P. and Lewis, J. W. (eds), *American Congregations Volume 1: Portraits of Twelve Religious Communities*, Chicago and London: University of Chicago Press.

Toulis, N. R. (1997), *Believing Identity: Pentecostalism and the Mediation of Jamaican Ethnicity and Gender in England*, Oxford: Berg.

Trebbi, D. (1993), 'Women-Church: Catholic Women Produce an Alternative Spirituality', in Robbins, T. and Anthony, D. (eds), *In Gods We Trust: New Patterns of Religious Pluralism in America*, second edition, New Brunswick, NJ: Transaction Publishers.

Virgo, T. (2001), *No Well-Worn Paths*, Eastbourne: Kingsway Publications.

Virgo, W. (1998), 'Sexes and the Family', Stoneleigh Bible Week audiotape, Hove: New Frontiers International.

Walker, A. (1998), *Restoring the Kingdom: The Radical Christianity of the House Church Movement*, fourth edition, Guildford: Eagle Publishing.

Walter, T. and Davie, G. (1998), 'The religiosity of women in the modern West', *British Journal of Sociology*, 49 (4), December, 640–660.

Woodhead, L. (2002), 'Women and Religion', in Woodhead, L., Fletcher, P., Kawanami, H. and Smith, D. (eds), *Religions in the Modern World*, London: Routledge.

Woodhead, L. and Heelas, P. (eds) (2000), *Religion in Modern Times: An Interpretive Anthology*, Oxford: Blackwell Publishers Ltd.

Woolever, C. and Bruce, D. (2000), *U.S. Congregational Life Survey*, Louisville, KY: U.S. Congregations.

Wraight, H. (2001), *Eve's Glue: The Role Women Play in Holding the Church Together*, Carlisle: Paternoster Press.

Wuthnow, R. (1988), *The Restructuring of American Religion: Society and Faith since World War II*, Princeton, NJ and Oxford, UK: Princeton University Press.

Chapter 14

Putting Congregational Studies to Work: Ethnography, Consultancy and Change

Martin Stringer

What is the Purpose of Congregational Studies?

In December 1999 I was approached by the minister of a number of Methodist churches in a north Birmingham circuit. Two of these churches had become very small and the congregations had become increasingly elderly. The churches were not 'inner city'. The circuit had already undertaken dynamic and exciting work with its inner city congregations. These churches were not in the wealthier outer ring of the circuit. They were ordinary Methodist churches, situated on two very stable and long-standing estates nestling under the M6. These churches were, in their own view, dying. They wanted to employ a lay worker to do something to stem this situation, although they were not quite sure what. On both estates the churches in question were practically the only Christian presence. The minister did not want to see the churches closed. It was clear that something had to be done. I was approached to provide a feasibility study both outlining the nature of the area, including its needs, and proposing options for the development of a project within the churches. I prepared a feasibility study and made a number of recommendations. The churches discussed these recommendations and chose the path they wished to develop. They approached the Methodist Church nationally and sought further funding. As part of this bid I was asked to develop one of the ideas that I had raised in the initial report, a concept I had proposed and given the title of 'sustainable church growth'. In the summer of 2002 the churches got their money and I was asked to join the Project Management Committee as a consultant and to work with the churches to develop their project and to provide both practical input and academic comment. It is in the light of this work that I will be addressing the possibility of applied congregational studies in Britain today.

Congregational studies in Britain, like so much of British theology, finds itself trapped between two distinct and very different institutions. On the one hand, we have the academic departments of theology and religious studies, many of which exist in secular institutions and all of which are driven by the need for academic excellence. On the other hand we have the churches. The mainstream denominations are declining and facing many different challenges, not least financial. They are unsure about the need for 'academic' research and have no spare money to pay for it. The newer churches may have money, but are generally suspicious of all that comes from the 'secular' academic traditions.

Thus congregational studies finds itself situated in relation to two somewhat unsympathetic institutions. The academy (and here I am including those in faith-based colleges and seminaries) focuses on a very specific understanding of 'excellence' in research that has a tendency to marginalize work that may be defined as 'congregational studies'. From this perspective the question will always be asked as to whether a detailed and essentially practical study of inner workings of two Methodist churches in north Birmingham could ever be understood as 'internationally relevant research' even if the project generated the most startling and internationally applicable findings (which is unlikely). The question for the academy is simply 'what is the point?' What is being contributed to 'knowledge' from such a study?

But the churches are equally likely to ask 'what is the point?' There is no question that churches, both local and national, have many questions and problems that they would clearly love to sort out. If they felt that they could call on the academic community to help them in this process then I have no doubt that they would. The fact that in Britain they do not shows that there must be some underlying problem. The most significant problem is, of course, money. The mainstream churches in Britain simply do not have the 'spare' money to employ fully qualified academics to undertake long-term research for them (although there have been some very notable exceptions). Where the churches do appear to be prepared to spend money on research, it is in sponsoring postgraduate work among their ministers. How much real value this brings back to the churches, apart from better-qualified staff, must remain an open question. Apart from money, however, I think there are more fundamental problems in the relationship between the churches and the academy in Britain today. Do the churches really know the questions that they want to ask? Do they trust academics to be able to answer them? Have academics concentrated far too much on 'internationally relevant' research at the expense of research that might actually be of value to the churches?

What, however, could the churches ask the academics to do? Why might a particular church approach the local department of religion and theology and ask for an expert in congregational studies? How much would it cost? How long would it take? Could the results ever be useful to the churches in question? Theology departments, I would guess, have little practical experience in consultancy work. Likewise, the churches have little practical experience in calling on consultants. When it does happen, therefore, it becomes very interesting, and the possibility of 'applied congregational studies' begins to emerge. What, however, does this 'applied congregational studies' actually look like, and can it really begin to address the problems faced by both the churches and the academy? These are the questions that I want to explore in this chapter.

The American Tradition: Who Pays the Piper?

Before attempting to answer this question I need to take a brief look at the situation in the USA. Earlier chapters in this volume explore the American tradition of congregational studies in far more detail than I am able to do here (see Chapter 2), and so my comments will be limited to the questions that I have so far been raising. One of the first things to note, of course, is that congregational studies in the USA has a far greater sense of purpose than I have suggested for the British context. There is one main reason for this. In the USA the vast majority of work that comes under the title of 'congregational studies' is funded by Christian organizations. These funding bodies are not always churches; in fact they appear very rarely to be churches as such. Rather they are trusts and research funds with specifically Christian foundations. These trusts were set up, at least in part, with the specific task of funding this kind of research. For this reason alone, therefore, the scholars involved in congregational studies have a clearer sense of purpose.

The question remains, however, as to whether, or to what extent, the work that is being produced in the USA can be defined as being 'applied'. The work that is being funded is certainly expected to be 'applicable'. This is a major element in achieving the funding in the first place. The organizations and trusts that fund congregational studies want to see 'outcomes'. They are not interested in research for the sake of research. Much of the material that is being produced from such research does inevitably 'contribute to knowledge' in the kind of abstract way that is expected of academic research in Britain. However, the funded research is expected to do more than that. Simply to find out more about the distribution of religious communities in Chicago is not enough. Even to describe the different ways in which these communities engage with their neighbourhoods only takes us a little further. This is not, of itself, what the funding bodies want to hear. These bodies are interested in the 'so what' question. What can the research on local religious communities and their interactions with their neighbourhoods tell us about how such congregations 'should' be engaging, or, alternatively, about how the national religious institutions can encourage greater engagement? There is a clear practical and, we might want to say, applied nature to this research.[1]

The work in congregational studies from the USA, therefore, has tended to lead to two distinct practical outcomes. In the first case the funders are looking for research that can guide national institutions and inform policy. These institutions need not be solely religious institutions. Much of the work is directed at the various denominational groups and suggests policy implications for these bodies. Much of it also addresses a far wider audience. How does a greater understanding of congregational/neighbourhood relations affect not just church policy, but the policy decisions of city, state and federal governments and their various departments? This is, as Chapters 1 and 2 in

---

[1] These comments are based on the work of the Religion in Urban America Project based at the University of Illinois in Chicago. See Livezey (2000) for details.

this volume make very clear, a contribution to a much wider discussion of civic society and it is in this context that the results of the research can be applied. There is some work of this kind being undertaken in Britain, although it is rarely done at the level of the congregation. However, the debate about civil society in Britain has never really taken off and this kind of contribution is still, I would suggest, in its infancy. This is also not really the kind of work that I am thinking of when I talk about applied congregational studies.

The other way in which American congregational studies could be said to be 'applied' is in the desire on the part of many of those involved in the studies to provide material that may actually be of use to the churches that are being studied. There is a clear sense of responsibility to the churches that are involved in the study, and which may be funding the study. This means that the researchers feel the need, or are perhaps obliged by the research contracts, to feed something back to the congregations concerned. This has led to a series of books that might best be described as 'how to' books. These texts take the results of congregational studies research and make it accessible to the average congregation in a form that should, in theory, help them to improve whatever it is that the book is about, from numerical growth through to the resolution of internal conflicts.[2] It would be interesting to analyse these data to see if there might be some more or less hidden ideal of a congregation that all these texts are encouraging their readers to aspire to, but that is not really the purpose of this chapter. It is significant only from the perspective of whether such writing can really be described as 'applied' congregational studies. Such self-help texts are obviously based on detailed and important research, and the results of that research are presented in a way that aims to help the local congregation; they are 'applied'. The question remains, however, of how many studies have looked at the way in which congregations handle these books and at the real processes of application involved.

I am not trying to say that the work of congregational studies in the USA is not 'applied', and I am certainly not saying that it is not significant for the British context. Far from it; this work has been extremely important and we in Britain have an incredibly long way to catch up. The point I am trying to make is to ask exactly what might be meant by the term 'applied' in the phrase 'applied congregational studies', particularly in the British context. I am not sure that the two primary applications presupposed by the American material really get to the heart of what I am trying to discuss. In order to develop this argument further, then, and to get back to the north Birmingham situation that I began with, I need to look at two traditions of 'applied' sociology in Britain and see if there is anything here we can learn for congregational studies.

Theory Testing: To Grow or Not to Grow

The first thoughts that I had when I was approached to be involved in the two Methodist churches in north Birmingham revolved around the idea of testing

---

[2] See, for example, Dudley *et al.* (1986), Mead (1994), and Becker (1999).

different theories of church growth. There were various reasons why this was the case. The first was the obvious fact that the two churches I was asked to comment on were very small in terms of congregation, one with fewer than ten members, and if they were to survive at all, then they would clearly have to grow in some shape or form. The second related to the situation that I actually found when I began the feasibility study. The first result of this study was the realization that the communities served by the congregations did not 'qualify' for any kind of service-led funding; the level of poverty or disadvantage among the people on these estates simply was not high enough. It would have been very difficult to make the case for any kind of community worker as such. It was also clear that these two churches, while being very small in terms of their regular congregations, actually had contact with a wide range of non-churchgoers. The buildings are well used by uniformed organizations, community groups and others, all of whom show a great deal of goodwill towards the congregations, even if the people involved never actually attend the churches. This provided an obvious market for potential growth.

The third reason why I was drawn towards the idea of testing ideas of church growth related to the way in which the process was developed. The congregations wished to put together a project in order to bring in a lay worker. They were not entirely clear what they wanted that worker to do, but it was always clear that the ultimate goal was to be church growth, or at the very least church survival. I was asked to put together a feasibility study and to make recommendations. Having done this, I was then asked to prepare a more detailed document to accompany the bid for the funding of the lay worker. As it was clear that we needed to show the Methodist Church that their money would be well spent, the form of the document I prepared was couched in terms of the testing of a particular theory of church growth. If this process works here, we were saying, then it could work elsewhere and could ultimately be rolled out across the whole of Methodism. These two churches, after all, were probably more typical of Methodism nationally than many inner city or large suburban churches that usually got the money on offer.

In choosing a theory to test I needed to relate my own ideas to those of other theories. There are currently a number of theories 'on the market', most of which have been developed out of previous 'congregational studies'. The best known is that of McGavran (1959) and the Church Growth Movement. This is rooted in the evangelical tradition and involves a process by which members of the congregation get alongside people in the community who are similar to themselves and invite them in to events and activities within the church. The whole process is presented in a very slick manner and has all the hallmarks of a major marketing strategy. It clearly works. It is based on solid research, and a significant number of postgraduate theses have been written over the years to look into the process. Whether it is ultimately distinct from other membership drives in other kinds of organization is an interesting question. It is presented from a conservative evangelical perspective and assumes a strong, self-confident, theologically literate community as its starting point. This method, therefore, was clearly not going to work for the two churches I was asked to work with. The congregational base had already been reduced too far, the congregations were inherently suspicious of any form of evangelicalism, and the preparatory work in building up the self-confidence of the congregations before the outreach could begin would, in my view, have taken far too long. A variation on this method that involves bringing in a team from outside to do the necessary work and to effectively plant a new congregation was also rejected as being potentially too destructive of what was already in place.

A second theory of church growth that I looked at begins from a very different perspective. This theory uses the label 'natural church growth' and, like the Church Growth Movement, is based in solid research of actual congregations (although in this case the data are international and not just American).[3] The principle in this method is to ask what it is that makes a 'successful' church. This is developed empirically by testing both successful and unsuccessful churches throughout the world and drawing up a list of features that are common to the successful churches and missing from the unsuccessful ones. The idea is that if we can work with a congregation on the markers of success then the congregation will grow of its own accord, naturally, as implied by the title. This process is actually very attractive and while I have my own personal doubts about the cross-cultural nature of those elements that define a 'successful church', I can see the process working within a congregation that is already well endowed with 'successful traits'. Whether the success comes simply from the development of the traits themselves, as proposed, or whether the process of self-critical analysis and reflection by the congregation as a whole, irrespective of the traits developed, is the factor that most leads to self-confidence and growth, would need to be tested by further research. My problem, however, like that with the Church Growth Movement, is that a congregation would need to be well advanced towards 'success' if the process itself were not going to be demoralizing and counter-productive.

In the end, I had to propound a new theory of church growth that played to the strengths of the congregations I was asked to work with, and which was able to function from an extremely low starting point. What I eventually proposed was a process I described as 'sustainable church growth' (Stringer, 2001). This was based entirely on my experience of growing up with an Anglican church in South Yorkshire. The church I grew up with was relatively small when we moved to the village but expanded considerably over twelve years through a whole series of mechanisms or processes, not all of which were obvious at the time. The congregation did not set out with a 'theory' or 'model'; it was often scrabbling around in the dark looking for what might work. Many things that were tried came to nothing. A few of the more successful ventures worked more by luck than judgement. What I did in preparing the supporting documentation for the bid was to reflect on that situation from my current perspective as an 'expert' on congregational studies, and to distil what I felt were the most important elements. The research lying behind my theory, therefore, was significantly less than that for any of the other theories or models considered. It was partly reflection on some kind of 'fieldwork experience'. It was partly the

---

[3] See Schwarz (1996).

application of what I would call 'sociological literacy', a gut feeling based on many years studying the sociology of small groups. It was entirely speculation, a possibility. I had no idea as I was writing it up whether it would really work or not. I hoped, I guessed, that it would.

If I was to sum up the essential features of my own theory of 'sustainable church growth', I would say that it is based on two basic principles. First, it is based on the assumption (clearly the case for the churches I was working with) that alongside those people who actually attend any church on a regular basis is a much wider group who have a strong sense of goodwill to the church but who do not actually attend. These may be other family members of the congregation or they may, as in the case of the North Birmingham Methodists, be other people who use the buildings for a very wide range of other activities during the week. The second principle is that people will be drawn into the core of the congregation if they are able to establish personal relationships with members of the core and if they are brought in through activities that are clearly of interest and relevance to them, in a way that the Christian faith may not necessarily be. Therefore I was suggesting that the congregations should build up partnerships with this 'extended congregation' in order to socialize, or to raise money or to serve the community, or whatever. It is through these other activities that the extended congregation slowly, but sustainably, get drawn into the core.[4]

My work with this congregation, therefore, having obtained the money on the basis of this 'speculation', must, in some way or another, be a process of testing the theory that I have proposed. Put very simply, we need to see if it works. If it does not, then we need to ask why; what was wrong with the original ideas that meant it did not work? Alternatively, what was unique about the particular situation that meant that it did not work here? In my experience it is usually the second question that will be asked before the first. If it does work, however, then what? Have we found a panacea, the final answer to the question of church growth? Do we shout aloud, publish our results and set out to prepare books or manuals for others to follow, letting every church in the land learn from our success? Is this really what applied congregational studies is about; is this its purpose?

Action Research: Making a Difference

Another approach to applied congregational studies is to follow what educational and social welfare research has defined as 'action research'.[5] This is a process of entering into a field situation with the explicit intention of

---

[4] I expand on this much more fully in the report I prepared for the congregations in question.

[5] Action research was particularly popular in the 1970s and 1980s; see Clark (1972). For a more recent discussion see Oja (1989), which focuses particularly on action research in education.

becoming involved and making a difference. The idea is to work with those
who are perceived to have the problem in order to find a joint solution that
could, possibly, be written up as a paper or larger text. There is no pretence at
objectivity within this kind of research. It is often undertaken from a very
explicit political point of view, and this has been its principal point of
contention. Should social science research be objective? Could it ever be, even if
it wanted to be? At least in most forms of 'action research' the question is
addressed head on and answered with a categorical 'no'.

So would it be possible for congregational research to be framed as 'action
research'? This is certainly the hope and the expectation of most of those
coming to work with me as students. There is no sense of distanced or objective
research involved in the original questions or the earliest drafts of a research
plan. It is clear that the vast majority of the students are fully involved in the
situation, often as ministers and hence as leaders within the situation. It is also
obvious that their primary aim is, through their research, to make a difference
to that situation. What is interesting is the implied assumptions made by most
of these students about the sequencing of research and action. It is
automatically assumed that the research will come first. Before any action
begins, it is suggested, we must first understand all the issues involved. The
research, therefore, is seen as a precursor to action, not really a part of it.
We need to understand how mixed-race congregations deal with issues of race
and ethnicity, for example, especially in relation to leadership, before we can
then make recommendations about the way in which congregations may be
helped to deal with these issues in the future. It is for this reason that so many
student studies appear to focus on the positive, on the examples of good
practice. If we can learn from those who do it well, then we can transfer that
knowledge to others.

This has a wonderfully appealing logic to it. Unfortunately, things rarely
work out quite like this in practice. If I take the example of the student looking
at mixed-race churches and explore this for a moment, then we can see one of
the major problems. The plan was to identify examples of good practice, and
then to undertake fieldwork in order to learn from these for the benefit of the
Church as a whole. Unfortunately, when the fieldwork began it was soon
realized that even the three churches chosen, despite their high reputations for
good practice on racial issues, were riddled with racial problems and tensions
and could not be taken as examples of good practice in any but the loosest or
most superficial of senses. The original plan was simply not going to work. This
is not the only example in which this process has become unstuck because
'good practice' is seldom as 'ideal' as we might at first presume, and because the
examples of 'good practice' are so unique as to be inapplicable to the majority
of cases.

It is of course possible to learn lessons from any congregation; they do not
have to be examples of best practice in order to be interesting. This was the
assumption of another student who was looking at collaborative ministry.
Three churches were chosen, not on the basis of good practice, but simply to
illustrate three different approaches to collaborative ministry. The examples
were studied in detail and the results brought together in a classification of

collaboration. Certainly recommendations for improvements in other congregations can be derived from this kind of work, and local churches could
implement those recommendations themselves. In order to complete the
process, however, the student would have to then study the implementation in
order to see whether the recommendations, once applied, would actually work.
This element of the research is that which is most often overlooked, especially
within the context of a three-year PhD. It is simply not practical to do this.

Another problem arises when the recommendations are not quite as clear
and straightforward as the student in question might have hoped. A further
student who has studied initiation practices in the Catholic Church of inner-
city Liverpool came to the conclusion of the thesis expecting to present a series
of practical and implementable recommendations for the churches of the
archdiocese. This was achieved. The recommendations, however, were felt to
be bland, and in the context of the thesis as a whole, irrelevant. What the
student had argued was that First Communion was caught up in a major
structural fault of the Catholic Church and that the recommendations, if any
were to be made, should not have been offered to local congregations but to the
whole institution of the Catholic Church.[6] This was a very different kind of
outcome from the one anticipated, and ultimately far more difficult to
implement. It is exactly this kind of conclusion, with its major political
implications, that ultimately gave action research in education and social
welfare such a bad press. The 'solutions' were seldom to be found at the local
level; they demanded major structural and political changes to the whole
system. This was a far more radical thing to be saying, and far more dangerous
when that system was providing the funding.

But is this real action research? Is the sequence of research leading to action
what action research was ever meant to be about? I would suggest not. In its
ideal form action research aims at merging action with research, working
towards solutions at the local level as part of the process of research itself. The
writing up of the research ideally follows the action; it is not a precursor to it.
This, perhaps, is the closest I can come to in terms of an ideal for my work in
north Birmingham. I have, of course, had to lay out a possible (and plausible)
theory of church growth in order to convince the Methodist Church to provide
the churches with money. I am not, however, simply setting out to try to prove
this theory right. My concern is with the people, with the specific situation of
these two churches and their future. I have no real idea whether the ideas I have
proposed will 'work'. I am not even sure that this is what the churches
themselves need. I simply wish to work with these two congregations in their
struggle, to offer what insights I can from my previous experience (both
practical and academic) and to work together for the best future for these
congregations in this part of Birmingham. If some interesting insights come out
of this process, as I am sure they will, then I will write them up and I will
publish them. If not, then I can always analyse the reasons for failure.

---

[6] For more details on the project, see Peter McGrail's contribution to this volume
(Chapter 6).

Collaborative Research: Juggling the Voices

This takes us on to the point where we have to ask about the role of the researcher within the process of congregational development that is being undertaken. Can the researcher simply be a neutral observer, turning up to all the meetings, keeping quiet and simply observing what is going on? The answer has to be 'no'. The whole basis of action research, and I would suggest any form of applied research, is that the researcher gets in there with everybody else, gets their hands well and truly dirty, and takes the credit and the blame alongside all those involved. The researcher, however, should probably not be the leader, and this is where the question of theory testing becomes particularly difficult.

For the first four or five meetings of the 'Management Committee' of the north Birmingham project, I largely sat and observed. The Management Committee was made up of representatives from each of the churches involved along with the minister, a couple of representatives from the circuit and myself. I knew what I wanted this group to do. I had set out the theory in two documents and I felt that their job was to implement that theory and to see if it worked. It soon became very clear, however, that, even if the other members of the group understood the 'theory' in the same way that I had set it out, they really had no intention of implementing it. Central to the theory, from my point of view, were the congregations themselves getting on with the work, making contacts with the extended congregation and bringing them closer into the church through a series of joint activities. Any worker that may or may not be employed was largely incidental to this process, essentially a facilitator of the wider activity. The Management Committee, however, had very different ideas. They had set out on the whole process in order to persuade the Methodist Church to pay for a worker and it was this worker, so they thought, who was to be the answer to all their prayers. This worker was the one who was to be brought in to 'do the work'.

This is perhaps a little unfair to the group. Their view was far more subtle than this, and it was clear that there was more than one voice within the group. The representatives from the church with only seven elderly members kept stressing, quite rightly, that their congregation simply was not able to undertake the work I was saying was important. They understood the theory, but the practice was going to be impossible. The representatives from the circuit (essentially the experts in employment matters, in the role of lay workers in Methodism, and in running projects) had not been part of the process that I had undertaken with the two churches as we worked towards the 'theory'. They were working on far more traditional models of 'lay workers' and they were imposing these models on the group. This was in no sense a deliberate ploy; it was simply the way in which they understood the situation. The minister came with other ideas, different understandings of the situation and the 'solution', that went back beyond my work with the churches to his original conception when he called me in to help. Each voice worked for its own understanding and model of action and it was the combined voices that led the Management Committee to form its decision. Within these discussions I also allowed my voice to play a role. I kept stressing what I thought was important, my own model of the theory. This, however, was not my enterprise. This was not a research project I had set up and funded to prove my own little pet theories. This was the responsibility of the congregations. It was, for one of the congregations at least, a matter of life or death for the churches involved, and they had to retain control. My contribution, as co-worker, not as 'researcher', was to make sure that ultimately, it was the congregation's voices that were heard and acted on.

As I write, the project itself has come to a temporary halt. The initial attempts to prepare a job description and to advertise for a worker only produced one reply and no appointment was made. The minister has since taken a sabbatical and the Management Committee has not met for some months. Nothing very much is happening, and once again I ask what my role, as consultant and researcher, may be at such a stage in the work.

Is this good research? I really could not say. In some ways it takes us back to the rather flippant comment that I made at the end of the previous section. Even if things go totally wrong and everything is a complete disaster, I, as researcher, will have something to write about in chapters such as this. In many ways it does not matter whether we implement the theory in any purist sense or not. Simply watching and being involved in the process will provide me with material to write about. Is this, however, the point? Once I get involved, once I make the decision that what is most important is not my theory but rather the voices of the congregations involved, does this cease to be a 'research project' in any meaningful sense? Am I not simply exploiting their situation by preparing papers? And if it is a research project, deliberately undertaken in a collaborative fashion rather than with me, as researcher, in charge, then whose research project is it? I am no more than the 'consultant'. The congregation is my 'employer'. I have an agreement that I can write papers and allow this situation to count as 'my research', but is it really mine? Is this not a collaborative act of research, with many voices and many different understandings of the nature of the project? Should I not allow others to have their voice within my texts? Should I not add their names to the list of 'authors' of each and every paper?

These are not questions that are unique to congregational studies. They arise whenever we engage in applied social sciences. I simply think that this is not an area that congregational studies, per se, has yet faced and addressed. These are questions that we need to ask, and questions that we need to find some kind of answer for before we progress much further.

Providing All the Answers?

So are congregational studies going to provide all the answers? Of course not. The question partially depends on what we mean by 'all the answers'. There are many different kinds of questions, both about the way in which congregations work and about the ethics involved in the study of congregations. Applied congregational studies bring both of these together and, I would suggest, make those elusive answers even more difficult to find. However, is congregational studies really about providing answers? Again, I think not. Congregational studies is, as I have suggested at the beginning of this chapter, part of a process, an alliance between the church and the academy, a mutual search for a better way of being church and living out our Christian (or Buddhist, or Hindu, or Muslim) life in the world of today. It is not about answers, at least not ultimate ones. We have to work together, tackling the questions and allowing the process of tackling those questions to throw up new questions as both the congregations and the world around us constantly change. Perhaps this is not the kind of answer that universities, driven by the need for research assessment and qualifications, would like to hear. It may not be, but I remain convinced, not least from my experience of working with two small, but living Methodist congregations in north Birmingham, that congregational studies should be the point at which sociology becomes the servant of the church.

References

Becker, P. E. (1999), *Congregations in Conflict: Cultural Models of Local Religious Life*, Cambridge and New York: Cambridge University Press.

Clark, P. A. (1972), *Action Research and Organizational Change*, London: Harper and Row.

Dudley, C. *et al.* (1986), *Handbook for Congregational Studies*, Nashville, TN: Abingdon Press.

Livezey, L. W. (ed.) (2000), *Public Religion and Urban Transformation: Faith in the City*, New York: New York University Press.

McGavran, D. A. (1959), *How Churches Grow*, New York: Friendship Press.

Mead, L. (1994), *Transforming Congregations for the Future*, Bethesda, MD: The Alban Institute.

Oja, S. N. (1989), *Collaborative Action Research, a Developmental Approach*, Basingstoke: Falmer.

Schwarz, C. A. (1996), *Natural Church Development: A Guide to Eight Essential Qualities of Healthy Churches*, Emmelsbull: C and P Verlags.

Stringer, M. D. (2001), 'Sustainable Church Growth, A Discussion', unpublished report prepared for the Handsworth Methodist Circuit.

Index

215